WordPress 3.7 Complete

Third Edition

Make your first end-to-end website from scratch
with WordPress

Karol Król

Aaron Hodge Silver

[PACKT] open source*
PUBLISHING   community experience distilled

BIRMINGHAM - MUMBAI

WordPress 3.7 Complete
Third Edition

First published: November 2006

Second edition: January 2011

Third edition: November 2013

Production Reference: 1191113

Published by Packt Publishing Ltd.
Livery Place
35 Livery Street
Birmingham B3 2PB, UK.

ISBN 978-1-78216-240-7

www.packtpub.com

Cover Image by Łukasz Siódmok (ls@la-ds.com)

Credits

Authors

Karol Król

Aaron Hodge Silver

Reviewers

Rodolfo Buaiz

Matthew Cohen

Patrick Cohen

Olivier Pons

Aaron Hodge Silver

Acquisition Editor

Kunal Parikh

Lead Technical Editor

Ritika Dewani

Technical Editors

Kapil Hemnani

Novina Kewalramani

Aparna Kumari

Shiny Poojary

Amit Ramadas

Gaurav Thingalaya

Project Coordinator

Rahul Dixit

Proofreaders

Bridget Braund

Lawrence A. Herman

Lesley Harrison

Indexers

Mehreen Deshmukh

Rekha Nair

Production Coordinator

Nitesh Thakur

Cover Work

Nitesh Thakur

About the Authors

Karol Król is a WordPress developer, PHP programming specialist, professional blogger, and writer. He has been building expertise in WordPress ever since his early years at the Silesian University of Technology, Poland, where he graduated with a Master's degree in Computer Science. Early in his career, he worked as a freelance website developer, and then launched a web design business together with a close friend. Later on, he decided to shift his interest towards popularizing WordPress as the perfect solution for all web-based projects and devoted his time to growing his writing career. To this day, his articles have been featured on websites, such as About.com, Lifehack.org, ProBlogger.net, Freelance Switch, Quick Sprout, and Six Revisions. Currently, his main two projects are providing Online Business Advice for Normal People through his main website (`http://newinternetorder.com/`) and taking active part in the Writers in Charge project (`http://www.writersincharge.com/`), and teaching other writers how to take charge of their writing career.

Karol spends most of his spare time making music, training Capoeira, cooking, and drinking wine.

I'd like to thank everyone at Packt Publishing for working with me and making this book a reality. Also, many thanks to everyone who supported me along the way. Last but not least, I'd like to thank ThemeFuse (`http://themefuse.com/`), one of the leading WordPress theme stores online, for providing guidance and delivering a custom theme design that I was able to use in this book.

Aaron Hodge Silver has been designing and developing new websites from scratch since 1999, just before his graduation from Columbia University. Early in his career, he worked for several web companies and startups, including DoubleClick and About. com. Since 2004, he has been self-employed through his company Springthistle Design and has worked with a staggering variety of companies, non-profits, and individuals to realize their website dreams. In his professional work, Aaron's focus is always on usability, efficiency, flexibility, clean design, and client happiness. WordPress is the best solution for many of Springthistle's clients, though Aaron also develops custom web applications using PHP and MySQL. Aaron was the author of the two previous editions of this book! You can find more about Aaron's professional work at http://springthistle.com.

In his free time, Aaron enjoys developing recipes in the kitchen, being active outdoors, and spending quality time with his family (both human and non human members).

About the Reviewers

Matthew Cohen is a Chief Product Officer at WooThemes. He is also a WordPress and web developer, musician, and blogger. He is a lover of punk rock, innovation, business and 80s/90s cartoons.

Olivier Pons is a developer who's been building websites since 1997. He's a teacher at Ingésup (École supérieure d'ingénierie informatique) at the University of Sciences (IUT) of Aix-en-Provence/France and École d'Ingénieurs des Mines de Gardanne, where he teaches MVC fundamentals, Symfony, PHP, HTML, CSS, jQuery/jQuery Mobile, Linux basics, and advanced VIM techniques. He has already done some technical reviews for Packt Publishing books, namely *Ext JS 4 First Look* by *Loaine Groner* and *jQuery Mobile Web Development Essentials Second Edition* by *Raymond Camden* and *Andy Matthews* among others. In 2011, he left a full-time job as a Delphi and PHP developer to concentrate on his own company, HQF Development (`http://hqf.fr`). He currently runs a number of websites, including `http://www.livrepizzas.fr`, `http://www.papdevis.fr`, and `http://olivierpons.fr` his own web development blog. He works as a consultant, teacher, project manager, and sometimes a developer.

www.packtpub.com

Support files, eBooks, discount offers and more

You might want to visit www.PacktPub.com for support files and downloads related to your book.

Did you know that Packt offers eBook versions of every book published, with PDF and ePub files available? You can upgrade to the eBook version at www.PacktPub.com and as a print book customer, you are entitled to a discount on the eBook copy. Get in touch with us at service@packtpub.com for more details.

At www.PacktPub.com, you can also read a collection of free technical articles, sign up for a range of free newsletters and receive exclusive discounts and offers on Packt books and eBooks.

http://PacktLib.PacktPub.com

Do you need instant solutions to your IT questions? PacktLib is Packt's online digital book library. Here, you can access, read and search across Packt's entire library of books.

Why Subscribe?
- Fully searchable across every book published by Packt
- Copy and paste, print and bookmark content
- On demand and accessible via web browser

Free Access for Packt account holders

If you have an account with Packt at www.PacktPub.com, you can use this to access PacktLib today and view nine entirely free books. Simply use your login credentials for immediate access.

Table of Contents

Preface

WordPress 3.7 Complete Third Edition will take you through the complete process of building a fully functional WordPress site from scratch. The journey goes all the way from teaching you how to install WordPress, to the most advanced topics such as creating your own themes, writing plugins, and even building non-blog websites. The best part is that you can do all this without losing your shirt along the way. Moreover, once you get some practice, you will be able to launch new WordPress sites within minutes (not a metaphor, by the way; this is as true as it gets).

This book guides you along the way in a step-by-step manner to explain everything there is to know about WordPress. We'll start with downloading and installing the core of WordPress, where you will learn how to choose the correct settings in order to guarantee a smooth experience for yourself and for your visitors. After that, the book will teach you all about content management functionality for your site from posts and pages to categories and tags, all the way to links, media, menus, images, galleries, administration, user profiles, and more. Next, you will find out what plugins and themes are and how to use them effectively. Finally, you'll learn how to create your own themes and plugins to enhance the overall functionality of your website. Once you're done with reading *WordPress 3.7 Complete Third Edition*, you will have all the knowledge required to build a professional WordPress site from scratch.

What this book covers

Chapter 1, Introducing WordPress, explains how WordPress is an excellent software that can run your website (blog or not). It's packed with excellent features and is so flexible that it can really do anything you want, and it has a wealth of online resources. Additionally, it's super easy to use, and you need no special skills or prior experience to use it. Last but not least, it is free!

Chapter 2, Getting Started, explains how to install WordPress on a remote server, change the basic default settings of your blog, write posts, and comment on those posts. It will also show you how to work with sites hosted on WordPress.com, which is one of the branches of the WordPress world.

Chapter 3, Creating Blog Content, teaches everything you need to know to add content to your blog and manage that content, be it about posts, categories, and comments, or tags, spam, and excerpts.

Chapter 4, Pages, Menus, Media Library, and More, explores all of the content WordPress can manage that's not directly about blogging. You can also learn about static pages, menus, bookmark links, the media library, image galleries, and more.

Chapter 5, Plugins and Widgets, discusses everything there is to know about finding the best plugins for WordPress and then using them effectively. Plugins are an integral part of every WordPress site's lifespan, so it's more than hard to imagine a successful site that isn't using any of them.

Chapter 6, Choosing and Installing Themes, describes how to manage the basic look of your WordPress website. You also learn where to find themes, why they are useful, and how to implement new themes on your WordPress website.

Chapter 7, Developing Your Own Theme, explains how to make your own theme. With just the most basic HTML and CSS abilities, you can create a design and turn it into a fully functional WordPress theme.

Chapter 8, Feeds, Podcasting, and Offline Blogging, explains what an RSS feed is and how to make feeds available for our WordPress blog. It also explores how to syndicate a whole blog or just posts within a certain category, and how to create your own podcast with or without the help of plugins. Finally, it goes on to discuss offline blogging and how it can speed up your web publishing experience.

Chapter 9, Developing Plugins and Widgets, teaches everything you need to know about creating basic plugins and widgets, how to structure the PHP files, where to put your functions, and how to use hooks. It also teaches about adding management pages and adding a widget that is related to a plugin.

Chapter 10, Community Blogging, explains how to manage a group of users working with a single blog, which is a community of users. Community blogging can play an important role in a user group or a news website. It also explains how to manage the different levels of privileges for users in a community.

Chapter 11, Creating a Non-blog Website Part One – The Basics, explores the endless possibilities of WordPress when it comes to using it to launch various types of websites. The chapter presents the first batch of our non-blog websites and explains in detail how to build them on top of a standard WordPress installation.

Chapter 12, Creating a Non-blog Website Part Two – Community Websites and Custom Content Elements, goes through some additional types of non-blog websites and also presents some technical aspects of building them (caution! code talk inside).

Chapter 13, Administrator's Reference, covers many of the common administrative tasks you may face when you're managing a WordPress-driven website. This includes backing up your database and files, moving your WordPress installation from one server or folder to another, and doing general problem-solving and troubleshooting. This chapter is the free one available online through a direct download link. Please hop over to our site to get it (`http://www.packtpub.com/sites/default/files/downloads/24070S_Chapter13_Administrators_Reference.pdf`).

What you need for this book

The prerequisites for this book include the following:

- A computer
- A web browser
- A text editor
- FTP software

Users may like a text editor that highlights code (such as Coda, TextMate, HTMLKit, and so on), but a simple text editor is all that's required.

Users may like to run local copies of WordPress on their computers, in which case they need a server such as Apache and MySQL installed (though WAMP and MAMP would take care of all that for them), but it's also not necessary as they could do the entire thing remotely.

Who this book is for

This book is a guide to WordPress for both beginners and those who have a slightly more advanced knowledge of WordPress. If you are new to blogging and want to create your own blog or website in a simple and straightforward manner, this book is for you. It is also for people who want to learn to customize and expand the capabilities of a WordPress website. You do not require any detailed knowledge of programming or web development, and any IT-confident user will be able to use the book to produce an impressive website.

Conventions

In this book, you will find a number of styles of text that distinguish between different kinds of information. Here are some examples of these styles, and an explanation of their meaning.

Code words in text are shown as follows: "For instance, using the <p> tags is not necessary in the text editor, as they will be stripped by default."

A block of code is set as follows:

```
// ** MySQL settings ** //
define('DB_NAME', 'wptestblog');
define('DB_USER', 'localdbuser');
define('DB_PASSWORD', '62dcx%^_0hnm');
define('DB_HOST', 'localhost');
```

When we wish to draw your attention to a particular part of a code block, the relevant lines or items are set in bold:

```
<div class="post post-item">
  <div class="post-title">
    <h2><a href="<?php the_permalink(); ?>"><?php the_title();
      ?></a></h2>
  </div>

  <?php if(has_post_thumbnail()) : ?>
    <div class="post-image alignleft">
      <?php echo '<a href="'.esc_url(get_permalink()).'"
        >'.get_the_post_thumbnail($post->ID, 'thumbnail').'</a>'; ?>
  </div>
  <?php endif; ?>

  <div class="entry clearfix">
    <p><em>by <?php echo get_post_meta($post->ID, 'book_author',
      true); ?></em></p>
    <?php the_excerpt(); ?>
  </div>
</div><!-- /.post-item -->
```

New terms and **important words** are shown in bold. Words that you see on the screen, in menus or dialog boxes for example, appear in the text like this: "To add a new page, go to your WP Admin and navigate to **Pages | Add New**".

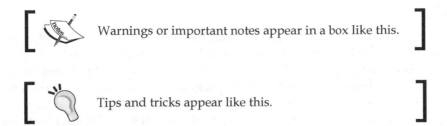

Warnings or important notes appear in a box like this.

Tips and tricks appear like this.

Reader feedback

Feedback from our readers is always welcome. Let us know what you think about this book—what you liked or may have disliked. Reader feedback is important for us to develop titles that you really get the most out of.

To send us general feedback, simply send an e-mail to feedback@packtpub.com, and mention the book title via the subject of your message.

If there is a book that you need and would like to see us publish, please send us a note in the **SUGGEST A TITLE** form on www.packtpub.com or e-mail suggest@packtpub.com.

If there is a topic that you have expertise in and you are interested in either writing or contributing to a book, see our author guide on www.packtpub.com/authors.

Customer support

Now that you are the proud owner of a Packt book, we have a number of things to help you to get the most from your purchase.

Downloading the example code for the book

You can download the example code files for all Packt books you have purchased from your account at http://www.PacktPub.com. If you purchased this book elsewhere, you can visit http://www.PacktPub.com/support and register to have the files e-mailed directly to you.

Errata

Although we have taken every care to ensure the accuracy of our content, mistakes do happen. If you find a mistake in one of our books—maybe a mistake in the text or the code—we would be grateful if you would report this to us. By doing so, you can save other readers from frustration and help us improve subsequent versions of this book. If you find any errata, please report them by visiting http://www.packtpub.com/support, selecting your book, clicking on the **errata submission form** link, and entering the details of your errata. Once your errata are verified, your submission will be accepted and the errata will be uploaded on our website, or added to any list of existing errata, under the Errata section of that title. Any existing errata can be viewed by selecting your title from http://www.packtpub.com/support.

Piracy

Piracy of copyright material on the Internet is an ongoing problem across all media. At Packt, we take the protection of our copyright and licenses very seriously. If you come across any illegal copies of our works, in any form, on the Internet, please provide us with the location address or website name immediately so that we can pursue a remedy.

Please contact us at copyright@packtpub.com with a link to the suspected pirated material.

We appreciate your help in protecting our authors, and our ability to bring you valuable content.

Questions

You can contact us at questions@packtpub.com if you are having a problem with any aspect of the book, and we will do our best to address it.

1
Introducing WordPress

Have you ever wanted to have a website at low cost, without the need to hire a team of developers and designers, without learning advanced PHP, and with almost unlimited extension possibilities? Or maybe you're more about getting into the world of website creation and becoming the next expert? If that's a yes to any of the above questions, WordPress is likely the platform you should look into.

These days, everyone has a good reason to have a website. It's not just large companies anymore. Individuals, families, and small or independent businesses all need to have one. Some individuals and small businesses don't have the financial resources to hire a website development company or a freelance web developer to create a website for them. In short, WordPress is an open source web software application that you can use to create and maintain an online website, even if you have the minimum of technical expertise.

Since it is a web application, WordPress does not need to be installed on your home computer, or any other machine under your control. It can live on the server (a kind of computer) that belongs to your website hosting company. It is also free, easy to use, and packed with excellent features. Originally, WordPress was an application meant to run a blog website, but it has now evolved into a fully-featured **Content Management System (CMS)**.

Actually, at the time of writing, WordPress powers over 60 million websites in total, or in other words, one of every six websites on the internet. And if that's not enough, the newest version of the platform has been downloaded over 14 million times. It seems that joining the team is, indeed, a wise thing to do.

In this chapter, we'll explore:

- The reasons that will make you choose WordPress to run your website
- The greatest advantages of WordPress
- Online resources for WordPress
- The complete list of features in the newest versions of WordPress

Getting into WordPress

WordPress is an open source blog engine. **Open source** means that nobody owns it, everybody works on it, and anyone can contribute to it. **Blog engine** means a software application that can run a blog. It's a piece of software that lives on the web server and makes it easy for you to add and edit posts, themes, comments, and all of your other content. More expansively, WordPress can be called a **publishing platform** because it is by no means restricted to blogging.

In fact, a number of big (by today's standards) online agencies use WordPress to run their sites. Outlets such as The New York Times, The Wall Street Journal, Forbes, and Reuters all use WordPress as the base of their web publishing platforms.

Originally, WordPress was a fork of an older piece of software named **b2/cafelog**. WordPress was developed by Matt Mullenweg and Mike Little, but is now maintained and developed by a team of developers that includes Mullenweg.

Over the years, the platform has evolved a lot and, even though a massive amount of new functionality got introduced, WordPress still remains one of the easiest to use web publishing platforms out there.

Using it for a blog or website

There are generally two popular types of websites for which WordPress is meant to be used:

- Normal websites with relatively static content—pages, subpages, and so on
- Blog websites—chronologically organized, frequently updated, categorized, tagged, and archived.

However, as experience shows, these days WordPress is successfully used to run a wide variety of other sites as well, such as

- Corporate business websites
- E-commerce stores

- Membership sites
- Video blogs
- Photo blogs
- Product websites, and more

For those of you unfamiliar with blog websites and blogging terminology, let's take a look at the basics.

Starting your journey, what is a blog? A **blog** is a website that usually contains regular entries such as a kind of log. These entries can be of various types, such as commentary, descriptions of events, photos, videos, personal remarks, tutorials, case studies, long opinion pieces, or political ideas. They are usually displayed in reverse chronological order, with the most recent additions on the top. These entries can be organized in a variety of ways — by date, by topic, by subject, and so on.

One of the main characteristics of a blog is that it's meant to be updated regularly. Unlike a site where the content is static, a blog behaves more like an online diary, wherein the blogger posts regular updates. Hence, blogs are dynamic with ever-changing content. A blog can be updated with new content and the old content can be changed or deleted at any time (although deleting content is not a common practice).

Most blogs focus their content on a particular subject — for example, current events, hobbies, niche topics, technical expertise — or else they are more like personal online diaries.

Originally, a blog was short for **weblog**. According to Wikipedia, the term weblog was first used in 1997, and people started using blogs globally in 1999. The terms weblog, **weblogging**, and **weblogger** were added to the Oxford Dictionary in 2003, though these days most people leave off the "we" part.

Understanding the common terms

If you are new to the world of blogging (or the "blogosphere," which is a fairly popular expression these days), you may want to familiarize yourself with the following common terms.

Post

Each entry in the blog is called a **post**. Every post usually has a number of different parts. Of course, the two most obvious parts are title and content. The **content** is text, images, links, and so on. Posts can even contain multimedia (for example, videos and audio files). Every post also has a publication timestamp, and most also have one or more categories, tags, comments, and so on. It is these posts, or entries, that are displayed in reverse chronological order on the main page of the blog. By default, the latest post is displayed first, in order to give the viewer the latest news on the subject.

Categories and tags

Categories and **tags** are ways to organize and find posts within a blog and even across blogs. Categories are like topics, whereas tags are more like keywords. For example, for a blog about food and cooking, there might be a category called **recipes**, but every post in that category would have different tags (for example, soup, baked, vegetarian, dairy-free, and so on).

The purpose and correct usage of tags and categories is one of the more discussed topics among bloggers. Although there are basic guidelines, as the ones presented previously, every blogger develops his or her own approach after a while, and there are no "written in stone" rules.

Comments

Most blogs allow visitors to post comments about the posts. This gives readers the opportunity to interact with the author of the blog, thus making the whole enterprise interactive. Often, the author of the blog will respond to comments by posting additional comments with the single click of a reply button, which makes for a continuous public online conversation or dialog.

Comments are said to be one of the most important assets for a blog. The presence of a big number of comments shows how popular and authoritative the blog is.

Theme

The **theme** for a blog is the design and layout that you choose. In most blogs, the content (for example, posts) is separate from the visual layout. This means you can change the visual layout of your blog at any time without having to worry about the content being affected. One of the best things about themes is that it takes only seconds to install and start using a new one. Moreover, there are a number of free or low-cost themes available online. However, you need to be careful when working with free themes from uncertain developers. Often, they contain encrypted parts and code that can hurt your site and its presence in Google. Always look for user reviews before choosing a theme.

Plugin

WordPress **plugins** are relatively small pieces of web software that can be installed on a WordPress site. They extend the native functionality to do almost anything that the technology of today allows. Just as with WordPress itself, the code within plugins is open source, which means that anyone can build a new plugin if they only have the required skillset. Every WordPress website or blog can work with an unlimited number of plugins (although it is not a recommended approach). The most popular functionalities introduced through plugins include spam protection, search engine optimization possibilities, caching, social media integration, interactive contact forms, backups, and more.

Widget

In short, **widgets** are a simplified version of plugins. Furthermore, they display a direct, visible result on your blog by using small content boxes (depending on the exact widget you're using, this content can be very diverse). The most common usage of widgets is to have them showcased within the sidebars on your site. Typically, your current theme will provide you with a number of widget areas where you can display widgets (as mentioned, many of these are located in the sidebar). Some of the common usages for widgets are to display content such as categories and tags, recent posts, popular posts, recent comments, links to archived posts, pages, links, search fields, or standard non-formatted text.

Menus

We need to talk some history to explain what the meaning of menus in WordPress is. Back in the day, WordPress didn't allow much customization in terms of tweaking navigation menus and hand-picking the links we wanted to display. This all changed in Version 3.0, when the new Custom Menus feature was introduced. In plain English, what it does is allow us to create completely custom menus (featuring any links of our choice) and then display them in specific areas on our sites (supported by the current theme). To be honest, this feature, even though it sounds basic, is one of the main ones that has turned WordPress into a fully-fledged web publishing platform and not just a blogging tool. I promise this will all sound much clearer in the upcoming chapters.

RSS

RSS is an acronym for **Really Simple Syndication**, and *Chapter 8, Feeds, Podcasting, and Offline Blogging*, addresses the topic of feeds in detail. For now, understand that RSS and feeds are a way to syndicate the content of your blog, so that people can subscribe to it. This means people do not actually have to visit your blog regularly to see what you've added. Instead, they can subscribe and have new content delivered to them via e-mail or through a feed reader such as **Feedly**.

Page

It's important to understand the difference between a page and a post. Unlike posts, pages do not depend on having timestamps and are not displayed in chronological order. They also do not have categories or tags. A **page** is a piece of content with only a title and content (an example would be **About Me** or **Contact Us**—the two most popular pages on almost any blog). It is likely that the number of pages on your blog remains relatively static, whereas new posts can be added every day or so.

Users

As mentioned in one of the paragraphs above, WordPress is now a complete web publishing platform. One of its characteristics is that it is capable of working with multiple user accounts, not just a single account belonging to the owner (main author) of the site. There are different types of user accounts available, and they all have different credentials and access rights. WordPress is clearly trying to resemble a traditional-world publishing house where there are authors, editors, and other contributors all working together. Even though the possibility to create an unlimited number of user accounts won't be that impressive for anyone planning to manage a site on his or her own, it can surely be a more than essential feature for big, magazine-like websites.

Choosing WordPress – the reason why

WordPress is not the only publishing platform out there, but it has an awful lot to recommend it. In the following sections, I've called attention to WordPress' most outstanding features.

A long time in refining

In web years, WordPress has been around for quite a while and was in development the whole time, getting better constantly. WordPress' very first release, Version 0.70, was released in May 2003. Since then, it has had 18 major releases, with a number of minor ones in between. Each release came with more features and better security.

Each major release comes with a codename honoring a great Jazz musician, and this has become a tradition in the WordPress world. For instance, the latest big version (Version 3.7) is codenamed **Basie**.

Active in development

WordPress is a constantly evolving application. It's never left alone to stagnate. The developers are working continually to keep it ahead of spammers and hackers, and also to evolve the application based on the evolving needs of its users.

Large community of contributors

WordPress is not being developed by a lonely programmer in a dark basement room. On the contrary, there is a large community of people working on it collaboratively by developing, troubleshooting, making suggestions, and testing the application. With such a large group of people involved, the application is likely to continue to evolve and improve without pause.

Amazingly extendable

In addition to having an extremely strong core, WordPress is also quite extendable. This means that once you get started with it, the possibilities are nearly limitless. Any additional functionality that you can dream of can be added by means of a plugin that you or your programmer friends can write.

Getting to know the WordPress family

WordPress as a platform and as a community of users has evolved in two main areas. The first one is gathered around WordPress.org—the native, main website of the WordPress project. The other is WordPress.com—a platform providing free blogs for every user who wants one.

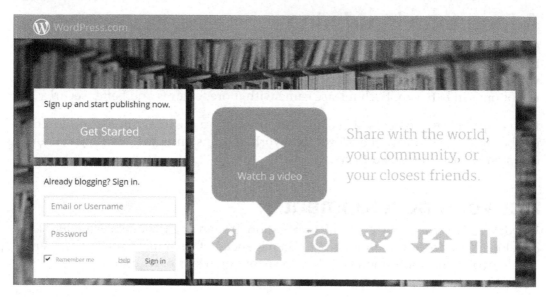

Essentially, WordPress.org is about developing the platform itself, about sharing new plugins, discussing the technical aspects of WordPress, and being all "techie" in general. WordPress.com (the image above) is a purely community-driven site where bloggers can meet with each other, and publish their content on free blogs based under the wordpress.com subdomain.

In *Chapter 2, Getting Started*, we will discuss all of the differences between having your blog on WordPress.com versus downloading the software from WordPress.org and hosting it yourself, but the basic difference is the level of control. If your blog is on WordPress.com, you have less control over plugins, themes, and other details of the blog because everything is managed and made worry-free by the WordPress.com service, which obviously has its pros and cons.

Digging into WordPress – the features

The following is a detailed list of many features of WordPress:

- Compliant with **World Wide Web Consortium (W3C) standards**
- Unlimited categories and subcategories
- Unlimited tags
- Automatic syndication (RSS and Atom)
- Uses XML RPC interface for trackbacks and remote posting
- Allows posting via e-mail and mobile devices (there are apps available for all major mobile platforms, including iOS and Android)
- Supports plugins and themes
- Imports data from other blogs (Moveable Type, Textpattern, Greymatter, b2evolution, and Blogger)
- Easy to administer and blog without any previous experience
- Convenient, fully functional, and built-in search
- Instant and fast publishing of content—no rebuilding of pages required
- Multilanguage capable
- Allows password-protected content
- Comments manager and spam protection
- Built-in workflow (write, draft, review, and publish)
- Intelligent text formatting via a **What You See Is What You Get (WYSIWYG)** editor
- Multiuser and multiauthor support for user accounts
- Feature-rich **Media Library** for managing photos and other non-text content
- Social media integration capabilities
- Dynamic and scalable revision functionality with post (edit) locking
- Built-in embed functionality through shortcodes
- Advanced **SEO (Search Engine Optimization)** features through plugins and themes

Getting familiar with the new feature list since 3.0

Since the last edition of this book was published, quite a staggering number of new features have been added to the WordPress software. If you're new to WordPress, this list may not mean a whole lot to you, but if you're familiar with WordPress and have been using it for a long time, you'll find this list quite enlightening.

- Internal linking available through the standard "add link" box
- Inclusion of the admin bar when browsing the blog while being logged in
- Full-screen mode for editing posts and pages
- Custom menus that can be included anywhere in the predefined areas within the current theme
- Faster page load times
- Faster upgrades
- Dropped support for Internet Explorer 6
- Inclusion of the single upload button (with file type detection)
- Drag-and-drop media uploading
- Responsive design of the admin panel (Dashboard)
- The possibility to select custom header images and custom background images from the Media Library
- Improved internationalization and localization features
- Renaming **HTML Editor** in the edit post/page screen to **Text Editor**
- New media manager makes it easier than ever to manage photos, videos, and other media files through a beautiful user interface
- Galleries can be created faster with drag-and-drop reordering and simplified controls
- New welcome screen in the Dashboard
- **High-Dots-Per-Inch (HiDPI)** compatible Dashboard design (also known as Retina-ready)
- Better accessibility for screen readers, touch devices, and keyboard users
- XML-RPC is always enabled by default and supports fetching users, managing post revisions, and searching

- All buttons updated to a modern shape (more rectangular)
- Autosave and post locking, together with the new revisions functionality for easy content editing
- In-line login feature to save expired user sessions
- Automatic maintenance and security updates in the background
- Automatic installation of language files (localization)
- New password meter to help users set secure passwords

Learning more

If you'd like to see detailed lists of all new features added since WordPress version 3.0, take a look at these links:

- `http://codex.wordpress.org/Version_3.1`
- `http://codex.wordpress.org/Version_3.2`
- `http://codex.wordpress.org/Version_3.3`
- `http://codex.wordpress.org/Version_3.4`
- `http://codex.wordpress.org/Version_3.5`
- `http://codex.wordpress.org/Version_3.6`
- `http://codex.wordpress.org/Version_3.7`

Also, you can read a fully explained feature list at `http://wordpress.org/about/features/`.

Learning more with the online WordPress resources

One very useful characteristic of WordPress is that it has a large, active online community. Everything you will ever need for your WordPress website can likely be found online, and probably for free. In addition to this, these days we can also find many paid resources and training programs that offer expert advice and training, revolving around many different possible usages of a WordPress site.

Staying updated through WordPress news

As WordPress is always actively developed, it's important to keep yourself up-to-date with the software community about their latest activities.

If you visit the Dashboard of your own WordPress site regularly, you'll be able to stay up-to-date with WordPress news and software releases. There are widgets on the dashboard that display the latest news and announcements, and an alert always appears when there is a new version of WordPress available for download and installation.

If you prefer to visit the website, the most important spot to visit or subscribe to is WordPress releases. Whenever there is a new release—be it a major release, an interim bug fix, or an upgrade—it will be present under the following link: `http://wordpress.org/news/category/releases/`.

Also, be sure to stay tuned to the main WordPress blog at `http://wordpress.org/news/`.

Some additional resources worth mentioning are:

- `http://wordpress.org/`: This is the absolute main hub for WordPress
- `https://wordpress.com/`: This is the main platform for free WordPress blogging
- `http://jobs.wordpress.net/`: This provides job listings for anyone searching for employment in various areas related to WordPress (or anyone searching for WordPress help)
- `http://wordpress.tv/`: This is a great source for top-notch WordPress tutorials, how-to advice, case studies, product demonstrations, and WordPress-related conference presentation recordings
- `http://central.wordcamp.org/`: **WordCamp** is a conference that focuses on WordPress and it takes place a number of times during the year in different locations around the world; this site is the central for the conference

Understanding the Codex

The WordPress **Codex** is the central repository of all the information the official WordPress team has published to help people work with WordPress.

The Codex has some basic tutorials for getting started with WordPress, such as a detailed step-by-step discussion of installation, lists of every template tag and hook, and a lot more. Throughout this book, I'll be providing links to specific pages within the Codex, which will provide more or advanced information on the topics in this book.

The Codex can be found at `http://codex.wordpress.org/Main_Page` (the following screenshot).

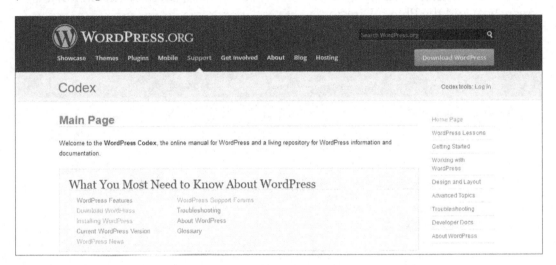

Getting support from other users

The online WordPress community asks questions and responds with solutions on the WordPress forum: `http://wordpress.org/support/`. That's an excellent place to go if you can't find the answer to a problem in the codex. If you have the question, probably someone else has had it as well, and WordPress experts spend time in the forum answering questions and giving solutions. There's also an **IRC (Internet Relay Chat)** channel where you can get additional support.

Using theme and plugin directories

There are official directories for themes and for plugins on WordPress.org. Although not every theme and plugin is available here, the ones that are here have been vetted by the community to some extent. Anything you download from these directories is likely to be relatively bug-free. Plugins and themes that you get from other sources can have malicious code, so be careful. You can also see what the community thinks of these downloads by looking at ratings, comments, and popularity.

Additionally, plugins in the **Plugin Directory** are automatically upgradable from within your WordPress Administration Panel, whereas other plugins have to be upgraded manually. We'll cover this in more detail in a later chapter. You can find the **Theme Directory** at `http://wordpress.org/extend/themes/` (the following screenshot) and the Plugin Directory at `http://wordpress.org/extend/plugins/`.

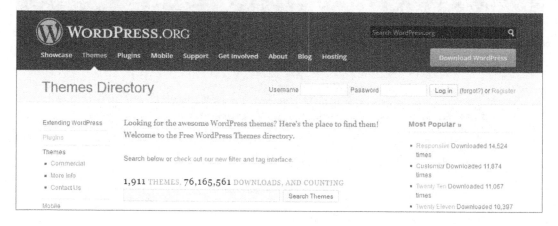

Summary

Having a website of your own is essential these days, whether you are an individual, a small business, or some other group. This is true whether you are blogging regularly, or just want some accurate static content up on the Internet. In this chapter, we reviewed basic information about blogging and common blog terms for those of you who are new to the concept.

WordPress is an excellent software application that can run your website (blog or not). It's packed with excellent features and is so flexible that it can really do anything you want, and it has a wealth of online resources. Additionally, it's super easy-to-use, and you need no special skills or prior experience to use it. Last, but not least, it is free!

In the next chapter, we will explore the choices and steps involved in installing WordPress and getting started.

2
Getting Started

This chapter will guide you through the process of setting up WordPress and customizing its basic features. You can choose between a couple of options regarding where your WordPress installation will be located. Keep in mind that WordPress is relatively small (under 10 MB), easy to install, and easy to administer.

WordPress is available in easily downloadable formats from its website, `http://wordpress.org/download/`. WordPress is a free, open source application, and is released under GNU **General Public License (GPL)**. This means that anyone who produces a modified version of the software released under the GPL is required to keep those same freedoms, that people buying or using the software may also modify and redistribute, attached to his or her modified version. This way, WordPress and other software released under GPL are kept open source. In this chapter, you will learn how to:

- Create a free blog on WordPress.com
- Install WordPress manually on your web host
- Perform basic setup tasks in the WordPress Admin panel (WP Admin)
- Publish your first content

Building your WordPress website – start here

The first decision you have to make is where your blog is going to live. You have two basic options for the location where you will create your site. You can

- Do it at `http://wordpress.com`
- Install on a server (hosted or your own)

Let's look at some of the advantages and disadvantages of each of these two choices.

The advantage of using WordPress.com is that they take care of all of the technical details for you. The software is already installed; they'll upgrade it for you whenever there's an upgrade, and you're not responsible for anything else. Just manage your content. The big disadvantage is that you lose almost all of the theme and plugin control you'd have otherwise. WordPress.com will not let you upload or edit your own theme, though it will let you (for a fee) edit the CSS of any theme you use. WordPress.com will not let you upload or manage plugins at all. Some plugins are installed by default (most notably Akismet, for spam blocking, and also plugins supporting Google sitemaps, caching, Carousel slideshows, and some social media buttons), but you can neither uninstall them nor install others. Additional features are available for a fee as well. Furthermore, you can sign up for WordPress.com Enterprise and get access to a range of optional plugins. The current list features more than 60 plugins (WordPress.com Enterprise is Available at http://en.wordpress.com/enterprise/). This chapter will cover creating a blog on WordPress.com, and you can learn about navigating around the WP admin in the next chapter. However, much of what this book covers will be impossible on WordPress.com.

The huge advantage of installing WordPress on another server (which means either a server that belongs to the web host with which you signed up, or a server you set up on your own computer) is that you have control over everything. You can add and edit themes, add and remove plugins, and even edit the WordPress application files yourself if you want (however, don't do that unless you're confident about your WordPress skills). You'll have to keep your own WordPress software up-to-date, but that's relatively simple, and we'll cover it in this chapter. The only disadvantage is that you have to do the installation and maintenance yourself, which, as you'll see, shouldn't be too intimidating. Moreover, some web hosts provide a one-click or easy-to-use installer, which lets you skip over some of the nitty-gritty steps involved in manual installation.

As I said, in this chapter, we'll discuss how to create a new blog on WordPress.com and how to start working with it on a daily basis. However, if you want to accomplish any of the more advanced topics from this book, you will have to install WordPress on your own server as opposed to using WordPress.com.

The following table is a brief overview of the essential differences between using WordPress.com versus installing WordPress on your own server.

	WordPress.com	Your own server
Installation	You don't have to install anything; just sign up	Install WordPress yourself, either manually or via your host's control panel (if offered)
Themes	Use any theme made available by WordPress.com	Use any theme available anywhere, written by anyone (including yourself)
Plugins	No ability to choose or add plugins	Use any plugin available anywhere, written by anyone (including yourself)
Upgrades	WordPress.com provides automatic upgrades	You have to upgrade it yourself when upgrades are available
Widgets	Widget availability depends on available themes	You can widgetize any theme yourself
Maintenance	You don't have to do any maintenance	You're responsible for the maintenance of your site
Advertising	No advertising allowed	Advertise anything and in any amount you like
Ownership	Even though the content belongs to you, WordPress.com can take down your blog at any moment if they consider it to be "inappropriate"	You have complete control over your site and no one can force you to take it down
Domain	Your site is available as a subdomain under .wordpress.com by default, but you can also upgrade to the Pro Bundle (for a fee) and use your own, manually registered domain	You can use any manually registered Internet domain

Using WordPress.com

WordPress.com (http://wordpress.com) is a free service provided by the WordPress developers, where you can register a blog or non-blog website easily and quickly with no hassle. However, because it is a hosted service, your control over some things will be more limited than it would be if you hosted your own WordPress website. As mentioned before, WordPress.com will not let you edit or upload your own themes or plugins. Apart from that, WordPress.com is a great place to maintain your personal site if you don't need to do anything fancy with your theme or the source code of your site in general. To get started, go to http://wordpress.com and click on the loud orange-and-white **Get Started** button. You will be taken to the signup page. In the following screenshot, I've entered my e-mail address (please triple-check when entering yours; it's where the confirmation e-mail will be sent), my username (this is what I'll sign in with), a password (note that the password measurement tool will tell you if your password is strong or weak; there's also a **Generate strong password** button available next to the field), and finally my blog address (WordPress.com also allows you to register a custom domain in place of the standard .wordpress.com subdomain):

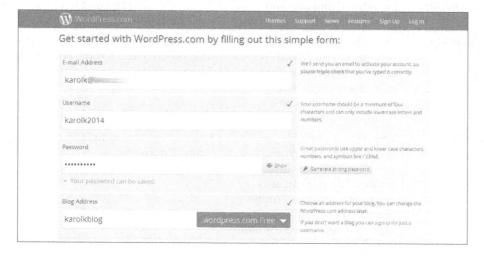

After providing all the required information and clicking on the **Create Blog** button, WordPress will try to sell you on one of their premium packages (**WordPress.com Premium** and **WordPress.com Business**). Some of the additional functionalities inside the premium packages include a free .com, .net, .org, or .me domain, advanced customization capabilities, access to a range of premium themes, the possibility to store videos directly on your WordPress.com account, additional disk space (the free account offers 3 GB), and direct e-mail support or live chat support.

For now, we're going to stick with the basic, free account. So just click the **Choose Basic** button and you'll be redirected to the final confirmation page that instructs you to visit your inbox and search for the activation e-mail that's just been sent. The e-mail itself is very clear and only requires you to click the big **Activate Blog** button. If you can't see the images, then you might need to check your e-mail software's settings. After clicking the big button, you're back at WordPress.com for some final setting up. The platform asks for things such as **Blog Title**, **Tagline** (optional), and **Language**.

When you're done with that and press the **Next Step** button, you'll be redirected to the theme selection panel. There are some free and paid themes available there. Additionally, after clicking on a specific theme you have some limited possibilities to customize it. Nothing too fancy, though. For more in-depth fine tuning, one of the WordPress.com premium packages is required.

Clicking on yet another **Next Step** button will finally allow you to create your first post. WordPress.com is 100 percent ready to welcome any standard type of content, including text, videos, photos, quotes (very popular these days), and links. If you don't want to do this right now, you can just click on the **Finish** button.

Publishing your first content on a WordPress.com blog

All you have to do in order to publish some content on your WordPress.com blog is click on the **New Post** link in the top menu:

When you do so, you're going to be presented with a prompt asking you what kind of content you'd like to publish. The current possibilities include:

- **Text post**
- **Photo**
- **Video**
- **Quote**
- **Link**

WordPress.com has some pre-formatted layouts prepared for each of these types, so it's always good to select the one that is the most accurate. For instance, for a standard text post, WordPress.com will ask you for a title (optional; posts on WordPress.com can be published without a title), the body of your post, and the tags (optional as well), and you'll also be able to add a photo to accompany your publication.

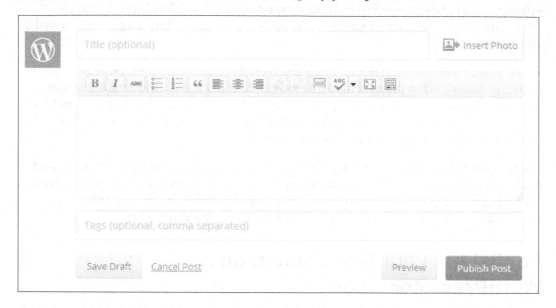

Once you're done editing your post, you can either save it as a draft (for further modifications), preview what it's going to look like on the blog, or publish it straight away with the **Publish Post** button.

Essentially, a WordPress.com blog can be managed just like any other WordPress site (content-wise), so you do get access to a Dashboard (explained later within this chapter), where you can edit and publish your content, too. The interface described above is a specially designed panel that can't be found on any other type of blog. In other words, you won't get it with a regular WordPress site (a standalone site on your own domain and hosting). Therefore, if WordPress.com is your preferred way of launching a blog, you can probably skip the next section of this chapter, which is exactly all about installing WordPress manually as a standalone site.

Installing WordPress manually

The WordPress application files can be downloaded for free if you want to do a manual installation. If you've got a website host, this process is extremely easy and requires no previous programming skills or advanced blog user experience.

Some web hosts offer automatic installation through the host's online control panel. One of these automatic installation methods is described later within this chapter.

Preparing the environment

A good first step is to make sure you have an environment setup that is ready for WordPress. This means two things: making sure that you verify that the server meets the minimum requirements, and making sure that your database is ready.

For WordPress to work, your web host must provide you with a server that does the following two things:

- Support PHP, which has to be Version 5.2.4 or greater
- Provide you with a MySQL database (full access); MySQL has to be Version 5.0 or greater

Additionally, these minimum requirements tend to change every once in a while. The most current requirements can always be found at http://wordpress.org/ about/requirements/.

You can find out if your host meets these two requirements by contacting your web host. If your web server meets these two basic requirements, you're ready to move on to the next step.

As far as web servers go, Apache is the best. However, WordPress will also run on a server running the Microsoft **IIS (Internet Information Services)** server (though using **permalinks** will be difficult, if possible at all).

Enabling mod_rewrite to use pretty permalinks

If you want to use permalinks, your server must be running Unix, and Apache's mod_rewrite option must be enabled. Apache's mod_rewrite is enabled by default in most web hosting accounts. If you are hosting your own account, you can enable mod_rewrite by modifying the Apache web server configuration file. You can check the URL, http://www.tutorio.com/tutorial/enable-mod-rewrite-on-apache, to learn how to enable mod_rewrite on your web server. If you are running on shared hosting, ask your system administrator to install it for you. However, it is more likely that you already have it installed on your hosting account.

Downloading WordPress

Once you have checked out your environment, you need to download WordPress from `http://wordpress.org/download/`. On that page, the `.zip` file is shown as a big blue button because that'll be the most useful format for the most people. If you are using Windows, Mac, or Linux operating systems, your computer will be able to unzip that downloaded file automatically. (The `.tar.gz` file is provided because some Unix users prefer it.)

A further note on location

We're going to cover installing WordPress remotely. However, if you plan to develop themes or plugins, I suggest that you also install WordPress locally on your own computer's server. Testing and deploying themes and plugins directly to the remote server will be much more time-consuming than working locally. If you look at the screenshots of my own WordPress installation throughout the book, you'll notice that I'm working locally.

After you download the WordPress `.zip` file, extract the files, and you'll get a folder called `wordpress`.

Upgrading from an earlier version of WordPress

If you are upgrading an existing installation of WordPress, you should probably leave this chapter and instead read the section on *Upgrading WordPress* in *Chapter 12, Creating a Non-blog Website Part Two – Community Websites and Custom Content Elements*.

Uploading the files

Now, we need to upload all these files to our web server using any FTP client (or simply put them in our local server directory on our local computer). FTP stands for File Transfer Protocol. There are several FTP clients available on the Internet, which are either freeware (no cost) or shareware (a small fee). If you don't already have an FTP client, try one of these:

- **Filezilla**: `http://filezilla-project.org/download.php?type=client` (for Mac or Windows)
- **Fetch**: `http://fetchsoftworks.com/` (for Mac only)
- **SmartFTP**: `http://www.smartftp.com/` (for Windows only)

You can also use the popular web-based FTP application net2ftp at
`http://www.net2ftp.com`. These services are useful if you don't want
to install a desktop application on your computer. You can also check if
your host provides browser-based FTP software.

A note about security

Whenever possible, you should use Secure FTP (called sFTP) rather
than regular FTP. If you're using sFTP, all of the data sent and
received are encrypted, whereas with FTP data are sent in plain text
and can be easily nabbed by hackers. Check both your FTP software
and your hosting options, and select sFTP if it's available.

Using your FTP client or service, connect to your FTP server using the server
address, username, and password provided to you by your host. Next, open the
folder where you want WordPress to live. You may want to install WordPress in
your root folder, which will mean that visitors will see your WordPress website's
home page when they go to your main URL – for example, `http://yoursite.`
`com`. Alternatively, you may want to install WordPress in a subfolder; for example,
`http://yoursite.com/blog/`.

On the left side, you will see the files from your local folder, and on the right side
you will see your remote folder. (Note: the FTP client you are using may have a
slightly different layout, but this is the general idea.)

Now select all of the WordPress files on your local machine from the left pane,
and drag all of them to the right pane. You can watch as your FTP client uploads
the files one at a time and they appear in the right panel. This could take a few
minutes, so be patient!

If you're installing WordPress on your local server, just be sure to place the
WordPress files in the correct `webroot` directory on your computer.

Once all of the files are done uploading, you're ready to do the installation.

Installing WordPress

Now it's time to install WordPress through the famous five-minute installation (the
fact that WordPress can be installed in five minutes or less is widely advertised on
the official WordPress website). If you access your WordPress URL via your browser,
you will see a short introduction message instructing you to create a file named `wp-`
`config.php` by clicking on the button labeled **Create a Configuration File**. After
doing so, you will be presented with another screen, informing you about all the
required details you'll need in order to complete the installation successfully.

Currently, these required details consist of the following:

- **Database name**: for example, `wptestblog`
- **Database username**: for example, `localdbuser`
- **Database password**: for example, `62dcx%^_0hnm`—the more complex the better, as usual with passwords
- **Database host**: for example, `1.1.1.1` – most of the time, you will be required to provide an IP address of your database host (if needed, you can take a look at this handy cheat sheet for an in-depth explanation of all the possibilities: `http://codex.wordpress.org/Editing_wp-config.php#Possible_DB_HOST_values`); in case of servers running locally on your own machine, the database host is most likely `localhost`

The big question, therefore, is where to get all this information from. Simple answer—your web host. Most of the large web hosts offer a way to create your own databases via an online control panel, with usernames and passwords of your choice. If you're not sure how to do this, just e-mail or call your hosting provider for assistance. Professional support teams will be glad to help you with this.

Once you have those four things, you can press the **Let's go!** button and proceed to the next step of the installation. This is what the main setup form looks like:

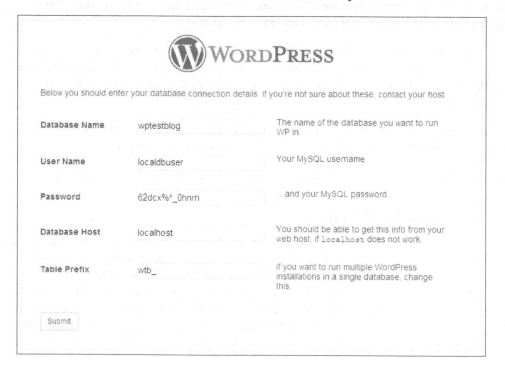

As you can see, I filled out mine with the details mentioned as an example a couple of paragraphs above. Of course, your details will be different. Also, one more thing worth pointing out: there's an additional field labeled **Table Prefix**. This is the default prefix that every table in your database will have before its name. The default value in that field is wp_. I advise you to change this to whatever two-letter or three-letter word you wish and end it with an underscore (_), just as a safety precaution against standard database attacks on known WordPress tables. The one I used is wtb_. One more additional reason for using a custom prefix is to enable you to take advantage of the WordPress multisite feature (if you plan to launch more than one site with a single WordPress installation, which is also possible). In such a case, you'll need to use different prefixes in your different installations.

After clicking on the **Submit** button, you will be redirected to the final confirmation page. All you have to do here is click on the **Run the install** button.

At this point, things can either go well, or not that well. In case of the latter, proceed to the next section, *Installing WordPress through a hand-built configuration file*. Luckily, such problems are rather rare. The best indication that the online installation is going well is the presence of the following screen:

This is the final setup page. Here, you get to set up the core details of your new site. (If you've ever installed an earlier version of WordPress, you'll notice some differences, such as the ability to choose your first username and password.) Now, fill out the installation form (you will be able to change all of these later, so don't be too worried about getting locked into your choices):

- **Site Title**: Fill in the name of your blog (it can be something simple, such as `Daily Cooking`, for example).

- **Username**: Note that the default username is `admin`, but for security purposes, you're better off picking something different. If someone ever tries to hack into your blog, he or she will be halfway there if he or she already know your username. Also worth pointing out is the fact that this account is the administrator account, which has the most privileges and access rights in all areas of the site.

- **Password**: Choose a secure password, one that has both the upper and lowercase letters, a number or two, and even a few punctuation marks.

- **Your E-mail**: Double-check that this is correct. This is the e-mail address WordPress will use to contact you about the blog, comments, and so on. If you do not get an e-mail from your WordPress site shortly after installing, check your spam folder.

- **Privacy**: This is the final checkbox, yet possibly one of the most important settings on this list. If you leave it checked (recommended), your site is going to be accessible through Google and other search engines. Unchecking it means banning your site from the search engines.

Now, click on **Install WordPress**. You're done with the installation.

You can click on **Log In** to get to the login page. Or you can always enter your WordPress Admin panel (also known as the WP Admin) by pointing your browser to `http://yoursite.com/wp-admin`. If you're not already logged in, this URL will redirect you to the login page.

Installing WordPress through a hand-built configuration file

Now, in some cases your web hosting account will prevent WordPress from creating a valid configuration file. It can be an issue caused by access rights limitations, for example. However, it's not a big obstacle because you can always create a configuration file by hand. To do this, just open the `wordpress` folder and find the file named `wp-config-sample.php`. Make a copy of this file and name it `wp-config.php`.

We'll modify this file together. Don't worry; you need not be a PHP programmer. Just open this file with a simple editor such as Notepad. The following is the copied text from the original `wp-config.php` file. Note that I've removed most of the comments, so that we can focus on the items we need to change.

```php
<?php
/** The name of the database for WordPress */
define('DB_NAME', 'database_name_here');

/** MySQL database username */
define('DB_USER', 'username_here');

/** MySQL database password */
define('DB_PASSWORD', 'password_here');

/** MySQL hostname */
define('DB_HOST', 'localhost');

/** Database Charset to use in creating database tables. */
define('DB_CHARSET', 'utf8');

/** The Database Collate type. Don't change this if in doubt. */
define('DB_COLLATE', '');

define('AUTH_KEY',         'put your unique phrase here');
define('SECURE_AUTH_KEY',  'put your unique phrase here');
define('LOGGED_IN_KEY',    'put your unique phrase here');
define('NONCE_KEY',        'put your unique phrase here');
define('AUTH_SALT',        'put your unique phrase here');
define('SECURE_AUTH_SALT', 'put your unique phrase here');
define('LOGGED_IN_SALT',   'put your unique phrase here');
define('NONCE_SALT',       'put your unique phrase here');

$table_prefix = 'wp_';
?>
```

Downloading the example code

You can download the example code files for all Packt books you have purchased from your account at http://www.packtpub.com. If you purchased this book elsewhere, you can visit http://www.packtpub.com/support and register to have the files e-mailed directly to you.

One thing to know about PHP is that any text that comes after a double slash (//), or between a slash-star and star-slash (/*   */), is a comment. It's not actual PHP code. Its purpose is to inform you what that line or that section is about. As you can see from the previous code, there are a number of settings that you can insert here, but they do resemble the ones we were filling out in the online installer just a minute ago. Let's walk through the most important ones.

Just as with the online installer, I took my database information, but this time I put it in the `wp-config.php` file:

```
// ** MySQL settings ** //
define('DB_NAME', 'wptestblog');
define('DB_USER', 'localdbuser');
define('DB_PASSWORD', '62dcx%^_0hnm');
define('DB_HOST', 'localhost');
```

Next, for security purposes, you really should put some unique phrases into the unique keys. The secret keys are used by WordPress to add random elements to your passwords and are also used in some other situations. This will help to keep your WordPress installation uniquely protected. No one else is likely to choose the same unique keys that you chose, and therefore, breaking or hacking into your site will be more difficult. You can get some secret keys generated by going to `https://api.wordpress.org/secret-key/1.1/salt/`. Once I did that, I got the following, which I can paste directly over the default code in `wp-config.php`:

```
define('AUTH_KEY', 'uu|6#00Pc/3h?Pg5:Zc#:S=;<3mdw-ai');
define('SECURE_AUTH_KEY', 'vy1.@Nr@Zb^G|0Vfz-|TH5&W');
define('LOGGED_IN_KEY', 'sryMVd'jVpiMWWQqx~!v XE5@fJMTt2[Z');
define('NONCE_KEY', 'i,+UPpMR>Mj3o}(B**^<T:/md,YFF76d]Kf');
define('AUTH_SALT', 'n.8Li=9OjV+_p|}e5yN2k<s{!KJs|[S&Zh');
define('SECURE_AUTH_SALT', 'I#2vPT^u[5vLX|'MzPg/J*y]RTfr');
define('LOGGED_IN_SALT', 'gR%QP^c*jfFUy,iQ}-0g_%;%H)pN0B5');
define('NONCE_SALT', '&L);.IH'v{]zYLO2:h_t#J0D-p)cvyc');
```

 Don't ever get the salt keys from anywhere else than `https://api.wordpress.org/secret-key/1.1/salt/`. This is an important security mechanism that protects your browser's session from being hijacked and then used for unauthorized access to your WordPress site.

Finally, we have the aforementioned table prefix. The `wp-config.php` file allows us to set this too. Again, here's my prefix of choice:

```
$table_prefix  = 'wtb_';
```

The WordPress codex has a long and detailed page that describes everything about editing your `wp-config.php` file: `http://codex.wordpress.org/Editing_wp-config.php`. Once you save the `wp-config.php` file and either upload it to your web host or put it on your local server, you can visit your site through your domain name (like `http://yoursite.com/`). You should be presented with the final setup page, the one visible in the preceding screenshot. All you have to do now is proceed according to the instruction described earlier in this chapter.

Learning more

If you'd like to see an even more detailed step-by-step guide for manual installation, take a look at this page in the WordPress Codex: `http://codex.wordpress.org/Installing_WordPress`.

Also, you can find more detailed installation instructions—as well as specifics on changing file permissions, using FTP, using languages, importing from other blogging engines, and more—in the WordPress Codex at the following link: `http://codex.wordpress.org/Getting_Started_with_WordPress#Installation`.

Installing WordPress through an autoinstaller script

Some web hosts provide their customers with access to a range of autoinstaller scripts for various web platforms, including WordPress. Most of these autoinstallers have quite similar functionalities and the actual process of installing a new WordPress site is similar as well. Here, we're going to focus on one of these scripts—**Softaculous**.

> This is yet another way of installing a WordPress site, and we're covering it here to make this book as complete as it can be; however, if you've already managed to install your site through the methods described earlier, this section won't be of any use to you at this point.

Softaculous is the preferred method of WordPress installation for many professional developers and bloggers. In some cases, it's the fastest method when dealing with a completely new hosting account maintained by a new web host. Softaculous is provided on hosting accounts running on many management platforms, such as cPanel, Plesk, DirectAdmin, InterWorx, and H-Sphere. Most likely, your hosting account (a commercial hosting account you've bought from a respected provider) is certain to be using one of these platform.

Here's an example of what cPanel—one of the platforms—looks like:

Although various platforms have different user interfaces, the core functionalities from a user's point of view remain mostly the same. To access Softaculous, just scroll down until you see the main icon labeled **Softaculous**. After clicking on it, you're going to be redirected to the control panel of Softaculous, where right in the center you can see the WordPress icon along with an **Install** button that becomes visible when you hover your mouse over the icon.

The whole idea of using this script is to make things quicker and more hassle-free; therefore, you don't have to take care of creating databases manually, setting configuration files, or anything else. Softaculous will handle all of this for you. The following is the site creation form:

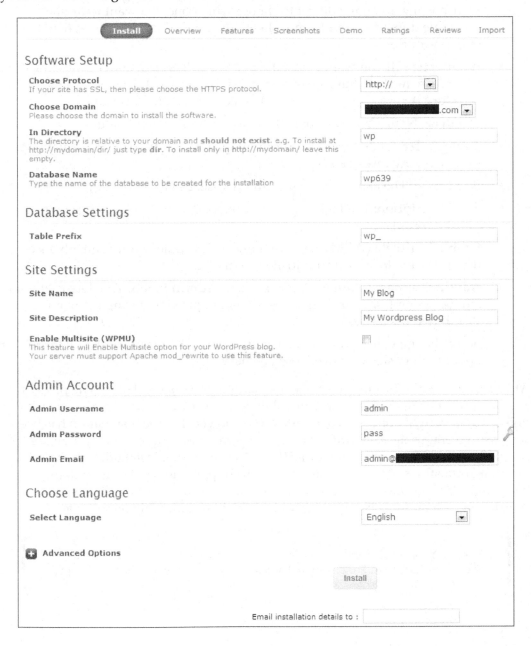

Here's a breakdown of all the fields and what details to fill them out with:

- **Choose Protocol**: You can stick with the default value of `http://`
- **Choose Domain**: If you have more than one domain assigned with your hosting account, you get to choose which one you want to use here; for single domain accounts (most likely the case), this drop-down field has only one option
- **In Directory**: If you want to install your WordPress site under a subdirectory, input its name here (just the name); if you want to install the site in the main directory (`http://yoursite.com/`), make sure the field is blank
- **Database Name**: You can confidently go with the default value
- **Table Prefix**: As discussed earlier in this chapter, change this to something unique (in my case, it's `wtb_`)
- **Site Name**: The name of your site (in my case, `Daily Cooking`)
- **Site Description**: The tagline (in my case, `Exploring cooking every day of the week`)
- **Enable Multisite (WPMU)**: Leave it unchecked unless you're an advanced user planning to launch a multisite installation
- **Admin Username**, **Admin Password**, and **Admin Email**: The details of your admin account, similar to the ones we had to provide during the manual WordPress installation
- **Select Language**: WordPress has many localized versions of the platform, not only English; you can choose one here

After clicking on the **Install** button the installation process will begin. The process itself requires no supervision and you will be able to access your site as soon as it finishes after roughly one or two minutes. You can check if the installation has been successful through the standard `http://yoursite.com/` and `http://yoursite.com/wp-admin/` URLs. In other words, this is the end of the installation process through Softaculous. As you can see, it's much simpler and quicker than doing it manually. Furthermore, Softaculous always installs the most recent version of WordPress, so you don't have to worry about getting something out of date.

 You can also encounter other auto-installer scripts, very similar to Softaculous. For example, Fantastico, Installatron, and SimpleScripts.

The WP Admin panel

WordPress installs a powerful and flexible administration area where you can manage all of your website content, and do much more. Throughout the book, I'll be referring to this in shorthand as the **WP Admin**.

Now that you've successfully installed WordPress, it's time for our first look at the WP Admin. There are some immediate basic changes that I recommend doing right away to make sure your installation is set up properly.

You can always get to the WP Admin by going to the following URL: `http://yoursite.com/wp-admin/`. If it's your first time here, you'll be redirected to the login page. In the future, WordPress will check to see if you're already logged in and, if so, you'll skip the login page.

To log in, just enter the username and password you chose during the installation. Then click on **Log In**. Note for the future that on this page there is a link you can use to retrieve your lost password.

Whenever you log in, you'll be taken directly to the **Dashboard** page of the WP Admin. Following is a screenshot of the WP Admin that you will see immediately after you log into the blog you just installed:

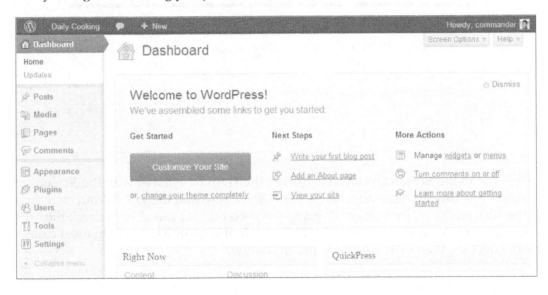

You'll see a lot of information and options here, which we will explore throughout this book. For now, we will focus on the items that we need to touch upon right after a successful installation. First, let's take a brief look at the top of the WP Admin and the **Dashboard** page.

The very top bar, which I'll refer to as the **top bar**, is mostly dark grey and contains

- A rollover drop-down menu featuring a set of links to **About WordPress** (some details about the current installation of WordPress), **WordPress.org**, **Documentation**, **Support Forums**, and **Feedback**

- A link to the front page of your WordPress website (in this example, the title of the whole site is **Daily Cooking**)

- Updates and activity section containing either links to the newest comments or to pending updates

- A rollover drop-down menu with handy links to **New Post**, **New Media**, **New Page**, and **New User**

- Your username linked to your profile, which is yet another drop-down menu containing a link labeled **Edit My Profile** and another one—the **Log Out** link

You'll also notice the **Screen Options** tab, which appears on many screens within the WP Admin. If you click on it, it will slide down a checklist of items on the page to show or hide. It will be different on each page. I encourage you to play around with that by checking and unchecking items, as you find whether you need them or not.

Right next to the **Screen Options** tab, there's the **Help** tab. Just as with the **Screen Options** tab, this one also appears on many screens within the WP Admin. Whenever you're in doubt regarding a specific screen, you can always check the **Help** tab for instruction. Going to the **Help** tab is always quicker, and in most cases more effective, than searching for solutions online.

On the left side of the screen is the main menu:

You can click on any word in the main menu to be taken to the main page for that section, or you can hover your cursor over a given link to see all the possible subsections you can visit. For example, if you hover your cursor over **Settings**, you'll see the subpages for the **Settings** section:

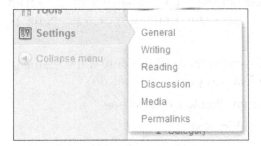

In this book, when describing to you which page within the WP Admin to go to, I'll write things such as "navigate to **Settings | General**" or "navigate to **Posts | Add New**". This always describes the path you should take to get there via the main menu.

The top menu and the main menu exist on every page within the WP Admin. The main section on the right contains information for the current page you're on. In this case, we're on **Dashboard**. It contains boxes that have a variety of information about your blog, and about WordPress in general.

Before WordPress 3, the first thing you'd have to do would be to change the password to something easier to remember. However, now that you can choose your password during installation, this is no longer necessary. Also, in the new versions of WordPress, when you log in for the first time, you're going to be presented with a welcome message, similar to this one:

In short, it's a welcome panel that allows you to access some of the crucial sections of the WP Admin with just one click. Once you click on the **Dismiss** link, the panel will no longer be displayed after login. In its current version, the panel allows you to do things such as

- Customize the current theme — but only if the theme provides some customization features (not all themes do)
- Change the current theme to a new one
- Write your first blog post
- Add an About page — usually, it's the most visited page on WordPress sites
- View your site
- Manage menus and widgets
- Turn comments on or off — by default they are on
- Learn more about how to get started with WordPress — which is an external link pointing to `http://codex.wordpress.org/First_Steps_With_WordPress`

For now, we're not going to focus on this welcome panel because first we need to understand what all of the above means in order to use it effectively. In this and the following chapters, we will get to know all the crucial methods of managing a WordPress site, and once we gain some experience, with time, this welcome panel can make our everyday work much quicker. Therefore, let's jump right into the general site settings section.

Changing general blog information

You may need to change and add some general blog information (such as blog title, one-sentence description, and so on) after a successful installation to get your website set up with the correct information. To get started with this, navigate to **Settings** in the main menu.

There are many options you can set here, most of which are pretty self-explanatory. We'll look at the most important ones, and you can explore the rest on your own. Obviously, you can change your blog's title; mine is called **Daily Cooking**, for example. You can also change the blog description, which is used in most themes as a subtitle for the blog, such as the subtitle of a book. The default description is **Just another WordPress site**. You'll probably want to change that. I'll change mine to "Exploring cooking every day of the week".

One of the few things you probably want to take a look at on this page is **Timezone**. Whether you have a blog (with timestamps on every post) or not, it's important that WordPress knows what time zone you're in, in case you want to schedule a page or post for the future, show users accurate timestamps, or even just make sure that e-mail notifications are correctly timestamped. Additionally, if you're planning to publish content internationally, meaning that your target audience is located in a completely different place than you, it's good to set the time zone to represent your target audience and not yourself.

The pulldown menu will show you different UTC settings, along with the biggest cities around the world. Just choose a city in your time zone. After you save the changes you made, the time that shows further down the page (next to **Time Format**) will change to the time you chose, so that you can check and make sure it's correct.

Another thing worth considering on this page is whether or not you want to allow user registration on your site. For most sites, this is not particularly useful, but if you're planning to make the site community-driven or utilize some form of crowdsourcing, this might be something worth considering. In this case, it's not advisable to give new users a user role higher than `Subscriber` (the default value).

When you're done making changes to this page, be sure to click on the **Save Changes** button at the bottom of the page.

Finally, there's only one more thing you should adjust in your new site's settings before publishing any content—the permalinks. As WordPress defines them, permalinks are the permanent URLs to your individual pages, blog posts, categories, and tags. By default, WordPress links to your new posts using a highly un-optimized URL structure. For instance, if you create a post titled "How to Cook the Best Meal Ever", WordPress will link to it as `http://yoursite.com/?p=123` (or something similar). The main problem with that structure is that it doesn't give any indication what such a page can possibly be about. Neither your visitors nor Google will be able to make a guess. In the case of Google, such a structure can also impact your future search engine rankings significantly. Therefore, to set a more optimized structure, you can go to **Settings | Permalinks**. Here are the available settings:

```
Common Settings

  ◉ Default                http://localhost/?p=123

  ○ Day and name           http://localhost/2013/03/20/sample-post/

  ○ Month and name         http://localhost/2013/03/sample-post/

  ○ Numeric                http://localhost/archives/123

  ○ Post name              http://localhost/sample-post/

  ○ Custom Structure       http://localhost
```

The best setting from a visitor's point of view, as well as from Google's, is the one labeled **Post name**. Going back to the example with the "How to Cook the Best Meal Ever" post, if you set the permalinks to **Post name**, the URL of this post will be `http://yoursite.com/how-to-cook-the-best-meal/`, which is a lot more clear and predictable.

You can always review the official info on permalinks anytime at `http://codex.wordpress.org/Using_Permalinks`. Further down the page, there are also the **Optional** settings for **Category base** and **Tag base**. By default, the category base is set to `category`. For example, if you have a category called "recipes," you can view all posts under this category by going to `http://yoursite.com/category/recipes`. Some site owners prefer to change this to something more user friendly, for example, the word `topics`. Even though it conveys the exact same message, it can be much easier to grasp for visitors who are not that familiar with the standards of content publishing on the web. In the end, it's your decision what you want your **Category base** to be. When it comes to **Tag base**, it rarely needs any adjustments.

Creating your first post

For this chapter, and the next few chapters, we'll be focusing on using WordPress to run a blog website. In a later chapter, we'll talk more specifically about using WordPress for a non-blog website.

So, with that in mind, let's add the first piece of content to your new blog—a blog post. (This won't be the very first post on the blog itself, because WordPress created a post, a comment, and a page for you when it installed. It will be your first post, however). To create a post, just click on **New Post** on the top menu. You'll be taken to the following page:

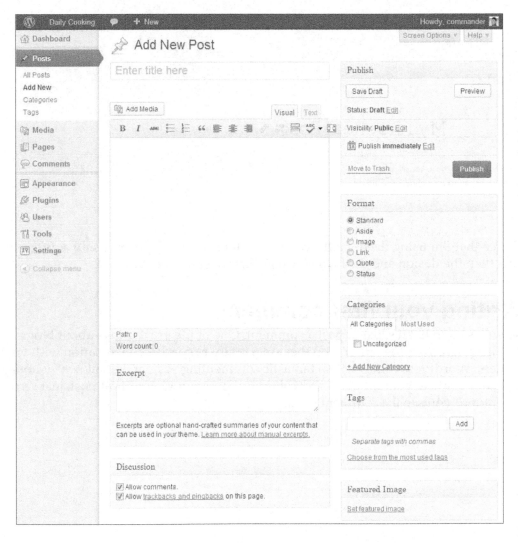

As you can see, there are a lot of options for your post (which we'll explore in more detail in *Chapter 3, Creating Blog Content*). For now, just worry about the basics. Every post should have, at minimum, a title and some content. So go ahead and write in some text for those two things. When you are happy with it, click on the **Publish** button.

You'll get a yellow note telling you that the post is published. Take a look at the front page of your site by clicking on the name of your site in the top bar. You'll see the following:

Notice that I'm using the default **Twenty Thirteen** theme. If you're using a different one, then the design and the layout of your first post will be different.

Writing your first comment

Now lets see what it's like to post a comment. One of the great things about blogs is that they give you, the writer, and the opportunity to spark a conversation with your readers. WordPress comes with a fantastic commenting system that allows visitors to add comments to your blog. To add your own comment to your first post, just scroll down until you see the comment form.

As you're already logged in, all you have to do is write something in the text area and click on **Post Comment**. The comment form you'll see is pretty basic and doesn't leave much place for error (the following screenshot):

Your visitors, however, those who are not logged into the WP Admin, will see a slightly different one (the following screenshot):

Later, we'll explore how you can control which comments show up right away and which comments have to wait for you to verify them as valid, as well as which fields are required for visitors.

Retrieving a lost password

If you have lost your password and can't get into your WP Admin panel, you can easily retrieve it by clicking on the **Lost your password?** link on the login page. A newly generated password will be e-mailed to you at the e-mail address you gave during the WordPress installation. This is why you need to be sure that you enter a valid e-mail address. Otherwise, you will not be able to retrieve your password.

Getting a Gravatar

One final thing that's worth discussing in this chapter is the matter of WordPress avatars. Although WordPress provides a number of possibilities in this area, the most popular one revolves around an external service — **Gravatar**. Gravatar started as a tool meant to provide people with the possibility to use the same profile picture (avatar) across the whole web. The name Gravatar actually stands for **Globally Recognized Avatar**.

What this means in plain English is that whenever you sign up with a web service, and if the service is Gravatar-compatible, so to speak, then it will pick your profile picture from Gravatar automatically, instead of forcing you to upload it manually from your computer. Apart from the profile picture, Gravatar also gives you a personal, online profile that anyone can see whenever he or she click on your (Gravatar) profile picture. Now, what does this all have to do with WordPress, right? Well, WordPress is one of those services and tools that widely support Gravatar in all possible areas of the platform. For example, if you create a new blog and use an admin e-mail address that's hooked to Gravatar, your profile picture in WordPress will immediately be replaced with the one provided by Gravatar. Moreover, if you ever comment on any WordPress blog with a Gravatar e-mail address, your profile picture will be set as the avatar for the comment itself.

To set your own Gravatar, just go to `http://gravatar.com/` and click on the **Sign in** button in the right corner of the screen. You'll be presented with a login form and a small signup link labeled **Need an account?** If you already have a WordPress. com account then you can safely log in with it. If not, click on the aforementioned **Need an account?** link, which will redirect you to the signup page. The fields are quite standard and include things like an e-mail address, your preferred username and password. Once you've completed the signup process, you can finally set your Gravatar. On the main **Manage Gravatars** page, there's a link labeled **Add one by clicking here!** — this is where you can upload a Gravatar.

The good thing about Gravatar is that you can choose where you want to get the picture from. You can either upload it from your computer, get it from some other place on the web (for example, from a direct link to your Facebook profile image), or use an image that you've uploaded to Gravatar previously. In the next step, Gravatar allows you to crop and adjust your image. When you're finally happy with the result, you can click the big button and proceed to the rating settings of your image. Every Gravatar can be classified as either **G rated**, **PG rated**, **R rated**, or **X rated**. The fact is that if you select anything other than G rated, your Gravatar won't be displayed on all sites; that's why it's a good practice to upload only appropriate images.

Once you're done with this step, your Gravatar is set up and ready to use. Gravatar also enables you to hook up more than one e-mail address to a single account, as well as use more than one image. This is actually a great feature because you can manage your every e-mail address and every kind of online presence you have with just one Gravatar account, a true timesaver. Now you can go back to your WordPress blog and see if your new Gravatar has appeared in the profile section within WP Admin (provided that you've used the same e-mail address for the account).

Summary

You have learned a lot of things from this chapter. Now you are able to install WordPress on a remote server, change the basic default settings of your blog, write posts, and comment on those posts.

You also have a basic understanding on how WordPress.com works, and how to handle your online image/brand by using Gravatar.

In the next chapter, we will learn about all the other aspects of a blog post that you can control and additional ways to add posts, as well as the intricacies of managing and controlling commenting and discussion on your blog.

3
Creating Blog Content

Now that your WordPress installation is up and running, you are ready to start creating content. In this chapter, you will first become familiar with the WP Admin's display and editing features and conventions. Then, you'll learn how to control all the information associated with a post, not just the title and content, but also images and media. You will also learn about comments—what they are for and how to manage them. Additionally, we will explore how to keep your content organized and searchable using tags and categories.

WP Admin conventions

In the WP Admin, you have the ability to manage a number of different types of content and content sorting types (objects), including posts, categories, pages, links, media uploads, and more. WordPress uses a similar format for various screens. Let's explore them in this section.

Lists of items

For every object in WordPress you might want to manage, there will be a page listing them. For example, let's have a look at what a list of posts might look like:

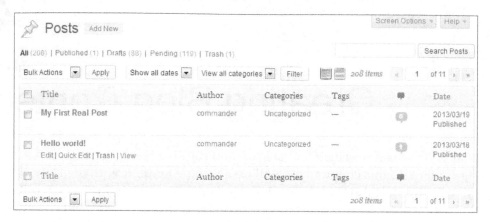

As you can see, the name of the object is at the top, and the list of items has columns. Let's take a look at the important elements:

- Each item in the list shows its **Title**. You can always click on an item title to edit it.

- If you hover your mouse over a specific row, as I hovered over Hello world! in the preceding screenshot, you will see four additional links. The first three links are always the same (**Edit**, **Quick Edit**, and **Trash**), while the fourth one varies between **View** and **Preview**, depending on whether we're dealing with an already published post or one that's pending. **Edit**, **Trash**, and **View/Preview** are pretty self-explanatory, but the **Quick Edit** link deserves an additional word. When you click on it, you will see a panel allowing you to perform some simplified editing (just the basic details and parameters, with no actual content editing).

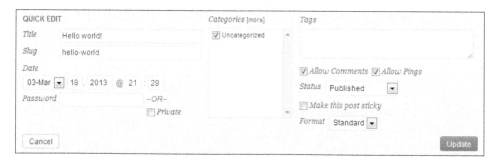

- You can make changes and then click on **Update**, or click on **Cancel** if you've changed your mind.

- The area above the list of posts lets you choose whether to view **All** (posts), **Published** (posts), **Drafts**, **Pending** (posts), or **Trash**.

- Just below those links is the **Bulk Actions** menu and its **Apply** button. Choose one or more posts by clicking on their checkboxes (or check the top checkbox to check every item). Then choose **Edit** or **Trash** from the **Bulk Actions** menu, and after clicking on **Apply**, you'll be able to bulk delete or bulk edit those posts. Additionally, further down the road, so to speak, when you install some third-party plugins, you'll notice that this **Bulk Actions** menu might contain more options on top of the standard two (editing and deleting).

- The filter menu lets you choose options from the **Dates** and **Categories** pull-down lists, and then click on the **Filter** button to only show items that meet those qualifications.

- The search field along with the **Search Posts** button provides yet another way of filtering through your posts to find the specific one you're looking for. This might not seem like a particularly useful feature at first, but once you have more than 200 posts published on the site, finding individual entries becomes quite a challenge.

- At the very top is the **Screen Options** dropdown. This tab, which appears on every screen, will allow you (on list pages like this one) to hide or show particular columns and choose the number of items to show per page.

Posting on your blog

The central activity you'll be doing with your blog is adding posts. A **post** is like an article in a magazine; it's got a title, content, and an author (in this case, you, though WordPress allows multiple authors to contribute to a blog). If a blog is like an online diary, every post is an entry in that diary. A blog post also has a lot of other information attached to it, such as a date, excerpt, tags, and categories. In this section, you will learn how to create a new post and what kind of information to attach to it.

Adding a simple post

Let's review the process of adding a simple post to your blog, which we carried out in the previous chapter. Whenever you want to add content or carry out a maintenance process on your WordPress website, you have to start by logging in to the WP Admin (WordPress Administration panel) of your site. To get to the admin panel, just point your web browser to `http://yoursite.com/wp-admin`.

Remember that if you have installed WordPress in a subfolder (for example, blog), your URL has to include the subfolder (that is, http://yoursite.com/blog/wp-admin).

When you first log in to the WP Admin, you'll be at the **Dashboard**. The **Dashboard** has a lot of information on it so don't worry about that right now. We'll discuss the **Dashboard** in detail later in the book.

The quickest way to get to the **Add New Post** page at any time is to click on **+ New** and then the **Post** link at the top of the page in the top bar.

This is the **Add New Post** page:

To add a new post to your site quickly, all you have to do is:

1. Type in a title into the text field under **Add New Post** (for example, Making Lasagne).

2. Type the text of your post in the content box. Note that the default view is **Visual**, but you actually have a choice of the **Text** view as well.

3. Click on the **Publish** button, which is at the far right. Note that you can choose to save a draft or preview your post as well.

Once you click on the **Publish** button, you have to wait while WordPress performs its magic. You'll see yourself still on the **Edit Post** screen, but now the following message would have appeared telling you that your post was published, and giving you a link **View post**:

If you view the front page of your site, you'll see that your new post has been added at the top (newest posts are always at the top).

Common post options

Now that we've reviewed the basics of adding a post, let's investigate some of the other options on the **Add New Post** and **Edit Post** pages. In this section we'll look at the most commonly used options, and in the next section we'll look at the more advanced options.

Categories and tags

Categories and tags are two types of information that you can add to a blog post. We use them to organize the information in your blog by topic and content (rather than just by, say, date), and to help visitors find what they are looking for on your blog.

Categories are primarily used for structural organizing. They can be hierarchical, meaning a category can be a parent of another category. A relatively busy blog will probably have at least 10 categories, but probably not more than 15 or 20. Each post in such a blog is likely to have from one up to, maybe four categories assigned to it.

For example, a blog about food and cooking might have these categories: **Cooking Adventures, In The Media, Ingredients, Opinion, Recipes Found, Recipes Invented**, and **Restaurants**. Of course, the numbers mentioned are just suggestions; you can create and assign as many categories as you like. The way you structure your categories is entirely up to you as well. There are no true rules regarding this in the WordPress world, just guidelines like these.

Tags are primarily used as shorthand for describing the topics covered in a particular blog post. A relatively busy blog will have anywhere from 15 to even 100 tags in use. Each post in this blog is likely to have 3 to 10 tags assigned to it. For example, a post on the food blog about a recipe for butternut squash soup may have these tags: **soup, vegetarian, autumn, hot**, and **easy**. Again, you can create and assign as many tags as you like.

Let's add a new post to the blog. After you give it a title and content, let's add tags and categories. While adding tags, just type your list of tags into the **Tags** box on the right, separated by commas:

Then click on the **Add** button. The tags you just typed in will appear below the text field with little **x** buttons next to them. You can click on an **x** button to delete a tag. Once you've used some tags in your blog, you'll be able to click on the **Choose from the most used tags** link in this box so that you can easily re-use tags.

Categories work a bit differently than tags. Once you get your blog going, you'll usually just check the boxes next to existing categories in the **Categories** box. In this case, as we don't have any existing categories, we'll have to add one or two.

In the **Categories** box on the right, click on the **+ Add New Category** link. Type your category into the text field, and click on the **Add New Category** button. Your new category will show up in the list, already checked. Look at the following screenshot:

If in the future you want to add a category that needs a parent category, select **— Parent Category —** from the pull-down menu before clicking on the **Add New Category** button. If you want to manage more details about your categories, move them around, rename them, assign parent categories, and assign descriptive text. You can do so on the **Categories** page, which we'll see in detail later in this chapter.

Click on the **Publish** button, and you're done (you can instead choose to schedule a post; we'll explore that in detail in a few pages). When you look at the front page of your site, you'll see your new post on the top, your new category in the sidebar, and the tags and category (that you chose for your post) listed under the post itself.

Images in your posts

Almost every good blog post needs an image! An image will give the reader an instant idea of what the post is about, and the image will draw people's attention as well. WordPress makes it easy to add an image to your post, control default image sizes, make minor edits to that image, and designate a featured image for your post.

Adding an image to a post

Luckily, WordPress makes adding images to your content very easy. Let's add an image to the post we just created. You can click on **Edit** underneath your post on the front page of your site to get there quickly. Alternatively, go back to the WP Admin, open **Posts** in the main menu, and then click on the post's title.

To add an image to a post, first you'll need to have that image on your computer, or know the exact URL pointing to the image if it's already online. Before you get ready to upload an image, make sure that your image is optimized for the Web. Huge files will be uploaded slowly and slow down the process of viewing your site. Just to give you a good example here, I'm using a photo of my own so I don't have to worry about any copyright issues (always make sure to use only the images that you have the right to use, copyright infringement online is a serious problem, to say the least). I know it's on the desktop of my computer. Once you have a picture on your computer and know where it is, carry out the following steps to add the photo to your blog post:

1. Click on the **Add Media** button, which is right above the content box and below the title box:

2. The box that appears allows you to do a number of different things regarding the media you want to include in your post. The most user-friendly feature here, however, is the drag-and-drop support. Just drag the image from your desktop and drop it into the center area of the page labeled as **Drop files anywhere to upload**.

3. Immediately after dropping the image, the uploader bar will show the progress of the operation, and when it's done, you'll be able to do some final tuning up.

4. The fields that are important right now are **Title**, **Alt Text**, **Alignment**, **Link To**, and **Size**. **Title** is a description for the image, **Alt Text** is a phrase that's going to appear instead of the image in case the file goes missing or any other problems present themselves, **Alignment** will tell the image whether to have text wrap around it and whether it should be right, left, or center, **Link To** instructs WordPress whether or not to link the image to anything (a common solution is to select **None**), and **Size** is the size of the image.

5. Once you have all of the above filled out click on **Insert into post**. This box will disappear, and your image will show up in the post—right where your cursor was prior to clicking on the **Add Media** button—on the edit page itself (in the visual editor, that is. If you're using the text editor, the HTML code of the image will be displayed instead).

6. Now, click on the **Update** button, and go and look at the front page of your site again. There's your image!

Controlling default image sizes

You may be wondering about those image sizes. What if you want bigger or smaller thumbnails? Whenever you upload an image, WordPress creates three versions of that image for you. You can set the pixel dimensions of those three versions by opening **Settings** in the main menu, and then clicking on **Media**. This takes you to the **Media Settings** page.

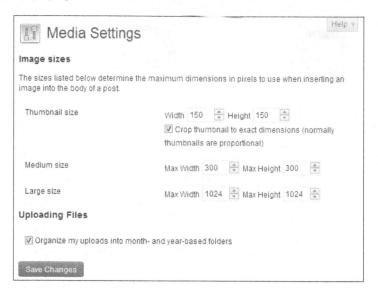

Here you can specify the size of the uploaded images for:

- **Thumbnail size**
- **Medium size**
- **Large size**

If you change the dimensions on this page, and click on the **Save Changes** button, only images you upload in the future will be affected. Images you've already uploaded to the site will have had their thumbnail, medium, and large versions created already using the old settings. It's a good idea to decide what you want your three media sizes to be early on in your site, so you can set them and have them applied to all images, right from the start.

Another thing about uploading images is the whole craze with HiDPI displays, also called Retina displays. Currently, WordPress is in a kind of a transitional phase with images and being in tune with the modern display technology; the Retina Ready functionality was introduced quite recently in WordPress 3.5. In short, if you want to make your images Retina-compatible (meaning that they look good on iPads and other devices with HiDPI screens), you should upload the images at twice the dimensions you plan to display them in. For example, if you want your image to be presented as 800 pixel wide and 600 pixel high, upload it as 1,600 pixel wide and 1,200 pixel high. WordPress will manage to display it properly anyway, and whoever visits your site from a modern device will see a high-definition version of the image. In future versions, WordPress will surely provide a more managed way of handling Retina-compatible images.

Editing an uploaded image

As of WordPress 2.9, you can now make minor edits on images you've uploaded.

In fact, every image that has been previously uploaded to WordPress can be edited. In order to do this, go to **Media Library** by clicking on the **Media** button in the main sidebar. What you'll see is a standard WordPress listing (similar to the one we saw while working with posts) presenting all media files and allowing you to edit each one.

When you click on the **Edit** link and then the **Edit Image** button on the subsequent screen, you'll enter the **Edit Media** section. Here, you can perform a number of operations to make your image just perfect. As it turns out, WordPress does a good enough job with simple image tuning so you don't really need expensive software such as Photoshop for this. Among the possibilities you'll find cropping, rotating, and flipping vertically and horizontally.

For example, you can use your mouse to draw a box as I have done in the preceding image. On the right, in the box marked **Image Crop**, you'll see the pixel dimensions of your selection. Click on the Crop icon (top left), then the **Thumbnail** radio button (on the right), and then **Save** (just below your photo). You now have a new thumbnail! Of course, you can adjust any other version of your image just by making a different selection prior to hitting the **Save** button.

Play around a little and you can become familiar with the details.

Designating a featured image

As of WordPress 2.9, you can designate a single image that represents your post. This is referred to as the **featured image**. Some themes will make use of this, and some will not. The default theme, the one we've been using, is named **Twenty Thirteen**, and it uses the featured image right above the post on the front page. Depending on the theme you're using, its behavior with featured images can vary, but in general, every modern theme supports them in one way or the other.

In order to set a featured image, go to the **Edit Post** screen. In the sidebar you'll see a box labeled **Featured Image**. Just click on the **Set featured image** link. After doing so, you'll see a pop-up window, very similar to the one we used while uploading images. Here, you can either upload a completely new image or select an existing image by clicking on it. All you have to do now is click on the **Set featured** image button in the bottom right corner. After completing the operation, you can finally see what your new image looks like on the front page. Also, keep in mind that WordPress uses featured images in multiple places not only the front page. And as mentioned above, much of this behavior depends on your current theme.

Using the visual editor versus text editor

WordPress comes with a visual editor, otherwise known as a **WYSIWYG** editor (pronounced wissy-wig, and stands for **What You See Is What You Get**). This is the default editor for typing and editing your posts. If you're comfortable with HTML, you may prefer to write and edit your posts using the text editor – particularly useful if you want to add special content or styling.

To switch from the rich text editor to the text editor, click on the **Text** tab next to the **Visual** tab at the top of the content box:

You'll see your post in all its raw HTML glory, and you'll get a new set of buttons that lets you quickly bold and italicize text, as well as add link code, image code, and so on.

You can make changes and swap back and forth between the tabs to see the result.

Even though the text editor allows you to use some HTML elements, it's not a fully fledged HTML support. For instance, using the `<p>` tags is not necessary in the text editor, as they will be stripped by default. In order to create a new paragraph in the text editor, all you have to do is press the *Enter* key twice. That being said, at the same time, the text editor is currently the only way to use HTML tables in WordPress (within posts and pages). You can easily place your table content inside the `<table><tr><td>` tags and WordPress won't alter it in any way, effectively allowing you to create the exact table you want. Another thing the text editor is most commonly used for is introducing custom HTML parameters in the `<img />` and `<a>` tags and also custom CSS classes in other popular tags. Some content creators actually prefer working with the text editor rather than the visual editor because it gives them much more control and more certainty regarding the way their content is going to be presented on the frontend.

Lead and body

One of many interesting publishing features WordPress has to offer is the concept of the lead and the body of the post. This may sound like a strange thing, but it's actually quite simple. When you're publishing a new post, you don't necessarily want to display its whole contents right away on the front page. A much more user-friendly approach is to display only the lead, and then display the complete post under its individual URL. Achieving this in WordPress is very simple. All you have to do is use the **Insert More Tag** button available in the visual editor (or the **more** button in the text editor). Simply place your cursor exactly where you want to break your post (the text before the cursor will become the lead) and then click on the **Insert More Tag** button:

An alternative way of using this tag is to switch to the text editor and input the tag manually, which is `<!--more-->`. Both approaches produce the same result. Clicking on the main **Update** button will save the changes.

On the front page, most WordPress themes display such posts by presenting the lead along with a **Continue reading** link, and then the whole post (both the lead and the rest of the post) is displayed under the post's individual URL.

Drafts, pending articles, timestamps, and managing posts

There are four additional, simple but common, items I'd like to cover in this section: drafts, pending articles, timestamps, and managing posts.

Drafts

WordPress gives you the option to save a draft of your post so that you don't have to publish it right away but can still save your work. If you've started writing a post and want to save a draft, just click on the **Save Draft** button at the right (in the **Publish** box), instead of the Publish button. Even if you don't click on the **Save Draft** button, WordPress will attempt to save a draft of your post for you, about once a minute. You'll see this in the area just below the content box. The text will say **Saving Draft...** and then show the time of the last draft saved:

At this point, after a manual save or an autosave, you can leave the Edit Post page and do other things. You'll be able to access all of your draft posts from **Dashboard** or from the **Edit Posts** page.

In essence, drafts are meant to hold your "work in progress" which means all the articles that haven't been finished yet, or haven't even been started yet, and obviously everything in between.

Pending articles

Pending articles is a functionality that's going to be a lot more helpful to people working with multiauthor blogs, rather than single-author blogs. The thing is that in a bigger publishing structure, there are individuals responsible for different areas of the publishing process. WordPress, being a quality tool, supports such a structure by providing a way to save articles as **Pending Review**. In an editor-author relationship, if an editor sees a post marked as **Pending Review**, they know that they should have a look at it and prepare it for the final publication.

That's it for the theory, and now how to do it. While creating a new post, click on the **Edit** link right next to the **Status: Draft** label:

Right after doing so, you'll be presented with a new drop-down menu from which you can select **Pending Review** and then click on the **OK** button. Now just click on the **Save as Pending** button that will appear in place of the old **Save Draft** button, and you have a shiny new article that's pending review.

Timestamps

WordPress will also let you alter the timestamp of your post. This is useful if you are writing a post today that you wish you'd published yesterday, or if you're writing a post in advance and don't want it to show up until the right day. By default, the timestamp will be set to the moment you publish your post. To change it, just find the **Publish** box, and click on the **Edit** link (next to the calendar icon and **Publish immediately**), and fields will show up with the current date and time for you to change:

Change the details, click on the **OK** button, and then click on **Publish** to publish your post (or save a draft).

Managing posts

If you want to see a list of your posts so that you can easily skim and manage them, you just need to go to the **Edit Post** page in the WP Admin and navigate to **Posts** in the main menu. Once you do so, there are many things you can do on this page as with every management page in the WP Admin, as we discussed at the beginning of this chapter.

Advanced post options

By now, you have a handle on the most common and simple options for posts, and you may be wondering about some of the other options on the **Edit Post** page. We'll cover them all in this section.

When you first visit the **Edit Post** page, some of the advanced options (**Excerpt**, **Send Trackbacks**, **Custom Fields**, **Discussion**, **Revisions**, **Author**, and **Format**) are "open" below the post content. If you never use them and want to clean up the look of this page, you can single-click each bar and they'll collapse. You can also rearrange them by dragging them to form a new order.

You can also use **Screen Options** (top right of the page) to uncheck certain boxes, and thus not display them at all.

Excerpt

WordPress offers theme designers the option to show a post's excerpt (instead of its full content) on pages within the theme.

Excerpt

Excerpts are optional hand-crafted summaries of your content that can be used in your theme. Learn more about manual excerpts.

This is how the excerpt works:

- If you enter some text into the excerpt box on the **Edit Post** page, that text will be used as the post's excerpt on theme pages that call for it

- If you do not enter any text into the excerpt box, WordPress will use the first 55 words of the post's content (which is stripped of HTML tags) followed by [...] (which is not a link)

- If you do not enter any text into the excerpt box, and the theme you are using does something special, the number of words and the final text could be different

You are never required to enter excerpt text. However, it is advisable that you do take advantage of this possibility. Excerpts can introduce big readability improvements to your site and make your content easier to grasp for the reader, provided that your current theme uses excerpts in one way or the other.

The more tag (`<!-- more -->`), which has been described in one of the previous sections in this chapter, should not be confused with the excerpt. It is different from the excerpt because you, not the theme designer, control its use. Additionally, the more tag is supported by every theme and has a slightly different task than the excerpt. It's meant to present the lead of the post, the part that's going to convince the reader to visit the complete post, while the excerpt is a summary of the post's contents.

Sending pingbacks and trackbacks

Pingbacks and **trackbacks** provide you with a way to communicate with other websites, and let them know that you've published a post mentioning them in one way or the other (usually through a link). For instance, they are useful if you write a blog post that is a response to an old post on someone else's blog and you want them to know about it.

The difference between pingbacks and trackbacks is that pingbacks are automatic whereas trackbacks are manual. In other words, WordPress always tries to send a pingback automatically whenever you link to another WordPress blog from any of your posts. Trackbacks are something you have to send manually, as WordPress will not do this for you. Apart from that, pingbacks and trackbacks are pretty much the same and produce a very similar effect.

If you want to notify a given blog via trackback, just copy the trackback URL from that person's blog post and paste it into the trackback box on your post's editing screen. An excerpt of your blog post and a link pointing back to your site will show up as a comment on their blog post, provided that the blog has trackbacks enabled. Sending an automatic pingback will also include a link pointing back to your site in the comments section. Again, that is if the blog you're targeting has trackbacks and pingbacks enabled.

Quite frankly, trackbacks are becoming somewhat out of date with the advent of pinging. Many WordPress themes are written to essentially disable trackbacks. As it turns out, most WordPress bloggers these days don't even bother to send trackbacks when the built-in mechanism of pingbacks handles it automatically.

Discussion

The **Discussion** box on the post editing screen has two checkboxes in it: one for allowing comments, and the other for trackbacks and pingbacks. When you first install WordPress, both these checkboxes will be checked by default. You have to uncheck them if you want to turn off the comments or trackbacks and pingbacks for the post.

If you uncheck the **Allow comments** box, visitors will not be able to comment on this blog post.

If you uncheck the **Allow trackbacks and pingbacks on this page** box, when other people mention your blog post and link to it on their own websites, your blog post won't notice and won't care. So, if you are using WordPress to run a non-blog website, this is the best option for you.

If the box stays checked, other people's pingbacks about this post will show up under your post along with comments, if any. If you're using WordPress to run a blog website, you'll want pingback to stay checked, especially if you want sites such as Technorati and other rating/authority sites to stay alerted.

If you want either or both of these boxes to be unchecked by default, go to Settings and then Discussion in the main menu. You can uncheck either or both of the boxes labeled **Allow link notifications from other blogs (pingbacks and trackbacks)** and **Allow people to post comments on new articles**.

The decision whether or not to support trackbacks and pingbacks on your site is entirely up to you. Even though they are both enabled by default, some bloggers quickly find that disabling them can make their everyday work much easier. The thing with pingbacks and trackbacks is that a large number of them, especially on popular blogs, are essentially spam. Basically, pingbacks and trackbacks are (were) the easiest way of getting a link from another site. Back in the day, no one was paying attention to what appeared in their pingback and trackback section, so every notification went through un-moderated in any way. These days, despite the fact that online publishers are much more aware of the situation, the spamming continues and it gets difficult to separate genuine pingbacks and trackbacks from the spammy ones. Hence, shutting them down altogether can make things easier in the long run.

To learn more about trackbacks and pingbacks you can visit the following sites:

- `http://www.wpbeginner.com/beginners-guide/what-why-and-how-tos-of-trackbacks-and-pingbacks-in-wordpress/`
- `http://codex.wordpress.org/Introduction_to_Blogging#Trackbacks`
- `http://codex.wordpress.org/Introduction_to_Blogging#Pingbacks`

Custom Fields

Custom Fields are WordPress' way of giving you the possibility to include some additional information in your blog post (information that you don't want to display directly on the frontend). In essence, Custom Fields are a kind of a semi-programming tool—they are not exactly "code" as understood by PHP programmers, yet they do give you a possibility to tweak your content in a certain, non-stock way. Many themes use various Custom Fields to style the individual aspects of posts. For example, some theme creators use Custom Fields to disable the sidebar on certain posts or include various typographic elements.

Another example, let's say you are a gadget reviewer and every blog post is a review of some new gadget. Every time you write a review, you're writing it about a product made by some company, and you'd like to have that company's logo associated with the blog post. You can make a custom field called `company_logo` and the value can be the path to the logo image.

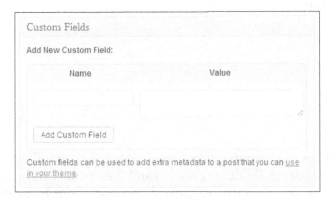

To display or make use of this custom field information, you either have to modify your theme files manually, or use a plugin.

 Read more about Custom Fields in the WordPress codex at `http://codex.wordpress.org/Using_Custom_Fields`.

Working with post revisions

Apart from many content formatting features, WordPress also allows some basic version control for your posts. What this means is that WordPress stores every subversion of your every post. Or in plain English, every time you click on the **Update** button, instead of overwriting the previous version of your post, WordPress creates a completely new one. Although this feature doesn't seem like the most useful one at first, it's actually very important for sites where the content is managed by more than one person. In such a scenario, it's easy to get the newest versions of the posts mixed up, so it's always good to have the possibility to return to the previous one.

In WordPress 3.6, the **Revisions** functionality has been completely revamped and a lot of new features have been introduced that make working with your content much more efficient. To take full advantage of the functionality, what you need to do is, first, enable **Revisions** in the upper slide-down **Screen Options** menu on the post editing screen. Once you do so, a small boxed titled **Revisions** will appear at the bottom of the screen.

If you click on any of the links displayed inside this box, you will be taken to a page where you can compare individual revisions and then restore the one you want to work with from now on. The interface provides a main slider that can be used to select individual revisions of the post as shown in the following screenshot:

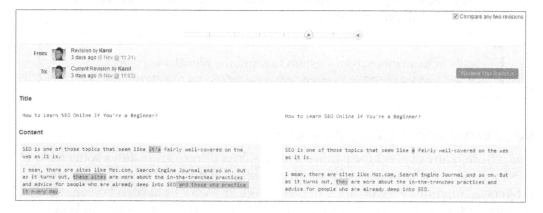

The revision functionality has two main versions. The first one, when the **Compare any two revisions** box isn't checked, lets you compare the revision that's currently selected (on the slider) to the revision directly preceding it. The second version is when the **Compare any two revisions** box is checked. In this case, you can select the revisions you want to compare individually, which allows you to essentially compare any two revisions just like the box suggests. The revision on the left is always the previous revision, while the one on the right is the next or current one (visible in the preceding screenshot). Every paragraph where there is a difference found will be highlighted in red and green, and every individual difference will have additional highlighting. Clicking on the **Restore This Revision** button will restore the revision on the right and you will be brought back to the post editing screen automatically.

On the other hand, if you feel that revisions won't be of any particular use to your site, you can simply not pay attention to the **Revisions** box. When you work with your content normally, not worrying about the revisions, WordPress will always display the most recent versions of your posts by default.

Changing the author of the post

This is a very basic feature in WordPress so let's only take a minute to discuss it. Basically, every post and page in WordPress has an author, which is quite obvious in itself. However, if you want to, you can change the assigned author of any given entry. In order to do it, just go to the post editing screen or the page editing screen and scroll down until you see the **Author** box. (If it's not visible, enable it from the pull-down **Screen Options** menu).

The box contains just one drop-down menu that lists every user account on your site. Just select a new author and click on the **Update** button. That's all. If you only have one user, the admin account, on your site, the box will contain one name.

Protecting content

WordPress gives you the option to hide posts. You can hide a post from everyone but yourself by marking it **Private** (although the user roles of admin and editor will still see it), or you can hide it from everyone but the people with whom you share a password by marking it as **Password protected**. To implement this, look at the **Publish** box at the upper right of the **Edit Post** page. If you click on the **Edit** link next to **Visibility: Public**, a few options will appear:

If you click on the **Password protected** radio button, you'll get a box where you can type a password. Visitors to your blog will see the post title along with a note that they have to type in a password to read the post.

If you click on the **Private** radio button, the post will not show up on the blog at all to any viewers, unless you are the viewer and you are logged in. The post will also appear if the person browsing the site is a logged-in editor (having the user role of Editor).

If you leave the post **Public** and check the **Stick this post to the front page** checkbox, this post will be the first post on the front page, regardless of its publication date.

Be sure to click on the **OK** button if you make any changes.

The pretty post slug

We've already talked about tuning the permalinks settings of your site in *Chapter 2, Getting Started*. Now is a good time to expand this knowledge and discuss a little about something called the post slug. One of the most accurate definitions in existence of what a post slug is comes from the WordPress codex itself. The one provided at `http://codex.wordpress.org/Glossary#Post_Slug` teaches us that the post slug is:

> *A few lowercase words separated by dashes, describing a post and usually derived from the post title to create a user-friendly permalink.*

In other words, the post slug is what comes after your domain name in the post's URL. For example, my post about **Making Lasagne** uses this URL: `http://mydomain.com/making-lasagne/`, where the last part, `making-lasagne`, is the slug. Just like the official definition says, WordPress chooses the slug by taking my post title, making it all lowercase, removing all punctuation, and replacing spaces with dashes. If I'd prefer it to be something else, such as `my-lasagne`, I can change it in the area just below the post's title:

Just click on **Edit** to change the slug. Readable URLs are something that Google search loves, so using them helps to optimize your site for search engines. It also helps users figure out what a post is about before clicking on the URL.

Custom post format settings

Since you will most likely start your WordPress journey with the default theme, **Twenty Thirteen**, I should probably say a few words about one more box that's visible on the post editing screen, the one titled **Format**.

Some themes provide basic, ready-made formatting styles for certain types of posts. Twenty Thirteen is one of those themes. In short, if you don't want to take care of styling your content manually, you can select one of the predefined styles and get great results in less than a minute.

Here are some examples. First we have a post saved as **Standard**:

Then the same post saved as **Quote**:

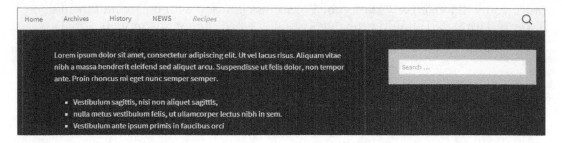

And finally, saved as **Status**:

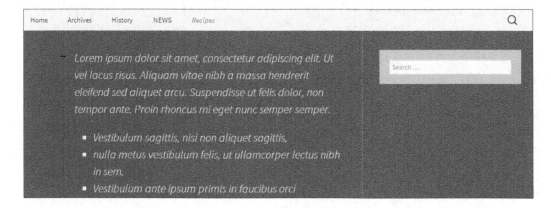

Those styles are, of course, entirely dependent upon your current theme, and usually, the more complex the theme, the more stark the differences between individual formats.

Additional writing options

In addition to simply logging in to the WP Admin, you have four other choices of ways to add posts to your blog.

Press This

WordPress offers a neat bookmarklet called **Press This**. You can put it into your browser's bookmarks or favorites, which will let you quickly write a blog post about the website you're visiting. You may have encountered this same feature as offered by Facebook, Delicious, and other social networking sites.

You just have to add **Press This** to your browser once, and then you can use it anytime. To add the **Press This** link to your browser in the WP Admin, go to the **Tools** page. On the top of the **Tools** page is the **Press This** box. Just use your mouse, and drag it up to your browser's bookmark bar.

Now you can use it! For example, if you're reading a newspaper website and you read an article you'd like to mention in a blog post, just click on the **Press This** bookmark (or favorite). A window will pop up with the **Edit Post** page in it and the URL of the site at which you're looking already written in as a link:

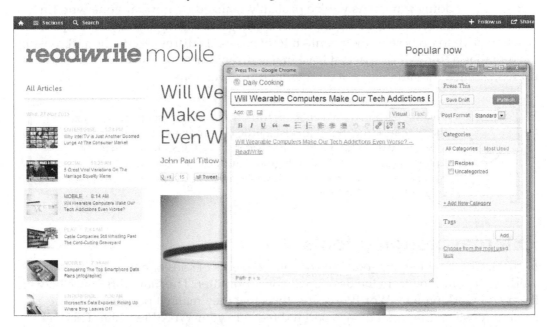

You can then write whatever additional text you want, add tags and categories, and then either save it as a draft or publish it right away.

Posting via e-mail

If you want to add a post to your blog without having to open the WP Admin and log in, you can set up your WordPress installation to accept posts sent via e-mail. First, you have to set up a special secret e-mail address that is accessible via POP. WordPress will check that e-mail address and turn any e-mails in it into posts. If you decide to set up this feature, you will have to be sure not to use this e-mail address for any other purpose!

Once you have the e-mail address set up at your mail server, go to your WP Admin and navigate to **Settings | Writing**. Scroll down a bit to the section labeled **Post by Email**. Now just enter the server, login name, and password into the **Writing Settings** page and be sure to click on the **Save Changes** button. Note that on this page, WordPress provides you with three random strings you could use for the e-mail address, so you might want to visit this page first to get one, set up your POP account, and then return to this page to set up **Post via e-mail**.

Even though posting via e-mail sounds like a good idea at first, it's actually not the safest way of doing things. As you've probably realized by now, anyone who finds out what your secret e-mail address is can easily get anything published on your site. All they have to do is send their content to that e-mail address. To be honest, posting via e-mail is a thing of the past, at least in its current form, unless WordPress comes up with some innovative way of doing it in future versions.

> Posting via e-mail in its default form is not the safest approach out there, that is true. But with just a little bit of creativity, you can do it in a way that still makes sense (safety-wise). Feel free to visit the following site for an in-depth guide: http://themefuse.com/blog/posting-to-wordpress-via-email-theres-a-safe-way-of-doing-this/.

External blogging tools

In short, external blogging tools are specialized pieces of software that allow you to work with your blog from the desktop of your computer. The main difference between them and working with WordPress directly is that they make it possible to create content (posts) offline, and then export it directly to your WordPress site. This has some great benefits, and the biggest of which is that you can write posts whenever inspiration hits you, not only when you have an Internet connection at your disposal (particularly handy for creating content while traveling). Another benefit is that your posts are stored as normal files, which you can copy wherever you want, send to someone via e-mail, or back up on Dropbox or other similar solutions.

The first question worth answering here is how are these tools better than writing a post in MS Word and then copying it into WordPress manually. Well, if you've ever tried doing this, you already know that most of your formatting, layout, as well as the graphics are sure to go missing. There's no such problem with external blogging tools, as they are optimized for working with WordPress right from the get-go.

The only bad news in this whole story is that the best tool available, **Windows Live Writer**, works on Windows only, so Mac users will have a little harder time here. If you're on Mac, you can consider alternatives such as **MarsEdit** (http://www.red-sweater.com/marsedit/) or **Qumana** (http://www.qumana.com/).

The best thing about Windows Live Writer is that, even though it's been created by Microsoft, it's absolutely free. You can download it at http://explore.live.com/windows-live-writer and then install it on any version of Windows. The tool itself is very easy to use and very efficient (when it comes to performance). Finally, Windows Live Writer doesn't require you to set up your site in any specific way before you can work with it. All you have to do is configure the Writer itself so it can connect to the site (basically, it only needs the address of the site, your username and password). I strongly encourage you to give it a shot.

Mobile apps for iOS and Android

This final method of posting content on WordPress is growing stronger every year, or even every month. The mobile usage of the Web is constantly rising, and this is only reflected in the way people interact with their WordPress sites or blogs.

It's not surprising that there's a great wealth of blogging tools and apps for the two most popular mobile platforms: iOS and Android.

Both systems have the native WordPress app available. You can get these apps at http://ios.wordpress.org/ and http://android.wordpress.org/.

The user interfaces of the apps have some minor differences depending on what device you're using to access the app with, but the core functionality remains the same. Here, we're going to use the iPad edition as an example.

The app is very user-friendly and virtually guides you through all the crucial steps of setting up a connection with your blog. You can add a new site from the **Settings** menu.

Once you do so, you get to use a standard set of features that let you in on a variety of actions you can perform on your site's content. You can create and edit posts, do the same with pages, moderate comments, and hop over to the site's WP Admin via a direct link.

Discussion on your blog – comments

Comments are an important part of most of the blogs. While you are the only person who can write blog posts, the visitors to your blog can add comments to your posts. This can fuel a sense of community within a blog, allow people to give you feedback on your writing, and give your visitors a way to help or talk to other visitors. The only downside of commenting is that unscrupulous people will try to misuse your blog's ability to accept comments, and will try to post spam or advertisements in your blog instead of relevant comments. Luckily, the WordPress community is always developing more ways of fighting spam.

Adding a comment

If you look at the front page of your blog, you'll see that every post has a link that says **Leave a Reply**. Clicking on that link will take you to the bottom of the post page, which is where comments can be added, as we saw in *Chapter 2, Getting Started*.

If you're logged in to the WP Admin, you'll see your name and a space to write your comment. If you're not logged in, you'll see a comment form that any other visitor will see. This form includes fields to fill in name, e-mail, and website, along with the commenting text area.

Once you type in the required information and click on the **Post Comment** button, the comment will be entered into the WordPress database along with all of your other blog information. How soon it shows up on the site depends on your discussion settings.

Discussion settings

The default comment form offered by WordPress makes two fields mandatory, those fields are **Name:** and **E-mail:**. As the administrator of this blog/site, you can change these requirements. First, log in to the WP Admin and navigate to **Settings | Discussion**. We explored the first box (**Default article settings**) earlier in this chapter.

Submission, notification, and moderation settings

Let's focus on the checkboxes on this page that relate only to **submission**, **notification**, and **moderation**. The boxes that are checked on this page will determine how much moderation and checking a comment has to go through before it gets posted on the blog.

The default settings are relatively strict. The only way to make a more strictly controlled discussion on your blog is to check **Comment must be manually approved**. This option means that no matter what, all comments go into the moderation queue and do not show up on the site until you manually approve them.

Let's look at the settings having to do with submission. These options control what the user has to do before he or she is even able to type in a comment:

- **Comment author must fill out name and e-mail**: As you noticed in the screenshot in the **Adding a comment** section, **Name:** and **Email:** are required. If you leave this checked, anyone posting a comment will encounter an error if they try to leave either of the fields blank. This doesn't add a huge amount of security because robots know how to fill out a name and an e-mail, and because anyone can put fake information in there. However, it does help your blog readers to keep a track of who is who if a long discussion develops, and it can slightly discourage utterly impulsive commenting. Also, visitors who have a Gravatar account (mentioned in the previous chapter) are quite willing to provide their e-mail addresses anyway. That's because using an e-mail address that's connected to Gravatar will result in their profile picture (avatar) being displayed along with the comment, making it much more personal and visible among all the other comments.

- **Users must be registered and logged in to comment**: Most bloggers do not check this box because it means that only visitors who register for the blog can comment. Most bloggers don't want random people registering, and most visitors don't want to be compelled to register for your blog. If you check this box, there's a good chance you'll get no comments (which may be what you want). Alternatively, if you're setting up a blog for a closed community of people, this setting might be useful.

- **Automatically close comments on articles older than X days**: Here, you can set any number of days after which the comments on your content will be closed. Although this feature might not seem like a useful one at first, it can actually be valuable to various kinds of news sites or other online publications where allowing comments on old events makes very little sense.

- **Enable threaded (nested) comments X levels deep**: This option is enabled by default, and it's yet another way of making your site more readable and user-friendly. Sometimes commenters want to be able to respond to someone else's comments, simply as part of an ongoing discussion. This is the feature that allows them to do so. Also, it gives you, the author, a great way of interacting with your audience through direct responses to every comment of theirs.

- **Break comments into pages with X top level comments per page and the X page displayed by default**: This feature won't be of any value to you unless you're getting more than 200 comments per post, so you can confidently leave it unchecked for now.

- **Comments should be displayed with the X comments at the top of each page**: This option has two main settings (older and newer), and it lets you select if want to display the newest comments first on the list or the oldest comments first.

Now let's look at the settings that have to do with moderation. These two options have to do with the circumstances that allow comments to appear on the site. They are by the **Before a comment appears** header:

- **Comment must be manually approved**: As I mentioned before, if this box is checked, every comment has to be manually approved by you before it appears on the site.

- **Comment author must have a previously approved comment**: If you uncheck the box above this, but check this one, you've relaxed your settings a little bit. This means that if the person commenting has commented before and had his or her comment approved, the person's future comments don't have to be verified by you; they'll just appear on the website immediately. The person just has to enter the same name and e-mail as the one in the previously approved comment.

Now let's look at the settings that have to do with notification. These options are under the **E-mail me whenever** header. These options are related to the circumstances of receiving an e-mail notification about the comment activity.

- **Anyone posts a comment**: This is generally a good setting to keep. You'll get an e-mail whenever anyone posts a comment—whether or not it needs to be moderated. This will make it easier for you to follow the discussion on your blog, and to be aware of a comment that is not moderated and requires deletion quickly.

- **A comment is held for moderation**: If you're not particularly interested in following every comment on your blog, you can uncheck the **Anyone posts a comment** checkbox and only leave this one checked. You will only get an e-mail about legitimate-looking comments that appear to need moderation and need your approval.

When to moderate or blacklist a comment

If you scroll down the page a bit, you'll see the **Comment Moderation** area:

Comment Moderation

Hold a comment in the queue if it contains 2 [ ] or more links. (A common characteristic of comment spam is a large number of hyperlinks.)

When a comment contains any of these words in its content, name, URL, e-mail, or IP, it will be held in the moderation queue. One word or IP per line. It will match inside words, so 'press' will match 'WordPress'.

This is an extension of the moderation settings from the top of the page. Note that if you've checked the **Comment must be manually approved** checkbox, you can safely ignore this **Comment Moderation** box. Otherwise, you can use this box to help WordPress figure out which comments are probably okay and which might be spam or inappropriate for your blog. You can tell WordPress to suspect a comment if it has more than a certain number of links, as spam comments often are just a list of URLs.

The larger box is for you to enter suspect words and IP addresses:

- Here you can type words that are commonly found in spam (you can figure this out by looking in your junk mail in your e-mail), or just uncouth words in general.

- The IP addresses you will enter into this box would be those of any comments you've gotten in the past from someone who comments inappropriately or adds actual spam. Whenever WordPress receives a comment on your blog, it captures the IP address for you so that you'll have them handy.

Scroll down a bit more, and you'll see the **Comment Blacklist** box:

Comment Blacklist

When a comment contains any of these words in its content, name, URL, e-mail, or IP, it will be marked as spam. One word or IP per line. It will match inside words, so 'press' will match 'WordPress'.

Unlike the **Comment Moderation** box we just saw, which tells WordPress how to identify the comments to suspect, the **Comment Blacklist** box tells WordPress how to identify comments that are almost definitely bad. These comments won't be added to the moderation queue and you won't get an e-mail about them; they'll be marked right away as spam.

Avatar display settings

The final box on this page is the **Avatars** box. Just as I already mentioned in the previous chapter, an avatar is an image that is a person's personal icon. Avatars in WordPress are provided through Gravatar, a service available at `http://gravatar.com/`, that lets you create your personal online profile, which is going to be then consistently used on other websites across the Web. By default, avatars will show up on your blog if you leave the **Show Avatars** radio button checked that's visible near the bottom of the discussion settings page.

The second box, **Maximum Rating**, will tell WordPress if it should not show avatars that have been rated too highly. Remember the rating we were setting while uploading a new picture to Gravatar? This setting here is the place where you can choose which pictures you want to allow on your own site.

The third box, **Default Avatar**, tells WordPress what avatar to use for visitors who do not come with their own Gravatar. When you installed WordPress, it created a comment for you on the first post, and also created a default avatar for you. You can see the default avatar, **Mystery Man**, in use on the **Hello world!** post:

Moderating comments

Now that we've thoroughly explored the settings for which comments need to be moderated, let's discuss what you actually need to do to moderate comments. Moderating means that you look over a comment that is in limbo and decide whether it's insightful enough that it can be published on your site. If it's good, it gets to appear on the frontend of your website; if it is bad, it's either marked as spam or is deleted and is never seen by anyone but you and the poster who wrote it.

To view comments waiting for moderation, log in to your WP Admin and navigate to **Comments** in the main menu.

If you have any comments waiting for moderation, there will be a little number in the main menu telling you how many comments await moderation.

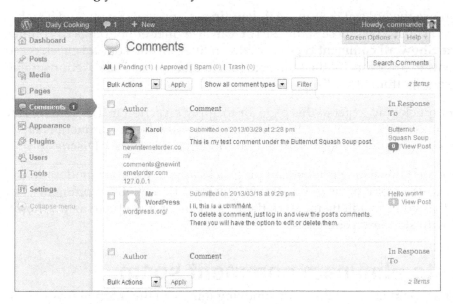

This main **Comments** page is fully featured, just like the **Posts** page. For each comment, you see the following information from left to right:

- Commenter avatar, name, website address, e-mail address, and IP
- Comment text, along with links to approve it so that it shows up on the site (the links appear when you hover your mouse over the comment), you can also mark it as spam, trash it, edit it, quick edit it, or reply to it

- Comment submission time and date

- The title of the post on which the comment was made (which is also a link to edit that post), a number in parentheses indicating how many approved comments are already there on that post (which is also a link that will filter the comments list so that it shows only comments on this page), and a link to the post itself (labeled as **View Post**)

Comments that are awaiting moderation have a yellow background, like the first comment in the preceding screenshot (you can also see my Gravatar).

You can click on the **Quick Edit** link for any post to open form fields right within this list. This will allow you to edit the text of the post and the commenter's name, e-mail, and URL.

You can use the links at the top — **All**, **Pending**, **Approved**, **Spam**, and **Trash** — to filter the list based on those statuses. You can also filter either pings or comments with the **Show all comment types** pull-down filter menu. You can check one or more comments to apply any of the bulk actions available in the **Bulk Actions** menus at the top and bottom of the list.

Another quick way to get to this page, or to apply an action to a comment, is to use the links in the e-mail that WordPress sends you when a comment is held for moderation (provided you've selected this option in **Settings | Discussion**).

Additionally, this listing is where all pingbacks appear for your moderation. From a blog owner's point of view, pingbacks look just like any other comments, which means that you can edit them, mark them as spam, or trash them as you normally would with standard comments.

How to eliminate comment spam

Comment spam is one of the most annoying things on the Internet if you're an online publisher. Basically, a spam comment is a comment that has been submitted for the sole purpose of getting a link back to a specific website. The main reason why people submit spam comments is search engine optimization — the number of links pointing to a site is a known SEO factor, and website owners around the world do whatever they can to get as many links as possible. Unfortunately for us, sometimes it means using various spam methods as well.

The way WordPress comments are set up by default makes it possible for anyone to get a link from your site just by submitting a comment and providing a website address in one of the comment fields. If they do so and the comment gets approved, the thing typed into the **Name** field of the comment becomes the text of the link and the **Website** becomes the link's destination.

The worst thing about comment spam is that once your site gets even remotely popular, you can start getting hundreds of spam comments a day; hence, dealing with them manually becomes almost impossible.

Unfortunately, fighting comment spam is not something built into WordPress by default. This means that you have to get some plugin(s) to enable this functionality. For now, let's focus on the most popular spam protection plugin of today—**Akismet**. The good thing about it is that it comes along with the standard WordPress installation, so you should be able to find it in the **Plugins** section in your WP Admin. We will cover plugins in detail later in this book, so now let's just review how to get Akismet working on your blog. If your blog is built on WordPress.com, then Akismet is already activated by default. For a standard, standalone blog, you'll have to activate it first.

You can learn more about the Akismet spam-fighting service at `http://akismet.com/`. Also, if you're interested in some alternative solutions, please visit these two official plugin pages: `http://wordpress.org/extend/plugins/antispam-bee/` and `http://wordpress.org/extend/plugins/growmap-anti-spambot-plugin/`.

Getting an Akismet API key

The Akismet plugin requires that you have a special API key. Getting this API key was a lot simpler just a couple of years ago. All you needed to do is go to WordPress.com, sign up for an account (even if you didn't intend to build a blog there), and you could get your API key from the Settings menu. Now there's a new path. The starting point is still quite similar, though. You need to go to WordPress.com and create a new account. Please follow the instructions in *Chapter 2, Getting Started*, in order to do it. Once your account is active, go to the signup page at Akismet.com and create a new account there as well. Here's the exact address: `https://akismet.com/signup/`.

This is what you'll see:

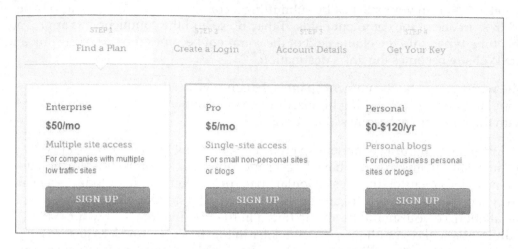

Apparently, Akismet wants to sell you some of their premium services, but luckily this isn't mandatory. Click on the **SIGN UP** button under the plan labeled as **Personal** and you'll immediately see a new button titled **Sign up with WordPress. com**. This is where you get to connect your WordPress.com account with your new Akismet account. Depending on the fact whether you're currently logged in to your WordPress.com account or not, you might see another signup page or a custom login page. In case of the former, just click on the **I already have a WordPress.com account** link. For the latter, type in your email address and password to log in to your WordPress.com account and then click on the **Authorize** button in order to finally connect both accounts together. When you do this, you're going to be redirected back to Akismet. Now this is tricky. The plan we've selected is based on voluntary donations. If you're not willing to spend any money, just take the slider that's in the center and slide it to the left, all the way to **$0.00/yr**. Apart from that, you just have to provide standard details like your first and last name.

CONTACT INFO		WHAT IS AKISMET WORTH TO YOU?
First name		$0.00/yr
Last name		Yearly contribution: $0

Your API key will arrive via e-mail to the address specified during registration. Select and copy that text. You may want to paste it into a text file to be sure you have it.

Activating Akismet

Now go back to your WordPress installation and navigate to **Plugins** in the main menu:

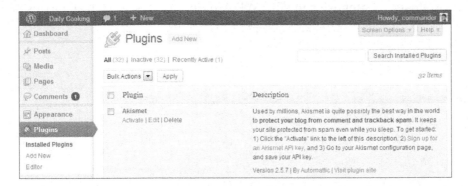

You'll see Akismet listed as the first plugin. Click on the **Activate** link. A yellow message bar will appear at the top of the page that says **Akismet is almost ready. You must enter your Akismet API key for it to work**. Click on that link and you'll be taken to a page where you can enter your API key you copied from WordPress.com:

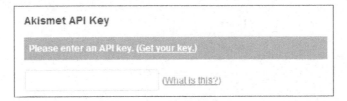

Paste your API key into the box. If you're feeling confident, you can also check the box below it to discard spam comments automatically. Akismet is relatively good at identifying which comment is actually spam, and checking this box will make those comments disappear. However, if you're concerned about Akismet misidentifying comments, leave this unchecked.

Now click on **Update options>>** and your blog is protected from comment spam!

Adding and managing categories

Earlier in this chapter, you learned how to add a category quickly while adding a post. Now let's talk about how to manage your categories in a bigger way. First, navigate to **Posts | Categories** in your WP Admin. You'll see the **Categories** page:

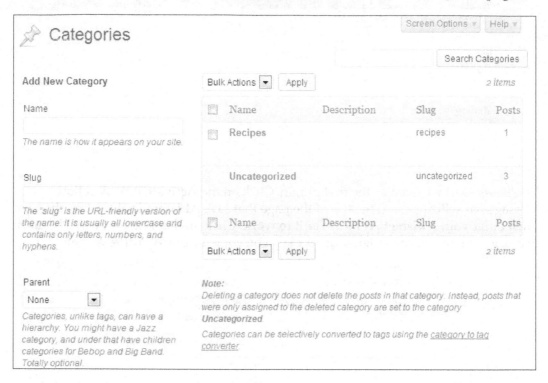

This is a useful page that combines the ability to add, edit, and review all your categories. As you can see, any category that you've added via the **Edit Post** page is listed. You can edit, quick edit, or delete any category by clicking on the appropriate link in the list.

If you add a category on this page, you can also choose its slug. The slug is the short bit of text that shows up in the URL of your site if you have pretty permalinks enabled. If you don't choose a slug, WordPress will create one for you by taking the category name, reducing it to all lowercase, replacing spaces with dashes, and removing any other punctuation mark.

Another thing you can do on this page is choose a parent category for any category. Some themes support displaying categories hierarchically, but not all do. In a good, modern theme, if you create a custom menu for categories, all child categories will be displayed as submenus.

The ability to create a hierarchy of categories is actually the main technical thing that separates categories from tags. Other than that, both elements are quite similar in construction, although they still have different purposes.

Summary

In this chapter, you learned everything you need to know to add content to your blog and manage that content. You learned about posts, categories, and comments. You discovered tags, spam, and excerpts. You also learned about adding and editing images, using the visual editor (and the text editor), changing timestamps, customizing excerpts, and the different ways of posting (for example, through e-mail or external blogging tools).

Your control of your blog content is complete, and you are well equipped to set your blog on fire!

In the next chapter, you'll learn about all the other types of content that you can manage on your website with WordPress.

4
Pages, Menus, Media Library, and More

You now have the blog part of your website fully under control. By now, you've probably noticed that WordPress offers you a lot more than simply posts, comments, tags, and categories.

In this chapter, we will explore and control all of the other content types that WordPress already has. You'll be able to create static pages that aren't a part of your ongoing blog, bookmark links that will drive visitors to other websites, add various types of media to your posts, and create appealing image galleries to display photos and other images. You'll also learn how to manage navigation menus and work with the basic layout customization features to further enhance the capabilities of your website.

Pages

At first glance, pages look very similar to posts. Both pages and posts have a title and a content area in which we can write extended text. However, pages are handled quite differently from posts. First of all, pages don't have categories, or tags. Moreover, posts belong to your blog, which are meant to be a part of an ongoing expanding section of your website, and are added regularly; pages, on the other hand, are more static and aren't generally expected to change that much.

In short, I would advise to treat pages as pieces of static content, and posts as series of articles published in a timely manner. In other words, pages are meant to hold content that is equally up-to-date no matter whenever it is read. Posts are often very time sensitive and present advice/news that's important today/now. For most blogs, posts are the pillar of their content and make up more than 90 percent of the site. Furthermore, posts appear in the RSS feed of a WordPress blog, while pages don't.

When you installed WordPress, a page was automatically created for you (along with the first post and first comment). You can see it by clicking on the **Sample Page** link in the main navigation menu at the top of your site, as shown in the following screenshot:

Adding a page

To add a new page, go to your WP Admin, and navigate to **Pages | Add New**, or use the drop-down menu in the top grey menu by clicking on **New** and then **Page**. This will take you to the **Add New Page** screen, as shown in the following screenshot:

The minimum you need to do in order to create a new page is type in a title and some content. Then, click on the blue **Publish** button, just as you would for a post, and your new page will become available under its unique URL.

You'll recognize most of the fields on this page from the **Add New Post** page. They work the same for pages as they do for posts. Let's talk about the one new section, the box named **Attributes**; consisting of elements such as **Parent**, **Template**, and **Order**.

Page Attributes

Parent

(no parent)

Template

Default Template

Order

0

Need help? Use the Help tab in the upper right of your screen.

Parent

WordPress allows you to structure your pages hierarchically. This way, you can organize your website's pages into main pages and subpages, which is useful if you're going to have a lot of pages on your site. For example, if I were writing this blog along with three other authors, we would each have one page about us on the site, but they'd be subpages of the main **About** page. If I were adding one of these pages, I'd first create a new **About** page, then create another page just for me named **About Karol**, and finally choose **About** as the parent page for this new page.

Template

Theme designers often offer alternate templates that can be used for special pages. However, the Twenty Thirteen WordPress theme—the default theme—doesn't come with any additional templates.

Other themes may come with a variety of templates, depending on what the theme designer thought you'd find useful. If you're creating your own WordPress theme, you can create any number of templates that have different layouts or have special content. Also, even when working with a stock theme, you can still tweak its structure and introduce your own custom page templates.

One of the common uses for a page template is to craft a custom home page with it—one that would present something else than just the standard listing of the most recent posts.

Order

By default, the pages in your page list on the sidebar or main navigation of your blog will be in alphabetical order by page title. If you want them in some other order, you can specify it by entering numbers in the **Order** box for all of your pages. Pages with lower numbers (for example, **0**) will be listed before pages with higher numbers (for example, **5**). You can test this easily by editing your **History** page and giving it the **Order** value of **5**. As a result, you'll see it after the **Sample Page** link in the top navigation menu. However, this isn't a very clear method of rearranging pages inside menus. You can do it much more easily with a functionality named **Custom Menus** (described later in this chapter). In the end, I would advise you to save all of your pages with the **Order** value of **0**.

Managing pages

To see a list of all the pages on your website in the WP Admin, navigate to **Pages | Edit** in the main menu. You'll see the **Pages** screen, as shown in the following screenshot:

By now, this list format should begin to look familiar to you. You've got your list of pages, and in each row are a number of useful links allowing you to **Edit**, **QuickEdit**, **Trash**, or **View** the page. You can click on an author's name to filter the list by that author. You can use the two links at the top, **All** and **Published**, to filter the pages by status (if you have pages saved as **Drafts** or **Pending Review**, they will also appear here). There's also filtering by date and category through the two drop-down menus just above the list of pages. Additionally, you can check boxes and "mass-edit" pages by using the **Bulk Actions** menu at the top and bottom of the list. You can also search your pages with the search box at the top.

Menus

As of WordPress 3.0, there are now Custom Menus available within the WP Admin. This wasn't always the case, but these days all modern themes support Custom Menus, and so does the default theme, Twenty Thirteen.

The Custom Menus feature lets you create menus with links to pages, category archives, and even arbitrary links to any URL (which also allows you to use links to your individual posts). Then, you can place your custom menu into your theme.

Adding a menu

Let's take a look at the menu's management screen. To get there, just navigate to **Appearance | Menus**:

To create your first menu, enter a title where it says **Enter menu name here**, for example, `Main`. After doing so, you can select individual pages from the panel on the left-hand side and click on the **Add to Menu** button to confirm:

You can add some custom links to the menu if you want to. This can be done after clicking on the **Links** heading on the left-hand side, and then filling out the required link information. To confirm, click on **Addto Menu**:

As you can see in the preceding screenshot, I'm using this opportunity to link to one of my posts.

Finally, you can add some category links. Click on the **Categories** heading on the left-hand side, and then click on the checkboxes next to the categories you want to have included. Click on **Add to Menu** to confirm, as shown in the following screenshot:

Then, be sure to click on **Save Menu** in the upper-right corner. The following screenshot is what my menu looks like now:

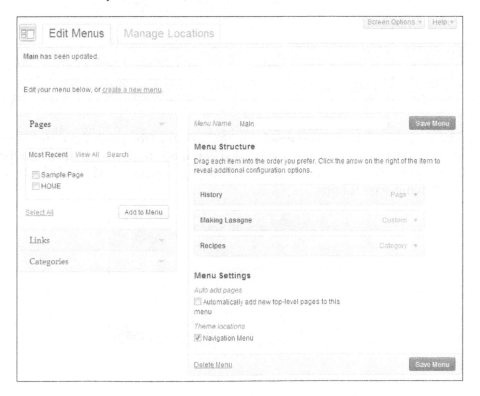

You can also drag items to the right-hand side to make them subitems of the item above. For example, I'll add my **Making Lasagne** post as a subitem under **Recipes**. Now, my menu looks like the following screenshot:

You can make more menus by clicking on the **create a new menu** link at the top to repeat the preceding process. Now you might ask,"I created my new menu, but how do I make it show up on my site?". Read on...

Displaying a menu

If you have a menu-enabled theme, then once you have one menu, a new box will appear on the menus page showing you the menu locations. Twenty Thirteen has just one menu location, and it's named **Navigation Menu**:

All you have to do to assign your newly created menu to the predefined menu area in Twenty Thirteen is to check the box labeled **Navigation Menu**, as shown in the preceding screenshot. After doing so, my primary navigation on the website looks like the following screenshot:

And when I hover my mouse over **Recipes**, I will also see my **Making Lasagne** post. So, as you can see in the following screenshot, Twenty Thirteen displays subitems in a rollover menu activated by the location of your mouse cursor:

Header

The functionality I'm about to describe is highly dependent upon your current theme, however, most modern themes these days support header customizations, so learning a few things about this feature will surely come handy to you sooner than later.

If you're starting your WordPress adventure with the default theme, Twenty Thirteen, in the **Appearance** section, you can see one link labeled **Header**. This is exactly where you can adjust the design of your site's header.

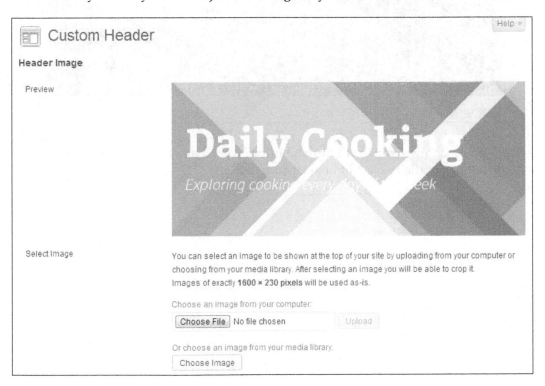

As you can see in the preceding screenshot, my header doesn't feature anything fancy at the moment, just the name (**Daily Cooking**) and the tagline (**Exploring cooking every day of the week**). But with just a little effort this can be changed in no time. Most themes will allow you to select any image to be placed inside the header. Twenty Thirteen has some specific requirements for this image, which you can see in the preceding screenshot. The suggested size is 1600 pixels wide by 230 pixels high, but you don't have to worry all that much about it because WordPress also provides some handy image editing tools. All you have to do here is use the **Choose Image** button and select one of the pictures from the media library (or upload a new one). WordPress will immediately redirect you to the aforementioned image editing tools where you can adjust and crop your image. The following screenshot is an example of what it looks like:

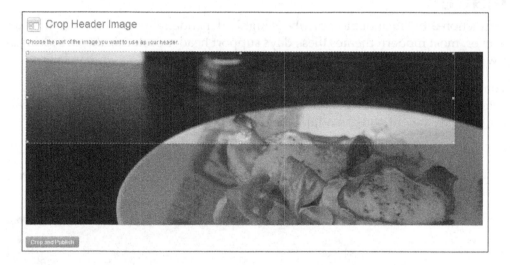

After clicking on the **Crop and Publish** button, we're back at the settings screen where we can handle two additional customizations:

The preceding screenshot is the place to decide whether or not to display the header text—the title of the site and the tagline—and select the default color for this text. I'm going to change this color to white to make the header text more visible. After clicking on the main **Save Changes** button, the header image is set. Here's what my site looks like now:

Much better, right?

Advanced site customization

Yet another feature in WordPress that's highly dependent upon your theme is the Customize Your Site module. If you still have the **Welcome** box enabled in your Dashboard's screen settings, you can access the module by clicking on the big **Customize Your Site** button, as shown in the following screenshot:

Another way of accessing this module is by visiting the following URL: `http://yoursite.com/wp-admin/customize.php`. The following screenshot is what you'll see (provided you're working with the default theme):

This module doesn't deliver any new functionality. It simply takes all the customization features and displays them in one, easy-to-grasp place.

By looking through the individual tabs on the left-hand side, you can adjust various aspects of your site that we've already talked about in this and the previous chapters. The tabs are listed as follows:

- **Site Title & Tagline**
- **Colors**
- **Header Image**
- **Navigation** (you can choose which menu you want to assign as the **Primary Menu**)
- **Static Front Page**

The best thing about this module is that it provides a live preview, which makes editing the basic aspects of your design much quicker. When you're done, you can either click on the **Cancel** button or the **Save & Publish** button.

Links

WordPress gives you a very powerful way of organizing external links or bookmarks on your site. This is a way to link other related blogs—websites you like, websites that you think your visitors will find useful, or just any category of link you want—to your blog. Speaking of categories, you can create and manage link categories that are separate from your blog categories.

The possibility to manage links is one of the old school features in WordPress. It's been available since forever. And that's probably why it's not available anymore (for WordPress 3.5 and above). At least not by default. What I mean is that everyone who had a site running on WordPress versions below 3.5 could access the link manager normally. So if such a person then updated WordPress to Version 3.5, the link manager remained intact. However, everyone who installs WordPress 3.5 from the ground up (as a completely new, fresh site) has link manager disabled. Nevertheless, the link manager is still worth discussing for a while as it remains to be one of the best ways to manage all external links (pointing to other sites) that you want to feature on your site.

First of all, if you don't see the **Links** section inside the left sidebar in the WP Admin (the following screenshot), it means your WordPress has the link manager disabled:

If that's the case, then you need to get one of the official WordPress plugins to enable it. The plugin is named **Link Manager** and you can get it at `http://wordpress.org/extend/plugins/link-manager/`. We will discuss how to work with plugins in the next chapter.

If, on the other hand, the **Links** section is visible in your WP Admin, you can proceed with the following. Navigate to **Links | All Links**, and you'll see something that looks like the following screenshot:

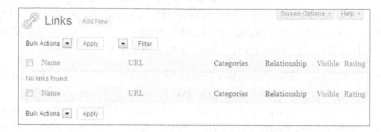

Currently there are no links there, but this is a standard WordPress content listing (just like the one for posts or pages), so you can create new links and manage existing ones in a familiar manner.

Adding a new link

In your WP Admin, navigate to **Links | Add New**. This will take you to the **Add New Link** page, which has a number of boxes in which you can add information about your new link, as shown in the following screenshot:

Of all the fields on this page, it's the top two that are the most important. You need to give your link a **Name**, which is the text that people will see and can click on. You also need to give a **Web Address**, which is the URL of the website. You can optionally add a **Description**, which will show up when visitors hover over the link and possibly in other places, depending on your theme.

If you're into the more advanced stuff, you can also check out the **Categories** and **Target** fields.

The **Categories** box in the preceding screenshot should look familiar because it's very similar to the **Categories** selection box for posts. However, **Link Categories** and **Post Categories** are completely separate from each other. You can assign a category to the new link that you're adding or create a new category by clicking on the **+ Add New Category** link. Your links will be organized by the categories on your website.

The **Target** box lets you choose whether your visitors will be taken to a new window or tab, when they click on the link. I generally recommend using **_blank** when sending people to an external website.

The other boxes on this page are used less commonly. You can use the **Link Relationship (XFN)** box to specify **XFN (XHTML Friends Network)** relationships between you and any individuals to which you link (you can get more info about XFN at: `http://gmpg.org/xfn/`). Finally, the last box at the bottom of this page, **Advanced**, will allow you to specify:

- An image that belongs with this link (for example, the logo of the company whose site to which you are linking)
- The RSS feed for the website to which you're linking
- Any notes you have about the site, beyond what you entered into the **Description** box
- A rating for the site from **0** to **9**

To make use of any of these pieces of information, you need to have a theme that recognizes and makes use of them.

At the top-right corner of the page is a **Save** box with a checkbox that you can check if you want to keep the link private; that is, if you don't want it to show up on your site to anyone but yourself.

For now, let's create a new link as a test. Pick your favorite website and input its name into the **Name** field and its URL into the **Web Address** field (in my case, it's the blog at `http://themefuse.com/blog/`). Next, create a new category using the **+ Add New Category** button. You can name it `My Favorite Sites`, like I did, as shown in the following screenshot:

Displaying links

The Twenty Thirteen theme doesn't come with any feature that actually shows your links. The easiest way to display them is to add a **Links** widget to your sidebar. Other themes may have other built-in ways to display links. We'll cover widgets in the next chapter.

Managing links and categories

You can manage your links just as you manage posts and pages by clicking on **Links**. From here, you can click on the name of a link to edit it, click on the URL to visit it, and see which categories you've chosen for it. Using the **View all categories** pull-down menu, you can filter links by categories, change their order, and do bulk deletes.

Just as with post categories, you can manage and add new link categories on the **Link Categories** page. You can access this page by navigating to **Links | Link Categories**:

This is a page that is very similar to the one available under **Posts | Categories**, only that here it's meant for the link categories, exclusively. Therefore, from this page, you can both add a new category using the form on the left-hand side, and also manage your existing categories using the table on the right-hand side, just like you did with post categories.

Media library

The media library is where WordPress stores all of your uploaded files—images, PDFs, music, videos, and so on. To see your media library, navigate to **Media** in the main menu (probably not a lot of media there at the moment):

The preceding screenshot shows the now-familiar management table/listing. My media library has only one photo. I uploaded it to place it inside the **Butternut Squash soup** post. As you can see from the preceding screenshot, it shows me the following:

- A thumbnail of the image. If this were another type of media, I'd see an icon representing the type of media.
- The title that I gave the file when I uploaded it, along with the format extension.
- The author of the file.
- Information about which post or page the file is attached to. This will be important when it comes to making an image gallery. The uploaded file will be attached to the post or page that you are editing while uploading a file.
- The number of comments waiting on the attached post or page.
- The date when the file was uploaded.

If you hover over the row with your mouse, links for **Edit, Delete Permanently,** and **View** will appear. You can click on the file's title or the **Edit** link to edit **Title, Caption, Description, Alt text,** and even the image itself. More on that in a bit.

You can also add a new file to your media library. Navigate to **Media | Add New** to get a page similar to the upload media page that you got while uploading a file for a post. When you click on the **Select Files** button and select the file to be uploaded, or drag-and-drop it directly from your desktop, it will upload it and then give you the same options you got when uploading an item through a page or post.

Enter a title, caption, and description if you want, and click on the **Update** button.

Your new item will appear in the media library and will be unattached to any post or page. However, you'll still be able to use what you just uploaded in any post or page.

To do that, click on the **Add Media** button as you did before on the **Add/Edit Post** or **Add/Edit Page** screen. However, instead of uploading a new file, select it from the media library (the default screen after clicking on the **Add Media** button), as shown in the following screenshot:

When you click on any image displayed on this **Insert Media** screen, you'll see the same set of options you got after uploading an image. Now, you can click on the **Insert into Post** button. The media item will now show as **Attached to** that post or page.

Media Manager

The aforementioned **Insert Media** screen that is visible on the preceding screenshot is also known as the **Media Manager**. This Media Manager is a relatively new feature in WordPress as it was introduced in Version 3.5. Its interface is a lot different than it was in the previous versions of the platform. It's certainly more visually attractive and, at the same time, much easier to use.

You can always access the Media Manager from within the **Add/Edit Post** or **Add/ Edit Page**screens by clicking on the **Add Media** button. We've already discussed two ways of using it: uploading new media and attaching media that has been previously uploaded. But that's not all. The Media Manager has a lot more interesting stuff under the hood.

First of all, if we take a look at the left sidebar, there are four links there (please review the preceding screenshot). Starting from the top, we have:

- **Insert Media**
- **Create Gallery**
- **Set Featured Image**
- **Insert from URL**

Also, later on, when you have some third-party plugins installed, you might find even more links in that sidebar, but for now, four it is.

Clicking on any of them will reload the center part of the screen to present a new range of features. The **Insert Media** tab—the default one—we've mostly covered already. It's where you can either upload new files or select existing ones from the media library. This tab also provides a handy search box and a filtering drop-down menu, as shown in the following screenshot:

The filtering dropdown won't be of much use right now, but once you have hundreds of different media in the media library, being able to sort through them will become invaluable. The filtering dropdown simply lets you display only media of a specific type (**Uploaded to this post**, **Images**, **Audio**, **Video**, and **All media items**). The search field is simply a search field, it works immediately as you type (there's no submit button).

The second tab, **Create Gallery**, is a completely new gallery creation mechanism. In its current form, it was also introduced in WordPress 3.5. The number of things we can do in this module is truly impressive. It's all explained in the next chapter.

The third tab in the Media Manager, **Set Featured Image**, is yet another way for you to assign a featured image to your posts. (The first method was from within the box on the post editing screen itself.) This is a simple task. All you need to do is click on the image you want to save as the featured one and then click on the **Set featured image** button in the bottom-right corner.

Finally, we have the last tab, **Insert from URL**. Apart from the possibility to upload your own images, WordPress also allows you to pick an image from the web and have it displayed on your site. As always in such situations, you have to be careful not to take a copyrighted image, but from the technical point of view, WordPress is capable of importing any image that you input into the main field.

As you can see in the preceding screenshot, I've used a link to an image on `flickr. com` (an image from my personal account, actually). There are some additional settings here that you should use. Apart from the **Caption** and **Alt Text** field (this is the text that gets displayed in case the image fails to load for whatever reason), there are also settings for the alignment and the URL destination of the link (if you want to link your image to something).

The important thing worth pointing out here is that WordPress doesn't import this external image into your media library. Instead, it hotlinks the image from the source. In other words, the image is still on another server. What this means for you is that you don't have any actual control over this image. It can be removed overnight or replaced with another image without your knowledge. That's why in 90 percent of cases, it's better to download the image you want to use and then upload it to the media library, instead of hotlinking it.

Adding an image gallery

Just like I've mentioned in the previous section, the gallery module that you can find inside the Media Manager provides a completely redesigned modern way of working with image galleries. Just to remind you, this new gallery module can be accessed by clicking on the **Add Media** button when editing a post or a page, and then clicking on the **Create Gallery** link in the left sidebar.

One of the most user-friendly aspects about creating image galleries in WordPress is that you can drag-and-drop multiple images at once, and WordPress will immediately start turning them into a gallery. However, before you can do that, you have to choose where you want to display your new gallery, and that's what we're going to do next.

Choosing a post or page

This is a very simple step, and we've been doing this previously, so here we go.

You can add a gallery (or multiple galleries) to any new or existing page or post. I, for example, went with one of my existing posts, which you can see in the following screenshot:

Note where I have left my cursor (it's right in the middle if you can't see it). I made sure to leave it in a spot on the page where I want my gallery to appear, that is, underneath my introductory paragraph.

Selecting/uploading images

You can start either by uploading some new images or selecting the ones already in your media library. If it's the former you're after, then simply click on the **Create Gallery** link on the left-hand side, grab some images from your desktop, and drag-and-drop them onto the upload area, as shown in the following screenshot:

If you want to work with some of your images that are already in the media library, then just click on the **Media Library** link as shown in the following screenshot. As an example, I've selected two images that I want to use (they have a checkbox in the upper-right corner):

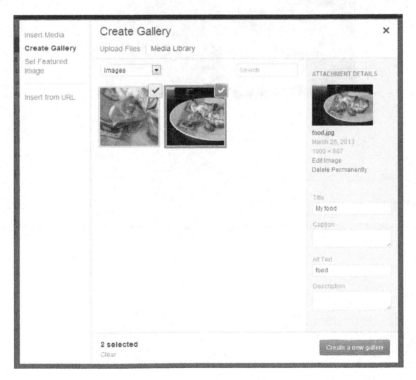

At this stage, you can adjust the titles and descriptions of the images if you want to, and then click on the **Create a new gallery** button. In the next step, you have the opportunity to rearrange your images by dragging them around the display area. You can also adjust the captions (the captions will be saved so they can be reused later on if you're creating a gallery using the same images). On the right-hand side, under **Link To**, there's a drop-down menu where you can change the link destination for each image. The way a gallery works in WordPress is when a visitor clicks on any image, they will be redirected either to the media file itself or to the attachment page (an individual page created for each image by default). Going with the default value of **Media File** is the recommended choice. The other two settings: the number of columns, and the **Random Order** checkbox, are pretty self-explanatory. When you're done just click on the **Insert gallery** button.

On the post editing screen, the gallery block itself doesn't look very attractive, which you can see in the following screenshot:

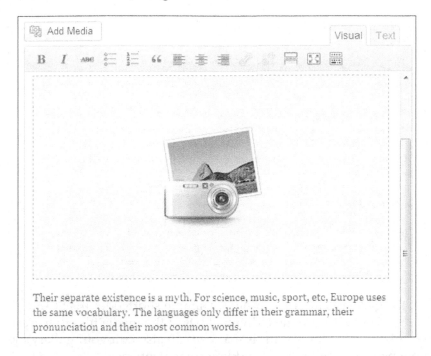

However, when you view the gallery on the frontend of your site, it's going to look great. The degree of its greatness depends closely on the theme you're using though. When you click on any of the images, you'll be taken to a larger version of the image.

Also, while on the post editing screen, you can edit any image and any gallery by clicking on the image itself and then on the Edit Image icon that's going to appear. The icon to delete the image is just next to it, as shown in the following screenshot:

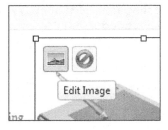

One more thing, if you're in the text view, you'll see the gallery shortcode instead of the visual gallery block:

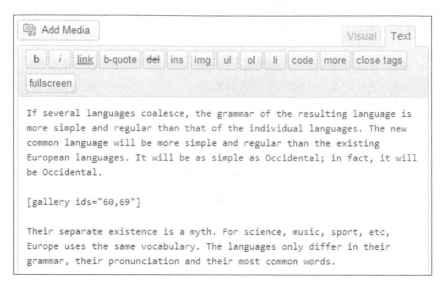

In this case, the gallery is inserted through a simple shortcode: `[gallery ids="60,15"]`. These IDs are the individual IDs of the media files that are a part of the gallery. What this means is that you can also edit your gallery by hand, simply by replacing the IDs or adding some new ones.

Because I'm uploading the photos while editing this particular post, all of these photos will be *attached* to this post, which is a nice way of indicating what images go where.

Learning more

The `[gallery]` shortcode is quite powerful! Take a look at the codex to get all of the parameters: `http://codex.wordpress.org/Gallery_Shortcode`.

Importing/exporting your content

The final thing I want to describe in this chapter is the feature of importing and exporting your content. By default, WordPress allows you to "take" content from other places and publish it on your site. There's a number of platforms supported, including former Blogger, LiveJournal, Tumblr blogs, and more. You can see the complete list by navigating to **Tools | Import** (it's also the starting point when importing content), as shown in the following screenshot:

Importing content

If you want to import content from any source, after you click on any of the links visible on the preceding screenshot, WordPress will prompt you to install some plugins to fully enable the feature. Plugins are the topic of the next chapter, but the way WordPress uses them for importing is really a hands-off approach so you don't have to know much about plugins themselves in order to be able to import content.

Now, importing content from each of the available platforms is a bit different, but the general process looks similar, so we're going to use another WordPress site as an example here (that is, we're going to import content from another WordPress site). The first step is to click on the **WordPress** link visible on the preceding screenshot. Immediately, you'll see a prompt to install the **WordPress Importer** plugin, as shown in the following screenshot:

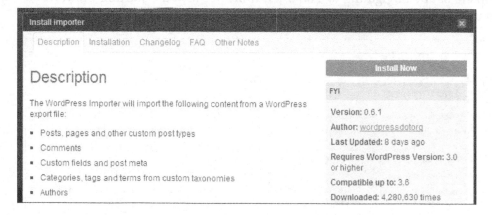

You can just click on the red **Install Now** button and the process will start automatically. When it finishes, you can navigate back to **Tools | Import**, click on the **WordPress** link again, and the following screenshot is what you'll see:

A very simple interface where all you have to do is take a WordPress export file and upload it to your site. The platform will take care of extracting the archive and importing the content in it. As a result, your site is going to be filled with new posts, pages, comments, custom fields, and navigation menus.

The main purpose of this feature is to help everyone who's migrating their sites from platforms, such as Blogger or LiveJournal. Imagine, if someone had a Blogger blog with over a hundred posts in it, going through each one individually and inputting it to WordPress by hand would be time-consuming. With this feature, it can be done in minutes.

Exporting content

Exporting content is even simpler than importing. To start, navigate to **Tools | Export**.

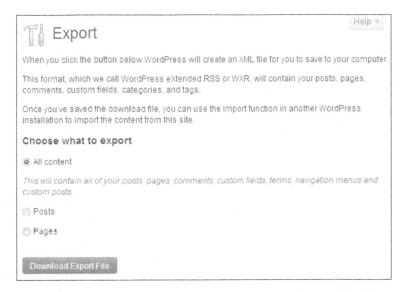

There's not much you can do here except select what you want to export and then click on the big **Download Export File** button to download the WordPress export file.

Selecting **All content** will export your posts, pages, comments, custom fields, terms, navigation menus, and custom posts. In a word, everything. Selecting just **Posts** or **Pages** is pretty much self-explanatory.

When you click on the **Download Export File** button, you will end up with a file that's just like the one we used when importing. This means that you can take it and create a mirror-copy of your site somewhere else under another domain name.

Summary

This chapter explored all of the content WordPress can manage that's not directly about blogging. You learned about static pages, menus, links, the media library, the Media Manager, image galleries, header and background settings, and more.

You are now fully equipped to use the WordPress Admin panel to control all of your website's content. Next, you'll learn how to expand your site's functionality by installing new plugins. This is exactly what we'll be discussing in the next chapter.

5
Plugins and Widgets

The topic of plugins and widgets has grown a lot in recent years. Nowadays, it's hard to imagine any WordPress site that could operate without at least a handful of (essential) plugins or widgets.

In this chapter, we will get to know what plugins are, why to use them, how to use them, where to get them, and how to be up-to-date and take notice of any new useful plugin that gets released into the community. We will also talk about some of the most basic and popular plugins in the WordPress world and why getting them might be a good idea. Finally, we'll learn how to work with widgets to make our sidebars even more functional and reader-friendly. Okay, let's get on with it!

Breaking down plugins – what are they?

Simply speaking, plugins are small scripts (files with executable PHP code) that allow you to include new functionality in your WordPress site—functionality that is not available or enabled by default.

One of the best things about WordPress is that it's a quite optimized platform. It makes your site load quickly and doesn't contain much redundant code. However, WordPress itself only offers the absolute essential range of features—the ones that are useful to everyone. At the same time, the platform provides a straightforward way of expanding the abilities of your site by introducing, you guessed it, plugins. The idea is simple, if you want your site to be able to handle a specific and new task, there's surely a plugin for that. Much like in the Apple world and the popular expression: *there's an app for that.*

Why to use plugins

The best thing about plugins is that you don't need any specific programming knowledge in order to use them. Essentially, they are just like standard applications for iOS or Android. You can install them and enjoy the things they have to offer without knowing what's going on inside.

Furthermore, the right combination of plugins can make your site more optimized, more user-friendly, more attractive, more social-media-friendly, properly backed up, protected against spam, and ultimately, unique. Plugins really are one of the best things about WordPress.

You see, before content management systems like WordPress were popularized, there was no easy way for site owners to introduce new functionalities on their sites. Doing so always required hiring a professional programmer and investing in the whole development process. Nowadays, this is no longer the case and virtually anyone can have an impressive site without losing their shirt.

Where to get plugins

The community behind WordPress plugins is a huge one. There's no one central plugin-building company, developers all over the world create plugins and then distribute them across the Internet. And very often, they receive no direct compensation whatsoever.

The best place to go for WordPress plugins is the official directory at http://wordpress.org/extend/plugins/.

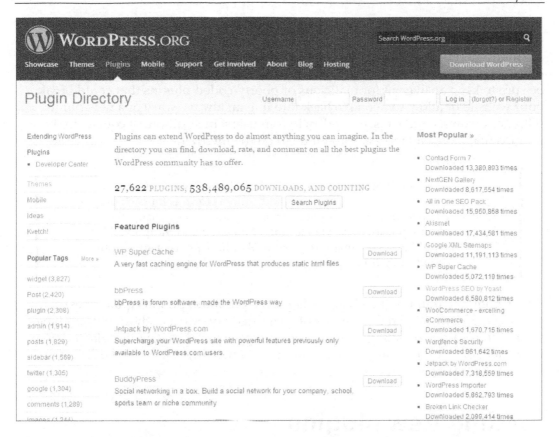

There are over 27,000 different plugins available in the directory at the time of writing and this number is constantly expanding with around 110 new plugins being added every week. This really is an impressive number considering the fact that many of those plugins are very advanced pieces of web software and not just simple, one-script add-ons.

There's a search field available in the center of the page in the directory (visible in the preceding screenshot), which allows you to search plugins by topic and by tag. You can also view a list of the most popular and featured plugins. In short, the official plugin directory is where you should always go first when looking for a plugin.

You can also do Google searches. I recommend searching for the problem you're trying to solve and see what plugins other users recommend and why. Often, there are multiple plugins that perform similar functions, and you will find the feedback of other WordPress users valuable in choosing between them. However, as you do this, be sure to keep an eye out for malicious or poorly-coded plugins that could break your website or allow someone to hack into it. I am always wary of a new plugin with no reviews, comments, or feedback from users, in addition, of course, to those plugins that have bad feedback about them on the Internet.

To get even more in-depth with your plugin investigation, you can also check out the changelogs and support forums for each plugin you're considering for your site (every plugin page inside the official plugin directory has a tab for the **Changelog** and **Support**). They should give you an idea of how well or how poorly a given plugin is coded, supported, and so on.

Apart from free plugins, there's also a big set of premium plugins (paid ones). However, you won't find them in the official directory. Most of those plugins have their own websites handling sales, customer support, and usage tutorials. If you're interested, one of the more popular premium plugins directories can be found at http://codecanyon.net/category/wordpress.

Finding new plugins

Generally speaking, if a given plugin proves that it's a quality solution and gains some popularity, it will be showcased on the home page of the official directory in the **Featured Plugins** section. But if you want to be up-to-date with things as they happen, you can pay attention to what's going on at: http://wordpress.org/extend/plugins/browse/new/

Additionally, a great way to discover new plugins is to become a regular at one of the popular blogs about WordPress. Although these blogs are not official creations (they are run by independent owners), they do provide an impressive range of knowledge and advice, not only on plugins but also on other aspects related to WordPress. The list includes:

- http://www.wpbeginner.com/
- http://digwp.com/
- http://yoast.com/
- http://wpmu.org/

- `http://themefuse.com/blog/`
- `http://wpengineer.com/`
- `http://net.tutsplus.com/category/tutorials/wordpress/`
- `http://wp.tutsplus.com/`
- `http://www.wprecipes.com/`

Installing a plugin – the how-to

The steps for installing a plugin are simple:

1. Find your plugin.
2. Install and activate it.
3. Configure and/or implement it (if necessary).

There are two ways to get the plugin into your WordPress installation:

- Install manually
- Install from within the WP Admin

The first option, installing plugins manually, generally requires a bit more effort than the second one, but sometimes it's the only way to work with some specific plugins (mostly premium ones). The second option, installing from within the WP Admin, is generally quicker and easier, but it's not possible in all cases. You need to be on a server that's configured correctly, in a way that lets WordPress add files (we talked about installing WordPress and server configuration in *Chapter 2, Getting Started*). Plus, the plugin you want to install has to be available in the WordPress Plugin Repository, that is, the official plugin directory.

In the following section, we'll go over the manual method first, and then handle autoinstallation.

Manual plugin installation

As an example here, I will install a popular plugin for handling site backups—Online Backup for WordPress. But the following procedure allows you to install any WordPress plugin you can get your hands on.

To install a plugin manually, you must start by downloading the plugin archive either from the official directory at `http://wordpress.org/extend/plugins/` or from some other website or source (usually when dealing with premium plugins).

In this case, the plugin is available in the official directory at:
http://wordpress.org/extend/plugins/wponlinebackup/

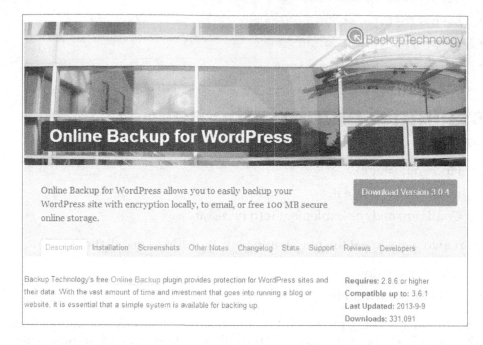

Just click on the orange-colored download button, and save the resulting ZIP file on your computer where you can find it again.

Before downloading any plugin, check the plugin compatibility. You can do it by looking at the parameter labeled **Compatible up to** that's visible on the plugin page (preceding screenshot). You can check which version of WordPress you are using on your site by taking a look into the **Updates** section of the **Dashboard** (available at http://yoursite.com/wp-admin/update-core.php).

Last checked on October 28, 2013 at 2:13 pm.   Check Again

You have the latest version of WordPress. Futu

At this point, if your server is set up correctly, you'll be able to upload the ZIP file directly by navigating to **Plugins** | **Add New** | **Upload**:

If this automatic uploader doesn't work for you, you can do this the old-fashioned way:

First unzip, that is, extract the ZIP file you downloaded so that it's a folder, probably named in this case, wponlinebackup.

Using your FTP client, upload this folder inside the wp-content/plugins/ folder of your WordPress installation. You'll also see the two plugins in that folder that WordPress came with — akismet and hello.php.

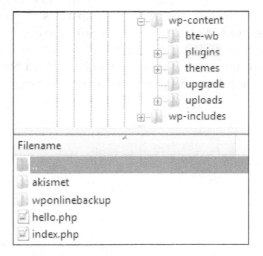

 If you need some assistance with FTP software, please review *Chapter 2, Getting Started*, where we talked about the topic of installing WordPress.

Now, go to your WP Admin and navigate to **Plugins**. You'll see the three plugins on this page. Just click on the **Activate** link in the **Online Backup for WordPress** row:

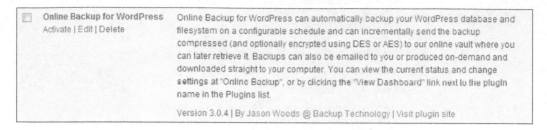

Now, you are ready for the final step, that is, configuring and ultimately making use of the plugin.

But before we shift our attention to this, let's discuss an easier method of dealing with plugin installation, which is actually the recommended way (if it's available in your situation).

Autoinstallation

If the plugin you want to install is available in the official plugin directory at http://wordpress.org/extend/plugins/ and your server configuration meets the requirements for Autoinstallation (your web host has to grant you the read/write/modify directory and file permissions; usually the case with the majority of serious hosting companies), then you can search for and install a new plugin from within the WP Admin. Just navigate to **Plugins | Add New**. If you already know the plugin you want, type its name into the search box.

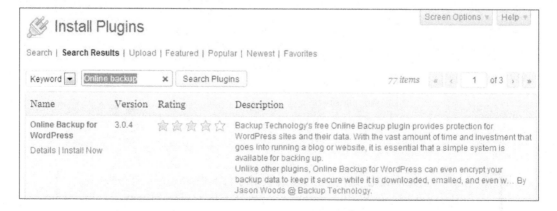

When you see the plugin, you can click on **Details** to see the plugin's details:

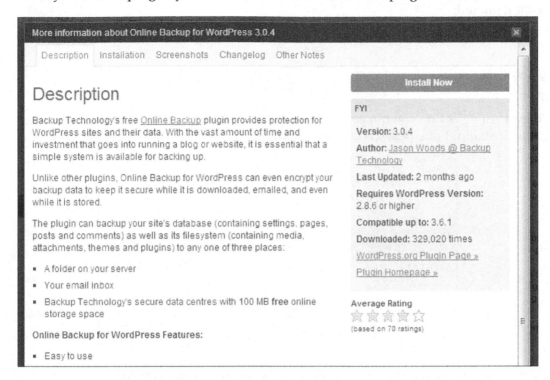

I recommend you always look at this information carefully. Be sure to watch for version compatibility. Just like with the manual installation method, there's a parameter labeled **Compatible up to** here as well. In some cases, you can risk installing a plugin that's a little outdated, but you should proceed with caution.

After the installation, you need to test the plugin carefully and verify that it's behaving correctly. Most of the time, if the **Compatible up to** parameter indicates an older version of WordPress, it doesn't necessarily mean that the plugin will fail to work with a newer version. It just means that it hasn't been thoroughly tested. Hence, the importance of performing your own tests. However, I strongly advise against installing any plugins that haven't been updated in more than two years. Luckily, whenever you encounter such a plugin, WordPress itself will warn you through this message on the official plugin page:

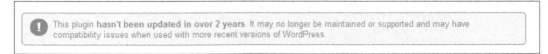

Inside the plugin details section in the WP Admin there's a parameter labeled **Last Updated**:

If everything is fine you can proceed by clicking the **Install Now** button, and you're done installing! The next screen you see will invite you to activate the plugin:

Installing Plugin: Online Backup for WordPress 3.0.4

Downloading install package from
http://downloads.wordpress.org/plugin/wponlinebackup.3.0.4.zip...

Unpacking the package...

Installing the plugin...

Successfully installed the plugin Online Backup for WordPress 3.0.4.

Activate Plugin | Return to Plugin Installer

In the case of this plugin, I do recommend you go ahead and activate it (the **Activate Plugin** link visible on the preceding screenshot). Some plugins are perfectly operational right after activation while others require some additional tuning up. Here are the three most likely scenarios:

- You may not have to do anything. Some plugins simply change the way WordPress does certain things, and activating them is all you need to do.
- You may have to configure a plugin's details before it begins to work. Some plugins need you to make choices and set new settings.
- There may not be a configuration page, but you may have to add some code to one of your theme's template files.

If you're unsure of what to do after you've uploaded and activated your plugin, be sure to read the readme file that came with your plugin, or look at the FAQ on the plugin's website.

Many plugin authors accept donations. I strongly recommend giving donations to the authors of plugins that you find useful. It helps to encourage everyone in the community to continue writing great plugins that everyone can use.

If for some reason the Autoinstallation process has failed then you will need to switch to the manual installation described in the previous section.

The must-have pack of plugins

Even though there are over 27,000 plugins available in the official directory, you surely don't need all of them on your WordPress site. There is a small set that we might call the "must-have pack". And obviously my list of must-have plugins can be different from the next guy's, so please treat the following information more as guidance rather than as a written-in-stone necessity. That being said, I am honest here, and despite the fact that some of my blogs feature more than 25 plugins working at the same time, the essential must-have list consists of only seven plugins. All these handle a specific task geared towards making a WordPress site better and more functional.

Backing up

Let's start with this one as we've already gone through the installation process of one of the top backing up plugins—Online Backup for WordPress. Now, backing up is probably the most important task for any website owner, and I'm saying this in all seriousness. For instance, can you imagine a situation in which you lose your whole site overnight with no ability to restore it? This might sound a bit hard to believe right now, but it does happen. If it's a personal blog you've been running then it's not that tragic. But for a business website, it's a completely different story.

This plugin allows you to handle website backups in an easy-to-grasp and hassle-free way. It doesn't require any initial setup (there are some settings but the plugin is already operational on the default ones), you can just go ahead and use it right away. Simply go to **Tools | Online Backup**. There, you'll be able to handle both database and filesystem backups, schedule backups to take place automatically, or perform them manually whenever you wish to.

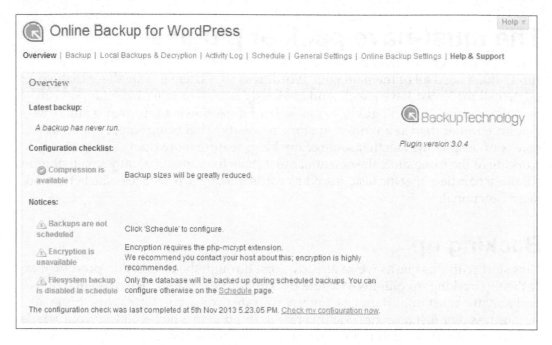

To get started, you can click on the **Backup** link visible in the top menu. On the following screen you can select what you want to backup (**Database** and **Filesystem**), and what you want to do with the backup once it's ready. The available options are:

- Get it sent to the Online Backup for WordPress Vault (an online service that's partly free, if you're interested)
- Download it to your local computer
- Have it e-mailed to you

My suggestion is to try downloading it for the first time. Once you click on the **Start Manual Backup** button, the backup process will begin and you will be informed about the result shortly afterwards. Later on, it can take a while if you have a lot of content on your site.

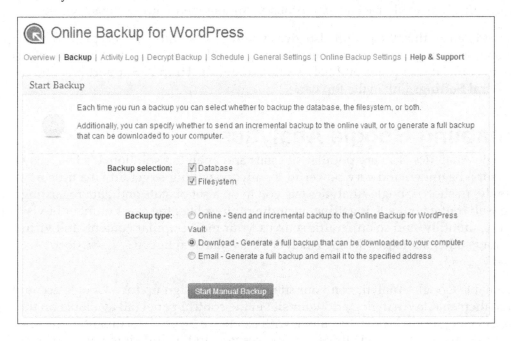

When the backup is ready you will be able to see it in the same **Backup** section:

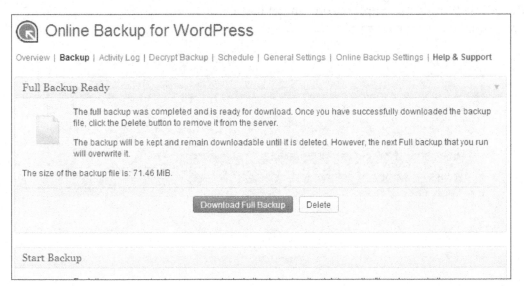

There is also an option of scheduling regular backups (go to the **Schedule** section through the link in the top bar). This is not 100 percent reliable though, so you should probably set up a reminder to check if your backup has been e-mailed to you or not. The frequency you choose should depend on how often you want to edit your site; weekly backups are probably frequent enough for most people.

Apart from all this, the plugin also gives you the possibility to encrypt your backups, so only you can access and then use them. To get the how-to on this feature, please see the official user guide and help section under the **Help & Support** link and the **General Settings** link in the top bar.

Enabling Google Analytics

Google Analytics is a very popular site stats and analytics solution. It's free, easy to use for a beginner, and very powerful for anyone willing to get into it a little more deeply. In short, Google Analytics lets you in on a set of stats and data regarding the web traffic your site is getting, including things like: the exact number of visitors (daily, monthly, and so on), traffic sources, your most popular content, and virtually myriads other statistics. Google Analytics is available at `https://www.google.com/analytics/`.

To enable Google Analytics on your site, you have to sign up for a Google account first, then enable Analytics, add your site in the control panel (all available on the official Google Analytics page, along with extensive tutorial documentation), and then take the tracking code that Google gives you and include it in your site. This last step is where the Google Analytics for WordPress plugin comes into play and makes the whole thing a lot simpler. You can get it at `http://wordpress.org/extend/plugins/google-analytics-for-wordpress/`.

Once you download and activate it, go to **Settings | Google Analytics** (in WP Admin). Although the plugin has a lot of settings, the only thing you must do in order to make it work is to authenticate the plugin to enable connection with your Analytics account. Just click on the **Click here to authenticate with Google** button. This will redirect you to a page on Google where you have to click another button, **Grant access**, and then you'll be taken back to your WP Admin. Now you can select your Google Analytics account and profile that you want to use for monitoring the site.

If you're having problems with this semi-automatic way of authentication, you can simply input your Analytics code (called the UA code) manually. This code is visible in your profile at Google Analytics (usually starts with UA- and is followed by nine numbers).

Once you're done with the authentication procedure, your site is fully connected to Google Analytics and the traffic stats are being collected. After a while, you can navigate to your profile in Google Analytics and see how your site's been doing in terms of visitor popularity. Also, to get a more immediate indication whether the tracking code has been set correctly or not, you can navigate to the new Real-Time traffic section inside Google Analytics.

Caching

To be honest, caching is a pretty complicated concept. If you speak "engineering" then here's the definition: In computer science, a cache is a component that transparently stores data so that future requests for that data can be served faster. What it means in plain English is that if you have caching enabled on your site, it will load faster and be much more accessible for your audience/visitors. Luckily, even though the concept itself is not that straightforward, the plugin that enables you to cache is.

Currently, the top of the line plugin is called W3 Total Cache, available at
`http://wordpress.org/extend/plugins/w3-total-cache/`.

And it's not just me recommending it, a number of major hosting companies
and experts say that it provides THE way to get your site optimized fast. More
than that, the plugin is also in use on some major blogs around the web, for
example, `http://css-tricks.com/`.

The installation procedure is the same as with any other WordPress plugin. But right
after you activate it, you'll see that the usage is quite different. For one, it's accessible
through a completely new section in the left sidebar.

It's labeled **Performance** and it's placed right below **Settings**. Probably less than
a second after you click it, you will realize that this plugin is a huge one. It could
probably have a completely separate book written about it. So here, I will only
share the quick start guide, so to speak.

Go to **Performance | General Settings** and browse through the page. There's
a number of checkboxes labeled as **Enable**. Just to get started with the plugin,
I advise you to enable the following blocks:

- **Page Cache**
- **Database Cache**
- **Object Cache**
- **Browser Cache**

And then click either of the **Save all settings** buttons. From now on, caching will be fully enabled on your site and your visitors should start experiencing performance improvements right away.

Obviously, we've only touched on the possibilities and customizations that this plugin brings to the table, so I encourage you to give it a closer look in your spare time.

Search Engine Optimization (SEO)

SEO is one of the most popular topics online (at least among website owners). The short truth is that working on your site's SEO, if done right, will raise its position in the search engines (like Google) and will bring you more visitors on a daily basis. The concept is pretty simple in theory, but the work involved in order to achieve this can become a full-time job. If you're not interested in devoting a big chunk of your time to SEO then at least get this plugin WordPress SEO, available at `http://wordpress.org/extend/plugins/wordpress-seo/` and have the basics handled. The plugin is very popular in the blogosphere. Among others, it's being used by blogs like `http://css-tricks.com/` and `http://www.viperchill.com/`.

Similarly to the previous plugin—W3 Total Cache—this one has a custom section within the WP Admin too. It's visible right below **Settings** and is called **SEO**.

The best way to get the core how-to on this plugin is to click the **Start Tour** button visible at the top of the settings page.

This tour will guide you through the most basic settings and features of the plugin. I really encourage you to spend a while optimizing your site with this plugin, because this work will surely pay off in the long run, or even much sooner.

There's a separate resource published by the author of the WordPress SEO plugin, Joost de Valk. It's where you should go to get true in-depth info on how to set up the plugin, and also what other things you can do to make your site more SEO-friendly. You can find it at `http://yoast.com/articles/wordpress-seo/`.

Securing your site

The issue of site security and hacker attacks is a serious thing online these days. You might be thinking that no one will try to harm your site in particular as you're not that popular yet, right? Well, the reality can be harsh in this case. Most hacker attacks are not about stealing your revenue or taking over your site as a whole, but they are about adding a small piece of code on your site that will link out to other external sites (most of the time either fraudulent sites or illicit content). The idea of such an attack is that you won't find out that it ever took place. This is the biggest danger.

Don't sweat though, there's a plugin to the rescue, BulletProof Security, available at `http://wordpress.org/extend/plugins/bulletproof-security/`.

Getting started with this plugin requires some basic setting up. First of all, download and activate it (the usual procedure). Next, navigate to the new section in the WP Admin labeled **BPS Security**:

Here, do the following things:

1. Click on the **Create secure.htaccess File** button visible in the first column as shown in the following screenshot:

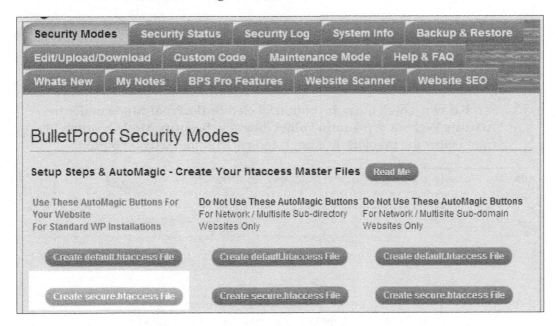

2. Scroll down, check the radio button labeled **BulletProof Mode** under the **Activate Website Root Folder .htaccess Security Mode** heading, and click on the Activate button:

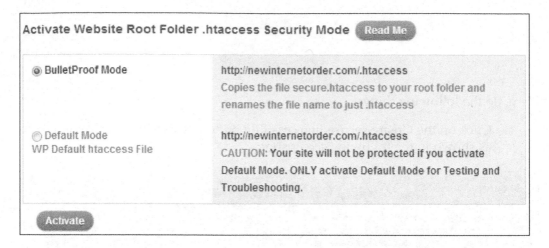

3. Scroll down, check the radio button labeled **BulletProof Mode** under the **Activate Website wp-admin Folder .htaccess Security Mode** heading (it's right below the previous heading), and click on the **Activate** button.

At this point, your site is fully protected against various hacker attacks. As usual, there are a lot more settings available in this plugin. However, I wouldn't advise playing around with them without reading the official documentation first. This type of protection is a very powerful mechanism and it's easy to make a mess if you're not careful.

Jetpack

This mysterious name is actually what one of the most popular plugins of today is called (it's being used by some mainstream blogs on the web; like Tim Ferriss' http://www.fourhourworkweek.com/). **Jetpack**, by the guys behind WordPress. com, offers a truly exceptional range of features and functionalities. The plugin consists of a number of modules that can be enabled or disabled one by one. This gives you full control over the features you want and don't want to use. Jetpack is available at http://wordpress.org/extend/plugins/jetpack/.

After downloading and activating it, you'll see a new section in the WP Admin, but this time, it's right below the Dashboard:

Inside, you can see all of the available modules and functionalities. Each comes with a **Learn More** button, **Configure/Deactivate** button, and a quick information on what the module has to offer.

In the current version, the modules are: **Notifications, Publicize, WordPress.com Stats, Jetpack Comments, Subscriptions, Likes, Carousel, Post By Email, Sharing, Spelling and Grammar, VaultPress, Gravatar Hovercards, Contact Form, Tiled Galleries, WP.me Shortlinks, Custom CSS, Shortcode Embeds, Mobile Theme, Beautiful Math, Extra Sidebar Widgets, Infinite Scroll, Phonon, JSON API, Mobile Push Notifications,** and **Enhanced Distribution**.

As you can see, the list is impressive, to say the least. I won't go over each of the modules here in detail because in total, it would probably require a chapter of its own. Instead, I encourage you to click the **Learn More** button that's next to each module and get a basic understanding of what they do. Quite possibly, the ones you'll find most useful are: **Publicize** (share your content automatically to various social media platforms), **WordPress.com Stats** (accessible stats), **Sharing** (social media share buttons that your visitors can use), **Spelling and Grammar** (an advanced spelling and grammar checker), **Contact Form** (let your visitors contact you directly), and **Shortcode Embeds** (an easy way of including YouTube videos and other external media in your content).

Switching to maintenance mode

The plugin that closes this short must-have list is called ThemeFuse Maintenance Mode, and it's available at `http://wordpress.org/extend/plugins/themefuse-maintenance-mode/`.

Sometimes when we're working on our sites, like for instance, playing with the theme, adjusting sidebars, testing out new layouts, and so on, we don't want to present our work-in-progress to the whole world. Instead, a much better solution is to make the changes only visible to us while the rest of the world sees a placeholder page, which informs them that there's something going on in the background and that the site will be available soon.

A page like the following screenshot:

This is exactly what the plugin in question allows you to do. The trick is that if you're a logged in administrator, you'll be able to see the site normally. But whoever comes across your site from the outside will see the placeholder page (it all happens automatically, you don't have to do anything else other than enabling the plugin).

Right after installing and activating the plugin, go to **Settings | ThemeFuse Maintenance Plugin** to adjust your coming-soon/placeholder page.

Available customizations include:

- **Upload Logo**: This specifies the possibility to upload a logo
- **Upload Background**: This specifies the possibility to upload a background
- **Date**: It specifies the date when the site is going to be back online
- **Text**: Text for the loader bar
- **Completed**: It shows a percentage value
- **Content**: It specifies some additional custom content to be displayed
- **Twitter username**: It is used to present a Twitter stream on the page

Be aware that the placeholder page will be visible until you deactivate the plugin. Therefore, once your work with the site is done, don't forget to go to the Plugins section in the WP Admin and deactivate the plugin. This will put your site back online for the whole world to see.

 If you're using the aforementioned W3 Total Cache plugin then it's a good idea to flush the cache right after enabling ThemeFuse Maintenance Mode (the **empty all caches** button in the main dashboard of W3 Total Cache as shown in the following screenshot). This will make sure that every visitor gets a consistent experience when browsing your site.

Widgets

Widgets are one of the native mechanisms in WordPress. Their main purpose is to provide us with an easy-to-use way of customizing the sidebars and footers of our site with the addition of extra content. Even though the most common placement of widgets is indeed the sidebar, the only actual rule is that a widget can be displayed inside a widget area. And a widget area can be anywhere a theme developer wants it to be. Common widgets contain:

- A monthly archive of blog posts
- A clickable list of pages

- A clickable list of recent posts

- A metadata box (containing log in/out links, RSS feed links, and other WordPress links)

- Recent comments posted on the blog

- A clickable list of categories

- A tag cloud

- A block of text and HTML

- A search box, and so on

These days, most themes are widget-enabled with one or more widget areas available for use. If I were to simplify this a bit, I'd say that widget areas behave like locations for menus.

To control the widgets on your new website, navigate to **Appearance | Widgets**:

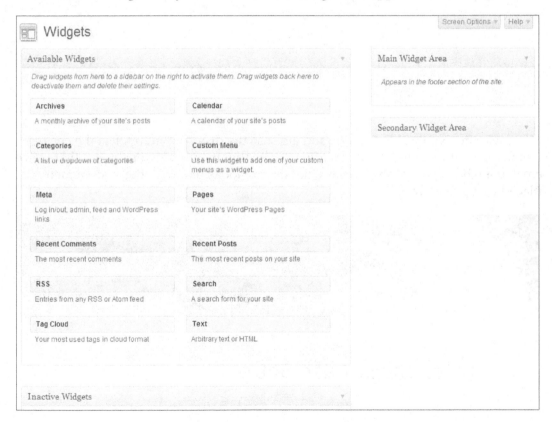

Twenty Thirteen comes with two widget areas. One of them is called the Main Widget Area and the other the Secondary Widget Area. Let's discuss them both.

The Main Widget Area appears in the footer section of the site, while the Secondary Widget Area sits in the sidebar on posts and pages. You can take any of the widgets visible on the left-hand side and drag and drop them in the right-hand area under Main Widget Area or Secondary Widget Area. For example, let's take the **Custom Menu** block and drag it all the way to the Secondary Widget Area. The result is as follows:

Now, we can give this block a title and also use the drop-down to select the custom menu we want to include in this widget. Currently, there's only one menu that we've created a while ago — **Main**. This is what the site looks like with the custom menu placed in the sidebar:

At this point, we have the main menu displayed two times on the site. One is in the top area and the other is within the sidebar. As you can see, if you want to place your custom menu somewhere on the site, you have two ways of doing so. You can assign it by going to **Appearance | Menus**, or use it as a custom menu widget and place it in any widget area that your theme supports.

Enabling any other type of widget is very similar to the process described above. All you need to do is drag the widget you like and drop it onto the area where you want to have it displayed. Then, once the widget is in place, you can adjust its settings and content.

When it comes to working in the **Widgets** section, you can click on the little down arrow at the right of any widget to expand the details and see the options. You can drag a new widget in from the collection of **Available Widgets** on the left. You can drag existing widgets up and down to change their order. You can delete a widget by expanding it and then clicking on **Delete**.

Experiment with putting widgets into different widget areas and then refresh your blog to see how they look. Always be sure to click on **Save** if you make changes to a widget.

Also, at the bottom of the screen, there's one more section labeled **Inactive Widgets**. Many widgets have their settings and parameters. And even if you don't want to display a particular widget on your site at the moment, or don't necessarily want to lose its settings in case you'd like to use the widget again in the future, this section is where you should put it. Just like the label says, it's where you can drag your widgets to remove them from the sidebar but keep them as inactive. This is also where you will find any widgets that were previously active in a sidebar, but that got deactivated automatically after switching to a theme that doesn't have the same sidebar naming convention.

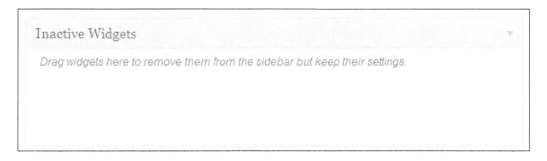

Summary

This chapter was all about expanding the features available on your site and making your content more attractive without the need to touch any source code. Basically, that's the whole idea behind plugins. Let's face it, most developers actually don't need plugins because they can code things on their own. However, for the rest of the world, plugins are what makes WordPress easy to use and attractive for everyone.

At this point we know how to control the content of our WordPress site, so now it's about time to learn how to control the display. In the next chapter, we will start discussing themes.

6
Choosing and Installing Themes

One of the greatest advantages of using a **Content Management System** (**CMS**) for your blog or website is that you are able to change the look and feel of your website without being knowledgeable about HTML and CSS. Almost every CMS allows users to customize the look of their site without having to worry about their content being changed. These managed looks are named themes. On other platforms (for example, Blogger, Joomla!, Drupal, and so on), themes are sometimes called templates or layouts.

Thousands of WordPress themes are available for download free of cost and thousands of more themes are available at a pretty low cost. Some of the free themes are developed by members of the WordPress community and listed on WordPress's main website, that is `http://wordpress.org/extend/themes/`.

Before you change the theme of your current site, you will want to know the following aspects:

- Some basic things about the theme you're considering
- Finding quality themes
- Choosing the theme that best suits your content and audience
- Installing a theme

In this chapter, we will discuss all of these topics. This chapter is a ground-up guide to using themes. In the next chapter, we will discuss the advanced topic of developing your own themes.

If you are using `WordPress.com` to host your WordPress website, you cannot upload themes to your site; you have to choose from the hundred or so themes that `WordPress.com` makes available to you.

Finding themes

There are dozens of websites that offer WordPress themes for you to download and implement on your own website. Many theme developers offer their themes for free, whereas some charge a small fee. Of course, if you cannot find a free theme that fits your needs, you can always hire a theme developer to create a customized theme for you, or you can be your own theme developer (refer to *Chapter 7, Developing Your Own Theme*).

WordPress Themes Directory

The first place you should always go to while looking for a theme is the official WordPress **Themes Directory** that is available at `http://wordpress.org/extend/themes/`. This is where everyone in the WordPress community uploads their free themes and tags them with keywords that describe the basic look, layout, and function of their theme. Have a look at the following screenshot:

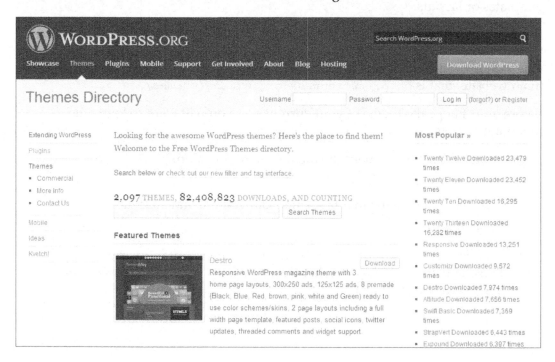

By looking at the list of popular themes on the right-hand side of the screen, you can see which themes are chosen most often. **Twenty Thirteen**, as you already know, is the default theme that WordPress uses automatically when you first install it.

To get a better idea of what a theme will look like than what's offered by the thumbnail, just click on the title of the theme (in my case it's **Responsive** that is available at `http://wordpress.org/extend/themes/responsive`). You'll be taken to the theme's detail page, as shown in the following screenshot:

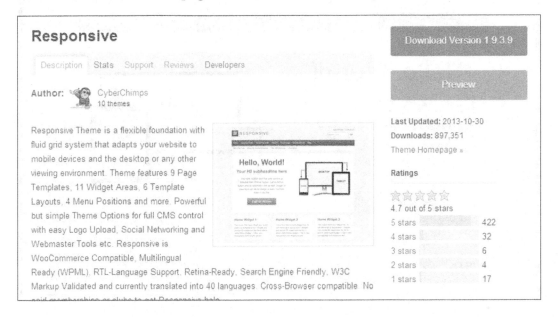

The preceding screenshot shows you the theme's description, all of the tags that apply to it, the average rating given to it by other users, and some comments on the theme. If you click on the **Preview** button, you'll get to see the theme actually in action. The theme in action will appear as shown in the following screenshot:

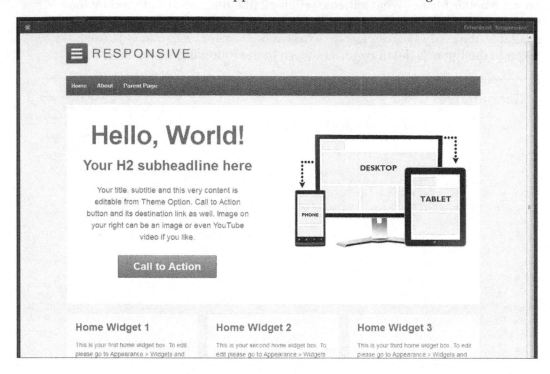

This preview is very useful. It not only shows you exactly what the theme will look like and what is included in the sidebar, but also includes examples of a variety of different HTML and element styles so that you can see how they'll appear. These elements include images, headings (1, 2, 3, 4, 5, and 6), paragraphs, lists, forms, tables, blockquote, code, and links.

If you browse through this site and find a theme you like, make a note of it; we'll discuss how to add it to your WordPress site later in this chapter.

It's also worth pointing out that each theme in the official directory comes with its own **Support** section and user **Reviews** section. You can view them by clicking on one of the links available in the bar just below the theme's name (highlighted in the following screenshot):

Main types of themes

As mentioned earlier, there are two main types of themes, namely free themes and premium (paid) themes. Also, if you don't consider price being a factor here, we can also divide themes into three additional groups, namely **standard themes**, **child themes**, and **theme frameworks**.

We will discuss child themes in detail in the next chapter, so for now, let's just say that a child theme is a theme that inherits the functionality of another theme, that is the parent theme.

Standard themes are themes meant to work in their original form while allowing some basic customizations and tuning up (just as the default theme, **Twenty Thirteen**).

Theme frameworks, on the other hand, are meant to be used as a base for custom theme development and some heavy customizations to make them fit the user's needs hand-in-glove. While going for theme frameworks probably sounds good from your perspective right now, the fact is that they are usually highly code-heavy products, which means that you can't really take full advantage of them if you don't possess any programming skill or don't have anyone on your payroll who does. We will discuss theme frameworks in the next chapter, when we start creating our own themes. In short, creating a theme from the ground up will have more educational value, but when it comes to getting the most out of your time and ending up with the most quality result, theme frameworks are the way to go.

At the end, standard themes are what most bloggers and site owners work with during their WordPress journeys. Especially if they don't need any advanced customizations or don't run purpose-specific websites, such as animated sites and interactive sites.

Finding more themes

If you can't find a theme in the directory that you like, you have other options. There are other sites with free themes and also sites that sell themes for a price. Most commercial themes are offered at two or three price points. The first price is simply the cost of buying the theme for your own use and can be anywhere from $30 to $100. Such a license allows you to use the theme on a single site. The second price is the price you pay if you want to be able to use the theme on multiple sites (domains) or when you need the project graphics (for example, Photoshop documents) and other development files. In this case, it's usually from $60 to $200. The last price point, although not that popular nowadays, is the exclusive license. You can get it if you want to be the only user of the theme. That can be anywhere from $500 to even $1,500, or more.

Let's focus on free versus paid themes here. While every theme in the official directory is free, the rest of the Internet is split in half on this. Some sites provide free themes exclusively while others offer paid ones exclusively. There's also a number of distributors who sit in between. I, personally, don't advise getting any free themes from anywhere other than either the official directory or one of the respected theme stores, which offer some free themes as a promotional method. The reason is simple. Only quality themes are allowed into the official directory, and I'm not just talking about the look or the design. What matters apart from the design is also the code structure and code quality. There's not one theme that features any mysterious blocks of code, such as encrypted code or suspicious external links that will ever find its way into the directory. That's what ultimately makes the official directory one of the best sources of free WordPress themes on the Internet.

When it comes to various free themes being released in theme stores, the story is quite similar. The "first league" of WordPress themes, so to speak, comprises of respected, serious companies. So even when they release a free theme, they can't afford it being low quality or lacking in any other way. Therefore, in most cases they are safe to use as well.

The last thing we can witness online are hundreds, if not thousands of free themes being released on random websites, promoted through paid advertising, "top themes" lists, advertorial articles, and so on. Let me say this again, I don't advise you to get any of those, even if the designs are attractive. The fact is that you'll never know what sits on the inside and what security breaches can be taken advantage of to hack into such a theme. They are also almost never supported by their creators and there's no theme documentation or updates. In short, it is not worth it.

If you want to learn more about why unknown-origin free themes are unsafe to use, feel free to visit the article available at http://newinternetorder.com/free-wordpress-themes-are-evil/

Finally, if you have some money you'd like to invest in your site and its' quality, consider getting a full-blown premium theme, or even a premium theme framework. As I've mentioned, the price range is around $30 to $100 depending on the manufacturer and the features the theme comes with.

You are welcome to check out any theme provider you wish, but just to make things quicker, the following is a go-to-first list of quality theme stores:

- **StudioPress**: http://www.studiopress.com/
- **ThemeFuse**: http://themefuse.com/
- **DIYthemes**: http://diythemes.com/
- **WooThemes**: http://www.woothemes.com/
- **WiniThemes**: http://winithemes.com/
- **Rockable Themes**: http://rockablethemes.com/
- **ThemeForest**: http://themeforest.net/category/wordpress

In general, the most good commercial theme sites let you see a preview of the theme in action before you buy it. Some also let you customize the theme before download. As with any other online shopping experience, do a little research before buying to make sure you'll be getting a quality theme with decent support. There are plenty of badly-coded themes out there, and even themes with malicious code. Before buying a theme, verify the source of the theme and see if you can find feedback or reviews from anyone else who has purchased it.

To find even more sites that offer themes, just do a Google search for WordPress themes or premium WordPress themes and you'll get over sixty million hits. Also, keep in mind that you can choose a basic theme now and customize it, or create your own from scratch later as you build skills by reading this book.

Some not-design-related theme basics

For you to be better informed while choosing and installing themes, let's have a quick look at some factors to consider, and what actually makes a theme.

The structure of a theme

A WordPress theme is actually a collection of files in a folder. There are no special or unusual formats, just a few requirements for those files in the theme folder. The only requirements for a folder to be a valid WordPress theme are as follows:

- It should have a `style.css` file and an `index.php` file
- The `style.css` file must have the basic theme information in its first five lines

There are a number of additional files that you'll find in most of the theme folders. They are as follows:

- The `screenshot.png` file is the little thumbnail that shows what the theme looks like
- The `images` folder is where all images associated with the theme live
- A variety of files that are used for different purposes, for example `header.php`, `footer.php`, `page.php`, `single.php`, `archive.php`, and so on

You don't have to worry about these details now, but knowing them will help you identify what is going on in the themes you download for now. This will also be useful in the next chapter when we discuss about making your own theme from scratch.

Also, don't worry if you download a theme and its directory structure looks very different from what's described here. Some theme developers decide to go with their own structure in order to provide some extra features and a more customizable environment. This is mostly the case with various theme frameworks and big premium themes that come with their pre-made child themes.

When you download a theme, you are actually just downloading a zipped folder.

Factors to consider when choosing a theme

As you look through all of the available themes, you'll see that there is quite a variety of both look and feel, and layout.

To be honest, picking the perfect theme involves effort and some thought. A couple of years ago, there were just a handful of quality websites and stores where you could get your hands on some themes. Now, there are hundreds to thousands of them.

This all results in a situation where there are multiple factors to consider when selecting a theme.

The purpose of the theme

As I've already mentioned multiple times in this and the previous chapters, nowadays, WordPress is perfectly capable of running any kind of site, and this is reflected in the number of available themes. Therefore, the first question to answer is what do you need the theme for?

Depending on the kind of site you're planning to launch, you should focus on different types of themes. The following are some of the popular possibilities:

- **Traditional blogs**: They are the ones where the content is laid out in a reverse chronological order, with only several pages of static content.

- **Photo blogs**: They are very much like the traditional blogs when it comes to content organization, but in this case, the content consists mainly of photos. This is a popular type of blog among photographers and other creative individuals.

- **Video blogs**: They are very much like photo blogs, except now, we're dealing with videos.

- **Small business sites and corporate sites**: Most small business sites don't feature a lot of posts like traditional blogs. They usually focus on static pages for providing the most important information about the business (such as contact data and offer). This type is most commonly used by local businesses, such as restaurants, cafes, hotels, and other similar "physical" businesses. Corporate sites are very similar in nature, but are much bigger and feature much more content.

- **Online magazines**: The main difference between traditional blogs and online magazines is that the latter feature a lot more content with usually as many as ten or more posts being published every day. This requires good content layout and clear presentation.

- **E-commerce sites**: Traditionally known as online stores or shops. An e-commerce store is any website that offers a shopping cart functionality and allows its visitors to buy a wide range of products, much like they'd do in a traditional store or supermarket.

- **Software or app sites**: These are websites devoted to promoting or selling one specific product. Nowadays, it's usually some kind of an app or other piece of software.

The trick while choosing a theme for your site is to understand its purpose and make your decision based not only on the appearance of the theme but also on the thing you need the theme for, its capabilities, as well as options for further customization. The easiest way to do this is to pay attention to the categories of themes on the site where you're looking for them. For instance, if you go to one of the popular theme stores such as `http://www.woothemes.com/product-category/themes/` or `http://themefuse.com/wp-themes-shop/`, you'll see that they both feature great mechanisms for filtering themes by purpose. The following screenshot shows how ThemeFuse does it:

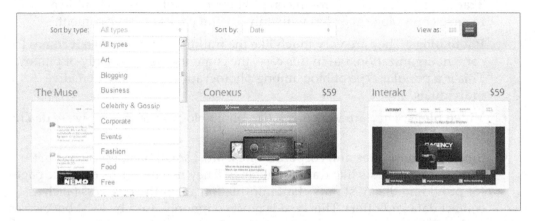

And the following screenshot is of WooThemes:

You can also do some research on the Internet and see what is the standard when it comes to the themes being used in your niche and for your type of site. For example, if you're thinking of launching a photo blog, check what sort of themes other photo blogs use. Do they feature a lot of sidebars? How big are the photos they publish? Are there a lot of static pages? And so on. The idea is this: Don't reinvent the wheel. If there's a significant number of sites that are similar to the one you're planning to launch, you should always try learning from them, and then make an educated decision when choosing your theme.

Theme licensing

If you're getting a theme from the official directory, this part doesn't concern you.

However, when getting a theme from a professional theme store, you usually have two or more options regarding the license. As I've mentioned earlier, the price range is usually $30 to $100. Now, there are many licensing models, but two of them are the most popular web-wide:

- **Standard, one-site license**: It allows you to launch one site using the theme. It's the recommended choice if you're just searching for a theme for yourself and not to use it on other people's sites as well. This is the cheapest kind of license.

- **Developer license**: It is targeted towards developers and people who want to launch more than one site with a theme. Additionally, the package usually includes PSD project files and other mid-development files (note that some one-site licenses include those as well). Developer licenses can be as much as two times more expensive than the standard, one-site licenses.

Up-to-date themes only

This is probably the most important parameter here. Your theme has to be up-to-date or it will fail to take advantage of all the newest features in WordPress. The only bad news is that you can't know for sure whether a theme is a modern one or not. You can only rely on the details provided by the theme seller. But as bad as this sounds, it's actually not that big problem because big theme stores can't afford to lie in their marketing materials. So, whenever you see a message that the theme is compatible with WordPress versions X.X, it's most likely true, provided you're getting a theme from a respected company.

Also, a good rule of thumb is to check when the last update took place. Depending on the theme store, this information can be displayed in various places so I can't give you any specific advice where to look for it. Nevertheless, if you're getting your theme from the official directory at http://wordpress.org/extend/themes/, you can find this detail in the right-hand sidebar on every individual theme's page (labeled **Last Updated**):

Themes that are customizable

When considering a theme, make sure to find answers to the following questions:

- Are the sidebars flexible? Can I choose how many sidebars I want to display?
- Is it widget-ready?
- Does it support custom menus?
- Is it complex or simple? Which do I prefer?
- How flexible is the content and layout? Can I choose the column count and widths?
- Does it offer a **Theme Settings** page where I can customize layout, category display, home page, and other options?

At this point in WordPress's development, I recommend rejecting any theme that does not support widgets or custom menus. This is because these days, a situation where you can use a theme right out of the box rarely happens, so having at least a couple of customization possibilities goes a very long way.

Themes with responsive structure

This is one of the new parameters among modern themes. Back in the day, if you wanted to make your site mobile-friendly, you needed to get some plugins and additional mobile themes, and then enable them to work at the same time. Now, with HTML5 and CSS3 you can use just one theme and be certain that it's going to look great on every possible device (from desktop computers, to laptops, to mobile devices). The keyword to all this is **responsive design/structure**.

Whenever a theme developer indicates that their theme is responsive, it means that it's compatible with all the devices people use to access the Internet these days. In a nutshell, whenever a theme is responsive, this fact will be surely mentioned on the official sales or download page.

Support, reviews, and documentation

This is especially important if you're getting a paid premium theme. Quite simply, since you're paying money, you naturally want to be sure that the product you're getting is a quality one that provides good customer service and well-designed functionality. Hence the importance of documentation, reviews, and customer support. It's as simple as this.

I do admit that selecting a theme can take a while, especially if you have to remember about all of the preceding aspects, but this is the work that will surely pay off. Let's not forget that you're going to be stuck with the theme you choose for at least a year or two (a common scenario), so you surely don't want to spend money on a low-quality product.

Installing and changing themes

Now that you've chosen the theme you want to use, you'll need to install it into your WordPress website.

You'll have the following two choices, as you did when adding new plugins:

- If the theme you want is in the WordPress theme directory, and if your server is set up properly, you can add the theme directly from within the WP Admin

- If either of those two conditions are not met, you'll have to download, extract, and then upload the theme by hand

Adding a theme within the WP Admin

As mentioned in the preceding section, you can add a theme directly from within your WP Admin if you've chosen a theme from the WordPress theme directory, if you're using a current-enough version of WordPress, and if your server settings allow. First, navigate to **Appearance**, and then click on the **Install Themes** tab, as shown in the following screenshot:

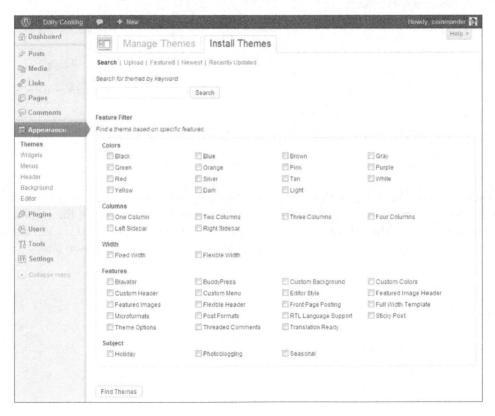

This will look similar to the **Add New Plugins** page because you have some subnavigation links at the top, namely **Search, Upload, Featured, Newest, Recently Updated** along with a search box. You also see checkboxes that will let you narrow down the type of theme for which you're looking (by color, by columns, by feature, and so on). The theme programmers tag their themes with this information and this is how the theme directory knows which themes meet these criteria.

I've already found a theme I like, so I'll put its name in the search box, as shown in the following screenshot:

If I click on **Live Preview**, I will see the same theme preview that I saw on the main theme directory page. Note that at this point, the theme preview will be the same as the preview on the **Themes Directory** page, rather than a preview of your own site's content. Until the theme is installed, you won't see a preview of your own site.

If I click on **Install** and then confirm by clicking on **Install Now**, this theme will be downloaded and added to my collection of themes, as shown in the following screenshot:

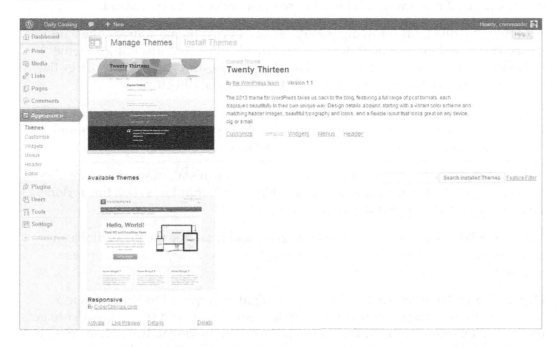

If I click on the thumbnail or the **Live Preview** link on the **Appearance** page, I will see a preview of the theme with my own content in it. If I like it, I can activate the theme in one of the following two ways:

- By clicking on **Activate Responsive** in the upper-right corner of the **Preview** window
- By clicking on **Activate** in the **Responsive** box on the main **Appearance** page

After activating, this theme will be used for my site instead of Twenty Thirteen, the default WordPress theme.

Downloading, extracting, and uploading

If you can't install a theme from within the WP Admin for one of the two aforementioned reasons, you'll have to use the mentioned steps instead.

Additionally, due to the growing popularity of external theme sources like various theme stores and independent developers, downloading and installing a theme manually becomes the default way of handling things, and gradually replaces the traditional approach of getting a theme from the official directory.

Therefore, to provide a good example when explaining the manual installation, I'm going to get a theme (a free one) from one of the premium theme stores and guide you through the process of having it installed.

It doesn't matter where you get your themes from, the installation procedure always starts once you have the theme downloaded to your computer. When this is done, you'll see a ZIP file on your desktop.

The theme I'd like to try out is called **Gadgetry** and it's a free theme available at ThemeFuse.com (`http://themefuse.com/wp-themes-shop/free-wordpress-theme/`).

Depending on the source of the theme, you might be required to either create a user account, make a purchase, or sign up to a newsletter, and so on, in order to get the theme. Of course, sometimes, there's just a direct download link. ThemeFuse has a pretty straightforward offer so I'm not going to describe the whole process in detail. I already have the theme's ZIP file so let's take it from there.

At this point, you can upload the ZIP file through the WP Admin by navigating to **Appearance | Install Themes | Upload**.

You can select the ZIP file and upload it that way. If that doesn't work, continue with the following steps to extract and upload the theme files.

1. If you're using Mac, the ZIP file may have automatically been unzipped for you, in which case you'll see a folder on your desktop instead of the ZIP file or in addition to the ZIP file (for example, `tfuse-download-gadgetry`). If not, just do the extraction or unzipping manually so that you have the theme folder on your desktop.

2. The following are the file contents of the `Gadgetry/tfuse-download-gadgetry` folder that I downloaded:

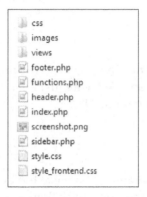

It's got a `style.css` file and an `index.php` file, and so I know it's definitely a valid theme.

Now, you need to upload the `themes` folder to your WordPress website. As you did in *Chapter 2, Getting Started*, you need to FTP to your server. Once there, navigate to your WordPress website's installation folder. Next, go to the `wp-content` folder, and then to the `themes` folder. You'll see one `themes` folder in here already, named `twentythirteen` (and possibly others as well). These are the themes that come pre-installed with WordPress.

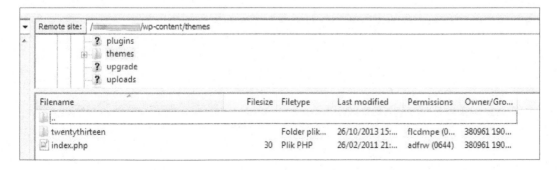

Upload the folder you just unzipped (for example, `tfuse-download-gadgetry`) into the `themes` folder on your server. That's it!

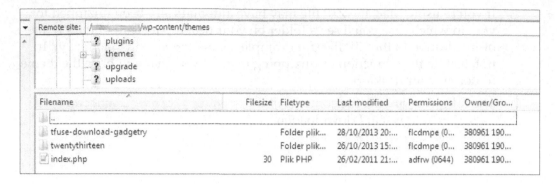

Now, when you go to **Appearance** in your WP Admin, the theme will appear. You can click on **Live Preview** and **Activate** just as if you'd added it from within the WP Admin (in the preceding section).

Summary

This chapter described how to manage the basic look of your WordPress website. You have learned where to find themes, why they are useful, what the basic differences between various themes are, how to select the perfect theme for your site, and how to install themes manually and through the WP Admin.

In the next chapter, you will learn step-by-step, how to build your own theme from scratch.

Developing Your Own Theme

7

You know how to find themes on the Web and install them for use on your WordPress site. However, you may not be able to find the perfect theme, you may want to create a thoroughly personalized theme, or you may be a website designer with a client who wants a custom theme.

In this chapter, you'll learn how to turn your own design into a fully functional WordPress theme that you'll be able to use on your own site. You'll also learn how to convert your theme folder into a ZIP file that can be shared with other WordPress users on the Web.

All you will need before we get started is have the following:

- Your own design
- The ability to slice and dice your design to turn it into HTML

We'll start out with tips on slicing and dicing, so that your HTML and CSS files are as WordPress friendly as possible, and then cover the steps for turning that HTML build into a fully functional theme.

Note that I assume that you are already comfortable writing and working with HTML and CSS. You don't need to be familiar with PHP because I'll be walking you through all of the PHP code.

This chapter covers only the very basics of theme creation. This topic actually deserves a whole book, and it has one! I highly recommend the book *WordPress Theme Development Beginner's Guide Third Edition* by *Rachel McCollin* and *Tessa Blakeley Silver, Packt Publishing*. This book covers in detail everything you possibly want to know about creating your own theme, including even such details as choosing a color scheme, considering typography, writing the best CSS, and laying out your HTML using Rapid Design Comping. If this chapter leaves you wanting more, go there!

Setting up your design

Just about any design in the world can be turned into a WordPress theme. However, there are some general guidelines you can follow—both in the design and the HTML/CSS build of your theme—which will easily convert the design into a theme.

Designing your theme to be WordPress friendly

While you can design your blog any way that you want, a good way to start would be with one of the standard blog layouts.

Note that while these different standard layouts have differing numbers of columns and column widths, they all have these essential parts:

- Header
- Main column
- Side column(s)
- Footer

WordPress expects your theme to follow this pattern, and so it provides functions that make it easier to create a theme that has this pattern. As you're designing your first blog theme, I suggest including these parts. Also, a design that stays within the same general design patterns of WordPress themes will most easily accommodate existing plugins and widgets.

That being said, a common situation in the WordPress world is to build custom home pages or landing pages (purpose-specific pages, mostly commercial) that feature completely different designs. Therefore, you might stumble upon websites that don't look like they're built with WordPress at first glance. Also, many modern theme frameworks give us the possibility to create such custom home pages as well as other custom page templates (more about them later within the chapter). This is all part of the trend to make WordPress capable of running any kind of website.

The two-column layout is the simplest and the easiest to implement as a WordPress theme, so we'll be using this layout as an example in this chapter.

Now, the example I'm actually using isn't an ordinary one. I got it from ThemeFuse (`http://themefuse.com/`)—one of the top WordPress theme stores out there. Basically, after a brief talk, one of the co-founders was happy to help me out and agreed to provide a custom and free design for everybody to use (you can find both the design and the complete WordPress theme that was built on it in the official code bundle for this chapter). Here's what it looks like:

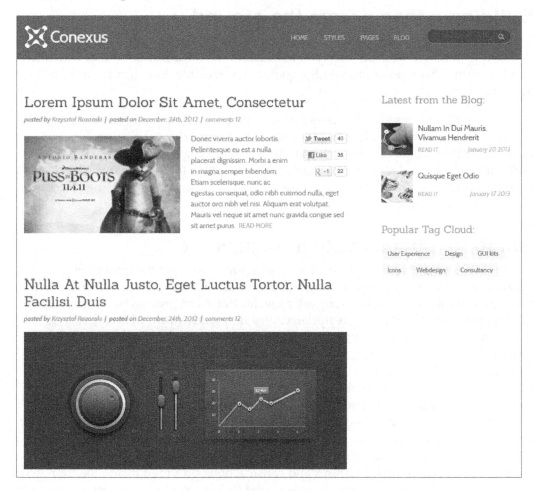

Now that the design is complete, we're ready for the next step, namely turning the design into code.

Two paths of theme development

Essentially, there are two paths you can follow while developing your new theme (as I mentioned in the previous chapter). You can either work from the ground up, that is, by building the HTML structure and the functional structure of the theme manually, or you can work on top of an existing theme framework, where you only have to adapt your design to work on the structure provided by the framework itself. Both these paths have their pros and cons though, as always.

Building a theme from the ground up

The main advantage is the massive educational value of this path. When you're developing a theme from scratch, you're learning the basis of theme construction and function. This kind of knowledge goes a long way for your future projects in WordPress.

On the other hand, it's also the longer of the two paths. In a professional production environment (among people designing and developing themes as a profession), creating themes from scratch is a highly time-consuming approach making it quite ineffective. And it's not that much about adapting the design (which always must be done, with theme frameworks as well), it's more about building the core functionality of a theme.

Building a theme with a framework

The main advantage of this approach is its time efficiency and the quality of the final result. For instance, if you're building a theme from scratch, you have to make sure to keep your theme up-to-date long after the development process has been finished. The thing is that WordPress gets updated very frequently (around once every 51 days) and many features change their purpose over time, get completely erased or replaced with new ones. In such a scenario, only modern themes that are kept up-to-date can take full advantage of those features. Updating your theme will obviously take a massive amount of work. That is where theme frameworks come into play. In essence, theme frameworks are themes with a very minimalist design and no visually attractive aspects. The purpose of frameworks is to make them the base of any future theme by acting as a parent theme. So the fact that the framework itself has no design allows every creator to introduce almost any design imaginable, while at the same time taking full advantage of the features and constructions provided inside the framework. Now, the strength of quality frameworks is that they get updated almost as frequently as WordPress plugins. In short, if you're using a framework, you don't have to worry about your theme going out of date. Whenever there's an update available, you can simply perform it and forget about the whole thing.

This brings me to the main disadvantage of using theme frameworks. Most of the time, theme frameworks are big and complex pieces of web software (PHP scripts). So if you want to be able to use them effectively, you'll have to spend a significant amount of time learning the framework. On top of that, if you decide to switch to a different framework later down the road, you'll have to learn it all over again (frameworks are usually very different from each other). As you can see, reaping the benefits of using frameworks has its price.

Nevertheless, if you're still interested, here are some of the popular theme frameworks (both paid and free ones):

- Thematic: `http://themeshaper.com/thematic/`
- Hybrid: `http://themehybrid.com/themes/hybrid`
- Gantry: `http://www.gantry-framework.org/`
- Whiteboard: `http://whiteboardframework.com/`
- Genesis: `http://my.studiopress.com/themes/genesis/`
- Thesis: `http://diythemes.com/`
- Some frameworks listed by WordPress: `http://codex.wordpress.org/Theme_Frameworks`

In the end, I advise you to create your first theme manually, just to learn the craft and get to know all the basic structures and mechanisms sitting inside WordPress. Then, as the next step in your mastery (if you're planning to work on other themes in the future), you can pick one of the popular theme frameworks, get deeply familiar with it, and use it as the base for your future themes from that point on. Such an approach will allow you to reach maximum time efficiency and save you the effort of dealing with the core set of functionalities that every theme needs, regardless of the design or purpose.

In this chapter I'm going to focus on the **from the ground up** approach as it is the one that offers more educational value. Also, if I were to give you an in-depth guide on building a theme with a specific framework, this guide wouldn't be usable for any other framework, so from the ground up it is!

Your journey with theme development starts once you have a graphic design prepared in Photoshop or some other similar tool. You can also take the code bundle for this chapter and work with the aforementioned design from ThemeFuse. Either way, the next step is to turn it into some HTML code.

Converting your design to code

The next step towards turning your ideal design into a WordPress theme is to slice images out of your design and write HTML and CSS files that put it all together. For the purpose of this chapter, I assume that you already know basically how to do this, and let's also assume we're working with a tableless layout! We'll cover some pointers on how to do your slicing and dicing in a way that will fit best into WordPress.

 If you'd like to learn how to do Rapid Design Comping, which is how to turn your design into HTML quickly and easily, be sure to check out the book *WordPress Theme Development Beginner's Guide Third Edition* by *Rachel McCollin* and *Tessa Blakeley Silver, Packt Publishing*.

Let's get down to business and take a look at the HTML structure that was built based on the design I'm using.

Examining the HTML structure

Following is the very basic layout of the HTML file for my food blog design; I'm showing it just to give you a general understanding of what we're going to be working on:

```
<!DOCTYPE html>
<html lang="en">
<head>
    <title>Title</title>
    <!-- other head elements -->
</head>
<body>
<div class="body_wrap">
    <div class="header_top"><!-- header of the site -->
    <div class="container">
        <div class="logo"><img src="images/logo.png" alt=""></div>

        <nav id="topmenu"><!-- topmenu -->
                <ul><li class="menu-level-0 mega-nav">Navigation
items</li></ul>
</nav>

        <div class="topsearch"><!-- search form --></div>
    </div><!--/ container -->
```

```
    </div><!--/ header_top -->

    <div id="middle" class="cols2">
    <div class="container clearfix">

        <div class="content" role="main">
        <div class="postlist">

            <div class="post-item"><!-- individual post -->
                <div class="post-title">
                <h2><a href="blog-details.html">Lorem Ipsum Dummy Text
</a></h2>
                <div class="post-meta">
                    posted by ... | posted on ...  | 
comments 12</div>
                </div>
                <div class="entry clearfix">
                <p>Lorem Ipsum More Dummy Text<a href="blog-details.
html" class="link-more">READ MORE</a></p>
                </div>
            </div>

        </div><!--/ post list -->
        </div><!--/ content -->

        <div class="sidebar" role="complementary"><!-- the sidebar -->

        <div class="widget-container widget_recent_entries">
            <h3 class="widget-title">Latest from the Blog:</h3>
            <ul>
                <li class="clearfix">Recent items</li>
            </ul>
        </div><!--/ widget_recent_entries -->

        <div class="widget-container widget_tag_cloud">
            <h3 class="widget-title">Popular Tag Cloud:</h3>
            <div class="tagcloud">
                    Tag-1 Tag-2
            </div>
        </div><!--/ widget_tag_cloud -->

        </div><!--/ sidebar -->
```

```
    </div><!--/ container -->
    </div><!--/ middle -->

    <div class="footer"><!-- the footer -->
        <div class="container clearfix">
            <div class="botmenu">
                <ul>
                    <li class="menu-level-0">2nd Menu</li>
                </ul>
            </div>
            <div class="copyright">...</div>
        </div>
    </div>

</div><!--/ body_wrap -->
</body>
</html>
```

You can see that I've separated out these four major parts:

- The header is in `div` with `class="header_top"`
- The side column is in `div` with `class="sidebar"`
- The main column is in `div` with `class="content"`
- The footer is in `div` with `class="footer"`

I'd like to call your attention to a few other things that have been done here:

- There's a standard place for the logo. Of course, the `logo.png` file can be replaced with another file that holds your actual logo.

- The `<nav id="topmenu">` element, the main navigation, is in an unordered list (`ul`). I did this because WordPress has a function that spits out the navigation of your site in the order you choose. When WordPress spits out the list, every linked item is in a list item tag (`li`).

- The sidebar is set with the attribute `role="complementary"`. Roles are one of the relatively new HTML parameters. Essentially, the role attribute describes the role that the element plays in the context of the document. In this case, the sidebar is complementary to the main content (and if you pay close attention you'll notice that the main part, the content, is indeed set to `role="main"`). In general, such attributes are meant to explain the purpose of elements in the HTML structure.

- Inside the sidebar, the recent posts list and the tag cloud are similar. There are going to be a number of items that you may want to add to your sidebar, including widgets. Many of these items will be lists with titles, so the HTML structure makes it possible.

- Within the `<div class="postlist">` element is a `<div class="post-item">` element. Even though this basic layout has just one post in it, I know that I'll want to show more than one post at a time. So this `<div class="post-item">` element will be repeated for each post.

Now that I've got my basic layout, I'm going to add a few more HTML elements to flesh it out a bit, including more information in `<head>` as well as the search box, and some additional CSS. Then, I'll fill up the sidebar, header, content, and footer with a bunch of dummy text so that it looks almost exactly like the theme's design in Photoshop. I'm not including the complete HTML here, but you can find it in the code bundle for this chapter (in the folder named HTML) if you'd like to do the same.

Examining the CSS

Generally, a very good practice in web development is to start your CSS design by resetting all the default styles used by various web browsers. The main issue and the reason why this is an important step is because most popular web browsers, or should I say every single one of them, has its own *default* set of CSS styles. And if you want your theme to look exactly the same in every browser, you have to start your work by resetting those styles, whatever they might actually be. The good thing about it is that you don't have to do it manually. You can just use one of the reset scripts available on the Internet. For the purpose of this description, I'm using the reset script by Eric Meyer (get it at: http://meyerweb.com/eric/tools/css/reset/). So, what we're doing first is just taking the following CSS and placing it at the beginning of our new `style.css` file:

```
html, body, div, span, applet, object, iframe,
h1, h2, h3, h4, h5, h6, p, blockquote, pre,
a, abbr, acronym, address, big, cite, code,
del, dfn, em, img, ins, kbd, q, s, samp,
small, strike, strong, sub, sup, tt, var,
b, u, i, center,
dl, dt, dd, ol, ul, li,
fieldset, form, label, legend,
table, caption, tbody, tfoot, thead, tr, th, td,
article, aside, canvas, details, embed,
figure, figcaption, footer, header, hgroup,
menu, nav, output, ruby, section, summary,
time, mark, audio, video {
    margin: 0;
```

```
        padding: 0;
        border: 0;
        font-size: 100%;
        font: inherit;
        vertical-align: baseline;
}
/* HTML5 display-role reset for older browsers */
article, aside, details, figcaption, figure,
footer, header, hgroup, menu, nav, section {
        display: block;
}
body {
        line-height: 1;
}
ol, ul {
        list-style: none;
}
blockquote, q {
    quotes: none;
}
blockquote:before, blockquote:after,
q:before, q:after {
        content: '';
        content: none;
}
table {
        border-collapse: collapse;
        border-spacing: 0;
}
```

Let's now take a look at the actual CSS, the things that build our design and not just reset it. First, we'll review the CSS that displays everything you see in the design. Note that I've got styles for all of the key elements such as the header, sidebar, main content area, and footer.

Also please notice that this is just *scaffolding*, so to speak. It only indicates the individual areas of the final CSS stylesheet. Listing the complete version here wouldn't be very helpful, as I'm sure that you're much more likely to copy and paste the code from the official bundle rather than rewriting it straight from here. Therefore, I'm including the complete version in the aforementioned code bundle and right now, I'm only presenting the individual areas of the CSS. This is just to make the whole thing easier to grasp once you look at the complete stylesheet. To be honest, the final CSS isn't actually that complex from a CSS-design point of view, but it is quite long since it was created mostly by ThemeFuse, and they want everything to look great (it's kind of their job). Here's the simplified version.

Let's start with the general structure and the typography settings. This will make our text formatting look nice:

```
/*=================================================*/
/* 1. GENERAL TYPOGRAPHY */
/*=================================================*/
/*---------------------------------*/
/* General Styles */
body {
    font-family: 'Cabin', sans-serif;
    color:#4f5e62;
    font-size:14px;
    line-height:1.6em;
    position:relative}

.body_wrap {
    width:100%;
    position:relative}
```

What follows next is a set of rules that will take care of the alignment, fonts, font sizes, block quotes, and other typical HTML elements:

```
/* Typography and structure
- setting general and text alignment (left, center, right, etc.)
- classes for clearing the alignment
- typography settings (fonts, font sizes, padding, etc.) for headings,
and other elements
- blockquotes display settings
- link formatting
- list formatting
- handling tables
- formatting forms and form fields */
```

Next, the structure of the site itself:

```
/*=================================================*/
/* 2. SITE STRUCTURE */
/*=================================================*/
/*---------------------------------*/
/* Header Top */
```

```
.header_top {
    width:100%;
    height:86px;
    background:url(images/header_top_bg.png) 0 0 repeat-x;
    top:0;
    z-index:2}

.header_top .container {
    width:940px;
    padding:17px 0 0 0}

.logo {
    overflow: hidden;
    height:50px;
    width:300px;
    float:left;
    z-index:2;
    position:relative}

.site-title {
    margin-top: 10px;
}

.logo img {
    max-width:100%}

/*----------------------------------*/
/* Topmenu */

/* topmenu Dropdown classes */

/*----------------------------------*/
/* Header */
.header {
    background-position:center top;
    position:relative;
    z-index:1}

/*----------------------------------*/
/* Middle content */

/* Layout: Full Width, Sidebar Left, Sidebar Right */
#middle {
    clear:both;
```

```
        position:relative;
        z-index:1;
        min-height:1px}

/* sidebar right */
#middle .content {
        width:624px;
        float:left;
        min-height:100px;
        margin:0 0 0 10px}

#middle .sidebar {
        width:250px;
        float:left;
        margin:0 10px 0 66px}

#middle.cols2 {
        padding:65px 0}

/*----------------------------------*/
/* Footer */
.footer {
        background:url(images/footer_bg.jpg) 0 0 repeat-x}

.footer .container {
        padding:50px 0 40px 0;
        color:#747e82}

.footer p {
        margin:0}

.botmenu {
        text-align:left;
        text-transform:uppercase;
        font-size:12px;
        font-weight:500;
        width:580px;
        float:left}

.copyright {
        float:right;
        width:360px;
        margin-left:20px;
        font-size:13px;}
```

Finally, we'll have to take care of the widgets, posts, comments, and other elements native to WordPress:

```css
/*====================================================*/
/* 3. EXTENDED TYPOGRAPHY and SHORTCODES
/*====================================================*/


/*====================================================*/
/* 4. WIDGETS STYLES */
/*====================================================*/

/* Sidebar Widget Container  */
.sidebar .widget-container,
.content .widget-container {
    position:relative !important;
    line-height:1.4em;
    color:#292929;
    padding:0}

.sidebar .widget-container {
    padding-bottom:40px}


/*====================================================*/
/* 5. POSTS */
/*====================================================*/
/*--------------------------------*/
/* Blog post list */
.entry {
    line-height:1.5em}

.post-item .entry,
.post-detail .entry {
    padding:0;
    color:#4f5e62}

.post-detail {
    padding-bottom:10px;
    margin-bottom:20px}
```

```
.post-page {
    background:none}
.entry .post-title h2 {
    color:#110d09;
    display:block}


/*----------------------------------*/
/* Pagination and Navigation */


/*----------------------------------*/
/* Comment list */
.comment-list {
    position:relative;
    padding:0 0 10px 0;
    margin-top:30px}


.link-add-comment {
    position:absolute;
    top:10px;
    right:5px;
    color:#e8890f;
    font-weight:bold;
    text-transform:uppercase;
    font-size:13px}


/*----------------------------------*/
/* Comment form */
.add-comment {
    margin:20px 0 40px 0;
    position:relative;
    background:#f2f2f2;
    border:1px solid #e6e6e6}


.contact-form {
    margin:40px 0}


/*----------------------------------*/
/* Print styles */
@media print {
    /* ... */
}
```

Inside this stylesheet, you will find many specific classes that aren't just my own creations, but rather come from WordPress itself. Here's what I mean. When WordPress spits out items that include page lists, category lists, archive lists, images, galleries, and so on, it gives many of these items a particular class name. If you know these class names, you can prepare your stylesheet to take advantage of them.

When you add an image to a post or page, WordPress gives you the option to have it to the right, left, or at the center of the text. Depending on what you choose, WordPress will give the image the class `alignleft`, `alignright`, or `aligncenter`. Those classes, for example, are handled in the /* Floating & Alignment */ section of our CSS stylesheet. Another thing is that when you add an image with a caption, WordPress gives it the class `wp-caption`. This particular thing is handled in the /* Images */ section of the stylesheet we're using. Another useful class is `current_page_item`. WordPress adds this to the list item in the pages menu, on the page that you are currently working. This gives you the ability to visually mark a page that the user is currently viewing. I'll mark it with a color change using the following code:

```
.sidebar .widget-container .current_page_item a {
    color:#e8890f;
    background-color:#f2f2f2;
    text-shadow:0 1px 1px #fff}
```

WordPress uses many other classes that you can take advantage of while building your stylesheet. I've listed a few of them in *Chapter 12, Creating a Non-blog Website Part Two – Community Websites and Custom Content Elements*.

Now that you've got your HTML and CSS lined up, you're ready for the next step, turning the HTML build into a WordPress theme.

Converting your build into a theme

You'll be turning your HTML build into a theme, which is composed of a number of template files and other scripts. We are going to first dig into the inner workings of a theme so as to get familiar with how it's put together. Then we'll actually turn the HTML build into a theme folder that WordPress can use. Finally, we'll replace the dummy text in your build with WordPress functions that spit out content. As I mentioned in an earlier chapter, doing development for your WordPress website on a local environment can make the whole process much smoother. Consider getting a server up and running on your home computer using WAMP, MAMP, or some other way to install Apache and MySQL.

Creating the theme folder

The first step to turning your HTML build into a theme is to create your theme folder and give it everything it needs to be recognized as a theme by WordPress. Let's look at an overview of the steps and then take them one by one:

1. Name your folder and create backup copies of your build files.

2. Prepare the essential files.

3. Add a screenshot of your theme named `screenshot.png`.

4. Upload your folder.

5. Activate your theme.

Let's take these steps one by one now:

- **Naming your folder and making backup copies**: You'll want to give your build folder a sensible name. I'm naming my theme `Conexus Kitchen` because it's a custom simplified version of the Conexus, a multipurpose theme by ThemeFuse, and since it is meant to run my cooking blog, the new name kind of makes sense. I'll name the folder `conexus-kitchen`.

  Now I suggest creating backup copies of your HTML and CSS files. As you'll eventually be breaking up your build into template files, you can easily lose track of where your code came from. By keeping a copy of your original build, you'll be able to go back to it for reference.

- **Preparing the essential files**: WordPress has only the following two requirements to recognize your folder as a theme:
  - A file called `index.php`
  - A file called `style.css` with an introductory comment

  Just rename your main design's HTML file to `index.php`, and that takes care of the first requirement.

  To satisfy the second requirement, your stylesheet needs to have an introductory comment that describes the basic information for the whole theme: title, author, and so on. Also, it has to be at the very top of the stylesheet. I've added this comment to my `style.css` file:

```
/*
Theme Name: Conexus Kitchen
Theme URI: http://themefuse.com/demo/wp/conexus/
Description: Conexus is created by ThemeFuse.
Version: 1.0
```

```
Author: ThemeFuse
Author URI: http://themefuse.com
Tags: gray, white, two-columns, editor-style, custom-menu
*/
```

The preceding structure has been created based on the template available at http://codex.wordpress.org/Theme_Development#Theme_Stylesheet. Whenever you're creating a new theme, it's always good to check the current recommended template beforehand.

When you add this comment section to your stylesheet, just replace all the details with those that are relevant to your theme.

- **Adding a screenshot**: Remember when we first learned how to activate a new theme that there were thumbnail versions of the themes in your **Appearance** tab? You'll want a thumbnail of your own design. It has to be a PNG file with the name screenshot.png. Just do the following:

  1. Flatten a copy of your design in Photoshop.
  2. Change the image width to **600** px and the height to **450** px.
  3. **Save for web** as a PNG-8.

> The preceding requirements (600 px by 450 px) are the current ones at the time of writing. To get the latest guidelines at any point in time please revisit the official codex at http://codex.wordpress.org/Theme_Development#Screenshot.

  4. Name your file screenshot.png and save it in your build folder.

- **Uploading your folder**: Using your FTP software, upload your template folder to wp-content/themes/ in your WordPress build. It will share the themes folder with twentythirteen and any other theme you've added as you installed WordPress. In the following screenshot, you can see my conexus-kitchen theme living in the themes folder:

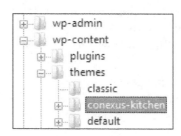

- **Activating your theme**: You've got the absolute basic necessities in there now, so you can activate your theme (though it won't look like much yet). Log in to your WP Admin and navigate to **Appearance**. There you'll see your theme waiting for you.

When you click on the thumbnail or the **Activate** link of your theme, an overlay window will appear on top of the page with a preview of what your site will look like. Don't be alarmed if it's not perfect. The stylesheet might not be pulled in correctly at this point.

Click on the link in the upper-right corner to activate your theme. This is another good reason to have a development server. You wouldn't want to have this incomplete theme active on a live site while you finish the final pieces!

Speaking of final pieces, your theme is now ready to have all of the WordPress content added.

Adding WordPress content

Right now, your `index.php` file is your only theme file. We'll be breaking it up into template files a bit later. First, we need to replace the dummy text with WordPress functions that will spit out your actual content into your theme.

The functions.php file

In short, the `functions.php` file is meant to set up your theme and provide some helper functions and settings to make the usage of the theme easier. Apart from that, this file also has many other applications that we're not going to be discussing here, as it is beyond the scope of this book.

In essence, `functions.php` is a kind of file that allows you to perform a very wide scope of modifications. Even though there is a set of standard things that should always be taken care of while dealing with a functions file, no one restricts you from doing virtually anything you wish.

For instance, you can create a classic PHP function such as `my_function_name()` and then call it from within one of your template files (such as `index.php`) through `<?php my_function_name(); ?>`, but this is just one of the possible scenarios.

Although this isn't a requirement, it's always good to start your `functions.php` file with the following lines of code (just as a good reference point):

```php
<?php
/**
 * CKitchen functions and definitions.
 *
 * @package WordPress
 * @since 1.0
 */
```

The preceding lines of code provide the essential info about the theme, the platform for which the theme has been built for (`@package`) and the version number (`@since`).

Next in line is the `$content_width` variable. Here's how to use it:

```php
if(!isset($content_width))
    $content_width = 624; //pixels
```

This parameter is often overlooked by many theme developers, despite the fact that it can mean a lot to the final form of the theme. It's simply the maximum width of the content area allowed in your theme (in pixels). For example, if you ever upload a picture that massively exceeds this value, it will always be scaled down to prevent messing up your site's layout. The exact value you should set depends on your CSS and design. The value `624` in the preceding example is just that, an example.

The next part in our `functions.php` file is the setup of the default features the theme is going to enable. Let's use a separate function to handle this:

```
function ckitchen_setup() {
    //Adds RSS feed links to <head> for posts and comments.
    add_theme_support('automatic-feed-links');

    //This theme uses wp_nav_menu() in two locations.
    register_nav_menus(array(
        'primary' => 'Primary Menu',
        'footer_menu' => 'Footer Menu',
    ));
}
add_action('after_setup_theme', 'ckitchen_setup');
```

The function `ckitchen_setup()` is going to be executed at just the right time, triggered by the action `after_setup_theme` called at the end to set up the basic features of our theme properly. Most of the code is pretty self-explanatory due to the comments, but there's just one thing I'd like to mention individually. This part (registering two menus):

```
register_nav_menus(array(
    'primary' => 'Primary Menu',
    'footer_menu' => 'Footer Menu',
));
```

This is a small piece of code that will let us assign any custom menu to appear as the primary menu and the footer menu later on. It is also what we'll use to set in our new theme. In addition, the preceding function allows you to register even more menu areas if you wish so, and all you'd have to do is add this line: `'secondary' => 'Secondary Menu'`.

Next, let's enable our stylesheet CSS file to load with our theme, or more accurately, to be "enqueued" and then load in precisely the right moment. Here's how to do it:

```
function ckitchen_scripts_styles() {
    $directory = get_stylesheet_directory_uri();

    wp_register_style('style', $directory.'/style.css');
    wp_enqueue_style('style');
```

```
    wp_register_style('screen', $directory.'/screen.css');
    wp_enqueue_style('screen');

    wp_register_style('googleFontsCabinSanchez','http://fonts.
googleapis.com/css?family=Cabin:400,500,400italic,600,700|Sanchez');
    wp_enqueue_style('googleFontsCabinSanchez');
}
add_action('wp_enqueue_scripts', 'ckitchen_scripts_styles');
```

As you can see, there are two stylesheets. One is the default one, that is, `style.css`, and the other one is `screen.css`, which is meant to ensure proper display on user devices with smaller screens. The last two lines take care of embedding some cool Google fonts that will improve the theme's typography.

Nowadays, the preceding code is the best practice for including various CSS styles and also JS scripts into our themes. You can still go with the traditional (alternative) approach through `<link rel="stylesheet" href="<?php bloginfo('stylesheet_url'); ?>" type="text/css" media="screen" />` placed inside the header section of your design, but it will lower the performance of your site as CSS styles and various JS scripts tend to take a long time to load. So, it's always better to deal with them through the modern `wp_enqueue_scripts` handle.

Finally, there are two calls to the WordPress function `add_theme_support()`, which lets WordPress know that the theme enables post thumbnails and custom menus.

The preceding code closes our first, template-like `functions.php` file. Later, we will add new lines to it to make it even more functional. Now, the interesting part is that there is no closing PHP tag in the functions file (that is, no `?>`). This is not a typo or anything. It's intentional. Since most of the file is pure PHP, we don't need this tag for anything.

```
<?php
/**
 * CKitchen functions and definitions.
 *
 * @package WordPress
 * @since 1.0
 */

if(!isset($content_width))
    $content_width = 624; //pixels
```

```
function ckitchen_setup() {
    //Adds RSS feed links to <head> for posts and comments.
    add_theme_support('automatic-feed-links');

    //This theme uses wp_nav_menu() in two locations.
    register_nav_menus(array(
        'primary' => 'Primary Menu',
        'footer_menu' => 'Footer Menu',
    ));
}
add_action('after_setup_theme', 'ckitchen_setup');

function ckitchen_scripts_styles() {
    $directory = get_stylesheet_directory_uri();

    wp_register_style('style', $directory.'/style.css');
    wp_enqueue_style('style');

    wp_register_style('screen', $directory.'/screen.css');
    wp_enqueue_style('screen');

    wp_register_style('googleFontsCabinSanchez','http://fonts.
googleapis.com/css?family=Cabin:400,500,400italic,600,700|Sanchez');
    wp_enqueue_style('googleFontsCabinSanchez');
}
add_action('wp_enqueue_scripts', 'ckitchen_scripts_styles');

add_theme_support('post-thumbnails');
add_theme_support('menus');
```

Just to remind you, this whole `functions.php` file can be found inside the code bundle for this chapter.

The <head> tag

First, we'll set up the header section of our HTML file. Let's start with the `charset` and the `device-width` parameters. Simply, here are the two lines to begin with right after the opening `<head>` tag:

```
<meta charset="<?php bloginfo('charset'); ?>" />
<meta name="viewport" content="width=device-width" />
```

The first one holds the character set that your blog uses. The other defines the width of the viewport used. Here, it's set to the width of the device being used (this allows everyone to view the site correctly, including desktop computer users, iPad users, Android phone users, and so on).

Next, you'll want WordPress to be able to place your blog's name in the title bar of your browser. So replace your dummy title with the following code in the title tag:

```
<title><?php wp_title( '|', true, 'right' ); ?><?php bloginfo('name');
?></title>
```

This will spit out the title of the current page, then the separator we've set (|), and finally the name of the site. Later, you may want to download the WordPress plugin, which will change <title> page by page, depending on what's appropriate.

You need to add another important chunk of code:

- To put header tags into your theme for the pingback URL
- Other miscellaneous WordPress stuff

Add the following lines to your <head> section:

```
<link rel="profile" href="http://gmpg.org/xfn/11" />
<link rel="pingback" href="<?php bloginfo( 'pingback_url' ); ?>" />
```

Finally, add the following line right before the closing </head> tag:

```
<?php wp_head(); ?>
```

Now add the body_class() function to the body tag, so it looks like this:

```
<body <?php body_class() ?>>
```

This is how your header looks:

```
<head>
<meta charset="<?php bloginfo( 'charset' ); ?>" />
<meta name="viewport" content="width=device-width" />
<title><?php wp_title( '|', true, 'right' ); ?><?php bloginfo('name');
?></title>
<link rel="profile" href="http://gmpg.org/xfn/11" />
<link rel="pingback" href="<?php bloginfo( 'pingback_url' ); ?>" />
<?php wp_head(); ?>
</head>
<body <?php body_class(); ?>>
```

The header and footer

It's time to start adding the content that you can see. Let's first replace the dummy text in the main navigation bar and header with WordPress content tags.

WordPress will generate a linked list of pages for you, as I mentioned earlier. Just replace your dummy text with this code, replacing the whole navigation tag:

```php
<?php
    wp_nav_menu( array(
            'theme_location'    => 'primary',
            'container'         => 'nav',
            'container_id'      => 'topmenu',
            'menu_class'        => 'dropdown',
            'link_before'       => '<span>',
            'link_after'        => '</span>'
    ));
?>
```

What's this code saying? Basically, it just calls the `wp_nav_menu()` function, which handles the whole process of displaying the menu correctly on its own.

Next, you can replace your dummy blog title and dummy blog description with the following two tags:

```html
<div class="logo">
    <h1 class="site-title"><a href="<?php echo esc_url(home_url('/'));
?>" title="<?php echo esc_attr(get_bloginfo('name', 'display'));
?>" rel="home"><img src="<?php echo get_template_directory_uri();
?>/images/logo.png" alt="<?php echo esc_attr(get_bloginfo('name',
'display')); ?>" ></a></h1>
</div>
```

These tags pull information from where you set the blog name and description in the WP Admin, and you can simply change them from **Settings | General**. As you can see, additionally, we're linking the logo to the home page—a standard practice in modern website design.

Now, the part of your HTML that describes the header looks as follows:

```
<div class="header_top">
<div class="container">
    <div class="logo"><!--logo-->
        <h1 class="site-title"><a href="<?php echo esc_url(home_
url('/')); ?>" title="<?php echo esc_attr(get_bloginfo('name',
'display')); ?>" rel="home"><img src="<?php echo get_template_
directory_uri(); ?>/images/logo.png" alt="<?php echo esc_attr(get_
bloginfo('name', 'display')); ?>" ></a></h1>
    </div>
    <!--menu-->
    <?php
        wp_nav_menu( array(
            'theme_location'   => 'primary',
            'container'        => 'nav',
            'container_id'     => 'topmenu',
            'menu_class'       => 'dropdown',
            'link_before'      => '<span>',
            'link_after'       => '</span>'
        ));
    ?>
    <div class="topsearch"><!-- additional search field-->
    <form id="searchForm" method="get" action="<?php echo home_
url('/'); ?>">
        <input type="text" name="s" id="stext" value="" class="stext">
        <input type="submit" id="searchSubmit" value="<?php
_e('Search','themefuse'); ?>" class="btn-search">
    </form>
    </div>
    <div class="clear"></div>
</div><!-- /.container -->
</div><!-- /.header top bar -->
```

Are you wondering why you should bother with some of this when you could have just typed your blog title, URL, and description to the theme? One reason is that if you ever want to change your blog's title, you can just do it in one quick step in the WP Admin and it will change all over your site. The other reason is that if you want to share your theme with others, you'll need to give them the ability to easily change the name through their own WP Admin panel. Keep in mind, anything, anything at all, that will change from site to site based on the site's purpose and content should not be hardcoded into the theme but should be to be dynamically generated.

Now when I refresh the site, my dummy text in the header has been replaced with actual content from my blog:

The two links visible in the header are live links coming from one of my custom menus. One additional thing you've probably noticed is that I also replaced the `logo.png` file to show something relevant to my cooking site.

Just to tie things up, I'm going to add the same code to my footer to close the main `<div class="body_wrap">` element, to display the **Proudly powered by WordPress** message, and to include the `wp_footer()` function/hook that's often used by many plugins in one way or the other, so every theme should feature it. My footer section now looks as follows:

```
<div class="footer">
    <div class="container clearfix">
        <div class="botmenu"><?php
        wp_nav_menu(array('theme_location' => 'footer_menu', 'link_
before'=> '<span>', 'link_after' => '</span>')); ?></div>
        <div class="copyright"><a href="http://wordpress.org/"
title="WordPress" rel="generator">Proudly powered by WordPress</a><br
/>
        Created with the CONEXUS KITCHEN theme by <a href="http://
themefuse.com">Themefuse</a></div>
    </div><!-- /.container -->
</div><!-- /.footer -->

</div><!-- /.body_wrap -->
<?php wp_footer(); ?>
</body>
</html>
```

As you can see, inside the footer, I'm also calling the other custom menu area I've created in the `functions.php` file. This is handled by the following line of code:

```
<div class="botmenu"><?php wp_nav_menu(array('theme_location' =>
'footer_menu', 'link_before'=> '<span>', 'link_after' => '</span>'));
?></div>
```

The sidebar

Now we can move along to adding WordPress-generated content in the sidebar, which still has just the dummy text:

Essentially, this part of our work is pretty simple. All we have to do is replace the dummy text with some WordPress functions that will handle displaying various bits of dynamic content; in this case, the archives.

Starting from the top, replace the dummy text showing the list of recent posts and the tag cloud with the piece of code that follows:

```
<div class="widget-container widget_archive">
    <h3 class="widget-title">Archives</h3>
    <ul>
        <?php wp_get_archives(); ?>
    </ul>
</div>
```

Just to note that by default, WordPress displays individual archive items as the `<li>` elements. So in order to place them correctly in our HTML structure, we have to use either the `<ul>` or `<ol>` tag, although the `<ul>` tags are much more common.

The classes you can see in the preceding code will make sure that our **Archives** links look just the way they should be (according to our main stylesheet).

Now, after all these modifications, the part of your HTML that describes the sidebar looks as follows:

```
<div class="sidebar" role="complementary">
    <div class="widget-container widget_archive">
        <h3 class="widget-title">Archives</h3>
        <ul>
            <?php wp_get_archives(); ?>
        </ul>
    </div>
</div>
```

Later in the chapter, we'll be making this a widget-ready area, but for now, we'll keep it like this. Remember, this approach is all about learning the structure of WordPress themes.

Save this file and reload your theme, and you'll see that your dummy text has been replaced with WordPress output for **Archives**.

I know it doesn't look like much, but after all, there's not that much content on the site at the moment.

The main column – the loop

The most important part of the WordPress code comes next. It's called the **loop**, and it's an essential part of your theme. The loop's job is to display your posts in reverse chronological order, choosing only those posts which are appropriate. You need to put all your other post tags inside the loop. The basic loop text, which has to surround your post information, is displayed using the following code:

```php
<?php if (have_posts()) : ?>
<?php while (have_posts()) : the_post(); ?>
    <?php get_template_part('listing', 'blog'); ?>
<?php endwhile; else: ?>
    <h5>Sorry, no posts matched your criteria.</h5>
<?php endif; ?>
```

The `get_template_part()` function call that's right in the middle fetches another file, `listing-blog.php`, which contains the rest of the loop, but for now, let's just focus on the main section here.

There are two basic parts of the loop:

- Individual post information
- What to do if there are no appropriate posts

The first part is handled by a standard PHP `while` loop that goes through every post and for each element calls the listing-blog.php file, which we'll discuss in a minute. The second part is a very straightforward piece of code, as it only displays a short message that there are no posts that can be displayed.

So let's take a look at the `listing-blog.php` file and try to figure out how the loop works. Here's the final version of the file:

```php
<div class="post post-item">
    <div class="post-title">
        <h2><a href="<?php the_permalink(); ?>"><?php the_title();
?></a></h2>
        <div class="post-meta">
        posted by <?php the_author_posts_link(); ?>  | 
            posted on <span class="post-date"><?php echo get_the_date();
?></span>  | 
        <a href="<?php comments_link(); ?>" class="link-
comments"><?php comments_number('no comments', '1 comment', "%
".'comments'); ?></a>
        </div>
```

```
        </div>

    <?php if(has_post_thumbnail()) : ?>
        <div class="post-image alignleft">
        <?php echo '<a href="'.esc_url(get_permalink()).'" >'.get_
the_post_thumbnail().'</a>'; ?>
        </div>
    <?php endif; ?>

    <div class="entry clearfix">
        <?php the_excerpt(); ?>
    </div>
</div><!-- /.post-item -->
```

If you give it a closer look, you'll notice that it's very similar to the static HTML version I shared earlier in this chapter. The only difference is that instead of the dummy text, there are calls to specific WordPress functions and commands. Let's take it from the top; the file starts with these two lines:

```
<div class="post post-item">
    <div class="post-title">
```

These are the exact two lines we used in the HTML version. Next, we have one line that displays the link and the title of the current individual post, instead of using the dummy text:

```
<h2><a href="<?php the_permalink(); ?>"><?php the_title(); ?></a></h2>
```

In it, the_permalink() handles the link, and the_title() handles the title. You have to admit that the standard naming of functions in WordPress is quite self-explanatory, by the way.

The next part handles the post details such as the author info, the date, and the comment links (which other visitors can click to submit their own opinion about the post):

```
<div class="post-meta">
    posted by <?php the_author_posts_link(); ?>  | 
    posted on <span class="post-date"><?php echo get_the_date(); ?></
span>  | 
    <a href="<?php comments_link(); ?>" class="link-comments"><?php
comments_number('no comments', '1 comment', "% ".'comments'); ?></a>
</div>
```

One interesting thing I'd like to point out here is the call to the
`comments_number()` function:

```php
<?php comments_number('no comments', '1 comment', "% ".'comments'); ?>
```

Here, you can see that there are three arguments passed, separated by commas:

- The first option tells WordPress the text that it has to display when there are no comments.
- The second option tells WordPress the text that it has to display when there is just one comment.
- The third option tells WordPress text that it has to display for more than one comment. The percent symbol (`%`) gets replaced with the actual number of existing comments.

Next, we have a small section for handling the thumbnail. Our theme simply displays the thumbnail that goes along with each post just to make it more recognizable within the listing. By the way, these thumbnails are created automatically once you upload an image to go along with a given post and assign it as the featured image.

```php
<?php if(has_post_thumbnail()) : ?>
    <div class="post-image alignleft">
        <?php  echo '<a href="'.esc_url(get_permalink()).'" >'.get_
the_post_thumbnail().'</a>'; ?>
    </div>
<?php endif; ?>
```

Finally, there's the most important part, displaying the actual post content (actually a shortened version of it). You can notice that I am only displaying the excerpts of the posts inside this loop (through the `the_excerpt()` function call, rather than showing the full contents of the post). However, if you want to go the other way, you can use the following instruction instead. This will display the full contents of the posts and not just the excerpts:

```php
<?php the_content('Continue reading <span class="meta-nav">&rarr;</
span>'); ?>
```

Once we have this part done, all we have to do is to take the first part of the loop (the short one, *not* the `listing-blog.php` file) and put it into our `index.php` file in the place where the main column lives. In my case, that's div with `class="postlist"`:

```
<div class="content" role="main">
    <!-- post list -->
    <div class="postlist">
        <?php if (have_posts()) : ?>
        <?php while (have_posts()) : the_post(); ?>
            <?php get_template_part('listing', 'blog'); ?>
        <?php endwhile; else: ?>
            <h5>Sorry, no posts matched your criteria.</h5>
        <?php endif; ?>
    </div>
</div>
```

I'm happy to say that this is it when it comes to the basic understanding of the loop. Of course, its structure allows you to do many more things and include many custom features. But for now, we are good with what we have here.

Okay, now save your `index.php` file and reload your website. Here's the theme in action:

Later in the chapter, I will show you how to create a custom page template, which will take advantage of the loop and use it for a slightly different purpose.

 If you'd like to learn more about the useful built-in WordPress template tags and functions you can implement while building up your theme, you can find it in *WordPress Theme Development Beginner's Guide Third Edition* by *Rachel McCollin* and *Tessa Blakeley Silver*, *Packt Publishing*.

Creating templates within your theme

You've now got a functional basic template for your theme. It works great on the main blog page and successfully loads content for anything you can click on in your site.

However, we want slightly different templates for other types of content on our site. For example, a **Single Post** page needs to have a Comments form where visitors can post comments; the **Page** page doesn't need to show the date, category, or tags; and the **Category** page should show the category name.

Before we can create other templates, we need to break up the main `index.php` file into parts so that these different templates can share the common elements. I've mentioned many times the importance of the header, sidebar, and footer. We're going to break them up now. First, let's take a quick look at how it works.

Understanding the WordPress theme

The WordPress theme is actually composed of a number of template files. This allows the different parts of the site (such as the frontend, blog archive, page, single post, search results, and so on) to have different purposes. Breaking the `index.php` file into template files allows us to not only share some common parts of the design, but also have different code in the different parts.

As I mentioned earlier, we'll soon be breaking up the four main pieces of the design (the header, sidebar, main column, and footer) so that WordPress can make good use of them. That's because while the header and footer are probably shared by all pages, the content in the main column will be different. Also, you may want the sidebar on some pages, but not on others.

We'll first create these template files and then move on to other, more optional template files.

Breaking it up

We're going to break up the index.php file by removing some of the code into three new files:

- header.php
- footer.php
- sidebar.php

header.php

First, cut out the entire top of your index.php file. This means cutting the doctype declaration, <head>, any miscellaneous opening tags, and the header div. In my case, I'm cutting out all the way from this initial line:

```
<!DOCTYPE html>
```

And I'm including these lines:

```
        </div><!-- /.container -->
    </div><!-- /.header top bar -->
```

Then, paste this text into a new file named header.php that you created within your theme folder.

Now at the very top of the index.php file (that is, where you just cut the header text from), write in this line of WordPress PHP code:

```
<?php get_header(); ?>
```

This is a WordPress function that includes the header.php file you just created. If you save everything and reload your website now, nothing should change. If something changes, you've made a mistake.

footer.php

Next, we will create the footer file. To create this, first cut out all of the text at the very bottom of the index.php file, from the <div class="footer"> div, and all the way through the </html> tag. In my case, this is the entire text I cut:

```
<div class="footer">
    <div class="container clearfix">
        <div class="botmenu"><?php
            wp_nav_menu(array('theme_location' => 'footer_menu', 'link_
before'=> '<span>', 'link_after' => '</span>')); ?></div>
```

```
        <div class="copyright"><a href="http://wordpress.org/"
title="WordPress" rel="generator">Proudly powered by WordPress</a><br
/>
        Created with the CONEXUS KITCHEN theme by <a href="http://
themefuse.com">Themefuse</a></div>
    </div><!-- /.container -->
</div><!-- /.footer -->

</div><!-- /.body_wrap -->
<?php wp_footer(); ?>
</body>
</html>
```

Paste the text you just cut into a new `footer.php` file that you create within your `theme` folder.

Now at the very bottom of the `index.php` file (from where you just cut the footer text), write in the following line of WordPress PHP code:

```
<?php get_footer(); ?>
```

This is a special WordPress function that includes the `footer.php` file you just created. Again, you should save everything and reload your website to make sure nothing changes.

The sidebar.php file

There is just one more essential template file to create. For this one, cut out the entire `div` containing your sidebar. In my case, it's the following text:

```
<div class="sidebar" role="complementary">
    <div class="widget-container widget_archive">
    <h3 class="widget-title">Archives</h3>
    <ul>
            <?php wp_get_archives(); ?>
        </ul>
    </div>
</div>
```

Paste this text into a new file in your `theme` folder named `sidebar.php`.

Now in `index.php`, add this function in the place you just cut your sidebar from:

```
<?php get_sidebar(); ?>
```

This will include the sidebar. In the case of my design, I will want the sidebar on every page. So it's not very crucial for it to be a separate file. I could have included it in the `footer.php` file. However, in some templates, including the default template that came with your WordPress installation, the designer prefers to not include the sidebar in some views such as the **Page** and single posts.

Your four template files

You've now got four template files in your `theme` folder, namely `header.php`, `footer.php`, `sidebar.php`, and the now-much-shorter `index.php`. By the way, my `index.php` file now has only a handful of WordPress functions and the loop. The following is the entire file:

```php
<?php get_header(); ?>

<!-- middle -->
<div id="middle" class="cols2">
    <div class="container clearfix">
        <div class="content" role="main"><!-- content -->
            <div class="postlist"><!-- post list -->
                <?php if (have_posts()) : ?>
                <?php while (have_posts()) : the_post(); ?>
                    <?php get_template_part('listing', 'blog'); ?>
                <?php endwhile; else: ?>
                    <h5>Sorry, no posts matched your criteria.</h5>
                <?php endif; ?>
            </div>
        </div>
                <?php get_sidebar(); ?>
    </div><!-- /.container -->
</div><!-- /.middle -->

<?php get_footer(); ?>
```

This whole cutting-and-pasting process to create these four files was just to set the scene for the real goal of making alternative template files.

Archive template

WordPress is now using the `index.php` template file for every view on your site. Let's make a new file—one that will be used while viewing a monthly archive, category archive, or tag archive.

To create your archive template, make a copy of `index.php` and name this copy `archive.php`.

Now navigate to a monthly archive on the site by clicking on one of the month names in the sidebar. At this point, it looks exactly like the main listing—the one handled by `index.php`.

Let's make one more change to the archive template. I'd like it to display a message that lets the users know what type of archive page they are on. Currently, the archive looks the same as the main index listing and this isn't the most optimized situation. To fix it, just add this code below the `<?php if (have_posts()) : ?>` line:

```
<h1>
    <?php if (is_category()) { ?>
    Archive for the '<?php single_cat_title(); ?>' Category
    <?php } elseif( is_tag() ) { ?>
    Posts Tagged '<?php single_tag_title(); ?>'
    <?php } elseif (is_month()) { ?>
    Archive for <?php the_time('F, Y'); ?>
    <?php } ?>
</h1>
```

Now, when I click on a month, category, or tag, I see a new heading at the top of the page that lets me know where I am:

Single template

The next template we need to create is for the single post view. To view a single post, you can usually just click on the post title. Right now, the single post page looks like the site's front page (because it's using `index.php`); except with just one post.

To get started, again make a copy of `index.php` and name the copy `single.php`. This is the template that WordPress will look for first when it's serving a single post. If it doesn't find `single.php`, it'll use `index.php`.

Without further delay, here's my `single.php` file. You should notice that the file features almost exactly the same elements as `index.php`. The only difference is that they are placed inside slightly different HTML elements to improve the way the contents of the posts are presented.

```php
<?php get_header(); ?>

<!-- middle -->
<div id="middle" class="cols2">
    <div class="container clearfix">
        <div class="content" role="main"><!-- content -->
            <article id="post-<?php the_ID(); ?>" <?php post_
class(array('post-item', 'post-detail')); ?>>
                <?php while ( have_posts() ) : the_post(); ?>
                    <div class="post-title">
                        <h1><?php the_title(); ?></h1>
                        <div class="post-meta">
                            posted by <?php the_author_posts_link();
?>   |  
                            posted on <span class="post-date"><?php
echo get_the_date(); ?></span>   |  
                            <a href="<?php comments_link(); ?>"
class="link-comments"><?php comments_number('no comments', '1
comment', "% ".'comments'); ?></a>
                        </div>
                    </div>

                    <div class="entry clearfix">
                        <?php if(has_post_thumbnail()) : ?>
                            <div class="post-image alignleft"><?php
echo get_the_post_thumbnail(); ?></div>
                        <?php endif; ?>

                        <?php the_content(); ?>
                    </div>
                <?php endwhile; ?>
```

```
        </article>

        <?php comments_template('', true); ?>
    </div>

    <?php get_sidebar(); ?>
  </div><!-- /.container -->
</div><!-- /.middle -->

<?php get_footer(); ?>
```

Three specific things that are worth pointing out here are:

- The `<article>` tag is present. The individual post's content is displayed inside this tag.

- The call to the `the_content()` function instead of the `the_excerpt()` function is made. This time, we're displaying the whole content of the post, not just the excerpt.

- The call to the `comments_template('', true)` function is made. It displays the comment form and the individual comments that have been submitted for this post.

Page template

The last template we're going to create is for the static page view. On my food blog site that would be the **History** page, for example:

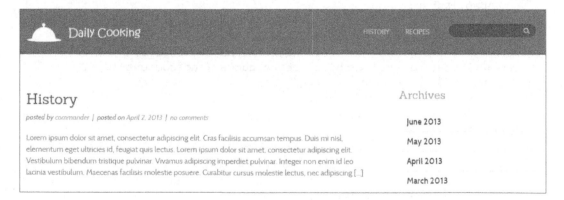

In short, I want to get rid of everything that is not essential. This includes the comment form, the publication date, the author info, and so on. To make this possible, let's start by creating a copy of index.php and naming it page.php. When you edit your version of the file, remove the code for the date, categories, and tags. With mine, what I did was use an additional `<article>` tag to display the contents of the page inside it. In the end, this is how my page.php file looks:

```php
<?php get_header(); ?>

<!-- middle -->
<div id="middle" class="cols2">
    <div class="container clearfix">
        <div class="content" role="main"><!-- content -->
            <article id="post-<?php the_ID(); ?>" <?php post_class(array('post-detail')); ?>>
                <div class="entry clearfix">
                    <?php while ( have_posts() ) : the_post(); ?>
                        <h1><?php the_title(); ?></h1>
                        <?php the_content(); ?>
                    <?php endwhile; ?>
                </div>
            </article>
        </div>

        <?php get_sidebar(); ?>
    </div><!-- /.container -->
</div><!-- /.middle -->

<?php get_footer(); ?>
```

Now my **History** page looks much cleaner.

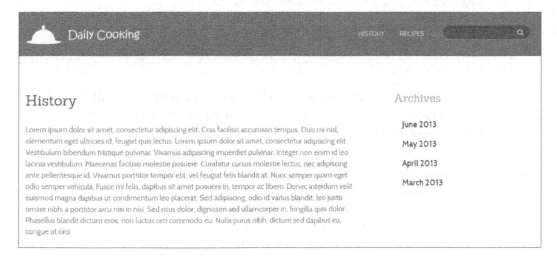

Generated classes for body and post

As you're modifying your theme to make accommodations for different types of pages, you should also know about the CSS classes that WordPress will put into your theme. One of them is classes in the body tag and the others are classes in the post div. If you look carefully at the code we've been using, you'll see these two functions:

- body_class()
- post_class()

The body_class() function adds a whole bunch of classes to the body tag, depending on the page you're viewing. For example, the main page of my site has these classes in the body:

```
<body class="home blog logged-in">
```

My Butternut Squash Soup single post page's body tag looks like this:

```
<body class="single single-post postid-15 logged-in">
```

If I wanted to style anything differently on different pages, I could do it largely with CSS without having to create another template.

The post_class() function does something similar with the post div, giving the div different classes depending on the characteristics of the post itself. For example, my Butternut Squash Soup post's div has these classes:

```
<article id="post-11" class="post-11 post type-post status-publish
format-standard hentry category-podcast category-recipes tag-hot tag-
soup tag-vegetarian post-item post-detail">
```

And my **History** page's post div has these:

```
<article id="post-46" class="post-46 page type-page status-publish
hentry post-detail">
```

By using these classes in my stylesheet, I could style every post differently depending on its category, tag, post type, and so on. Keep that in mind as you design your next theme!

This becomes extremely important while working with theme frameworks further down the road. Although modifications inside PHP files are allowed, most of the time, you can customize the design of your whole site just by working in the CSS and tweaking various classes (both the native ones in WordPress and the new ones that the framework uses). Situations where a whole new site working on a theme framework gets built purely in the CSS files are not uncommon.

Other WordPress templates

In addition to `archive.php`, `single.php`, and `page.php`, there are a number of other standard template files that WordPress looks for before using `index.php` for particular views. We're not going to create those files here, but you should feel free to experiment on your WordPress installation. These files are as follows:

- `rtl.css` is a custom CSS file that gets used, and included automatically whenever the website's text direction is right to left

- `archive.php` trumps `index.php` when a category, tag, date, or author page is viewed

- `single.php` trumps `index.php` when an individual post is viewed

- `single-{post-type}.php` trumps `index.php` when an individual post of a given custom type is viewed; for example, if you're using a custom post type to present quotes, you can create a file such as `single-quotes.php`, which will then be used for displaying single posts from the custom post type named **quotes**

- `page.php` trumps `index.php` while looking at a static page

- `search.php` trumps `index.php` when the results from a search are viewed

- `404.php` trumps `index.php` when the URI address finds no existing content

- `front-page.php` trumps `index.php` when the home page is viewed but only if you use a static front page (**Settings | Reading** in the WP Admin)

- `home.php` trumps `index.php` when the home page is viewed, which is the home page template by default; however, if you use a static front page (**Settings | Reading** in the WP Admin), this is the template for the page with the latest posts

- `taxonomy.php` trumps `index.php` when a custom taxonomy is viewed

- `attachment.php` trumps `index.php` when a single attachment is viewed

- `image.php` trumps `attachment.php`, which trumps `index.php` when a single image attachment is viewed

- A custom template page, selected via the WP Admin, trumps `page.php` when that particular page is viewed

- `category.php` trumps `archive.php`, which trumps `index.php` when a category is viewed

- `tag.php` trumps `archive.php`, which trumps `index.php` when a tag page is viewed

- `author.php` trumps `archive.php` when an author page is viewed

- `date.php` trumps `archive.php` when a date page is viewed

In addition, when you browse the official code bundle for this chapter, you'll see that many of the preceding files have been created and are actually available inside the bundle. We're not covering them here, however, as it would probably be too much information at this point.

 You can find a detailed flow chart of the template hierarchy here: `http://codex.wordpress.org/Template_Hierarchy`. You can get a more detailed discussion of creating these built-in template pages in *WordPress Theme Development Beginner's Guide Third Edition* by *Rachel McCollin* and *Tessa Blakeley Silver, Packt Publishing*.

In this chapter, we've experimented with the uses of quite a number of WordPress template tags. In *Chapter 12, Creating a Non-blog Website Part Two – Community Websites and Custom Content Elements*, I have listed more of the most useful template tags.

Next, we'll explore making custom templates for pages.

Creating and using a custom page template

WordPress allows you to create custom templates. These can be used only for pages (not for posts). A custom template allows you to display the content differently, or easily use built-in WordPress functions within a template.

Just to give you a good example of what custom page templates are and how they can benefit your site (no matter what theme you're using), let's create a custom version of the archives template. This is also what we will use to create a custom **Archives** page that should be much more useful to our readers than the standard one. Here's what the archives look like on my blog right now:

Archives

June 2013

May 2013

April 2013

March 2013

There are just a couple of small links in the sidebar that redirect the visitors to a standard monthly archive presenting posts published between **March 2013** and **June 2013**. Of course, later on, when there are more posts on your site, there will be many more links shown (exactly one link for each month of your site's existence).

Now, as far as the idea of archives goes, I have to admit, somewhat reluctantly, that WordPress was never good at this. One of the few problems with the platform as a web publishing solution was the fact that posts usually have very short life spans. Whenever you publish a post, it sits on the front page for a while and then it vanishes in the archives never to be seen again, no matter if it's still relevant or not. In the end, it's really hard for a new visitor to find these old posts on your site.

One of the few chances you have at reviving those old posts is mastering the art of **SEO (search engine optimization)** and driving some new traffic to your old posts through your SEO efforts only (it's the most popular solution). But luckily, it's not the only way around to fix this issue. Again, custom page templates are an interesting remedy here.

In the preceding screenshot, you can see that the default version of the archives is just a sidebar widget with some links to the individual months. The problem with such content organization is that it provides really a bad user experience. Archives, in general, are not about listing everything in one place; they are about providing a hub where the visitor can go and find some specific piece of content. For example, think about how archives work in your local library. This is what you want to eventually have on your site as well. So what we're going to do here is say no to the traditional archives template in WordPress and create a custom page template to handle the archives manually. Then, we're going to link to this archive from one of the menus. Here's how to do it.

On our new archives page, we want to achieve the following things:

- Display a piece of custom text, for instance, as a form of introduction or a notification message explaining what's in the archives
- Display a categories archive, which will be a list all the categories in use on the site
- Display a tag cloud, which will be a form of tag archive where all of the tags in use on the site are displayed one after the other (inline, not in a list format), and the font size increases for the tags that have been used more often than others
- Display a list of 15 latest posts or whatever number you wish
- Display a monthly archives block, the fact that they are displayed at the bottom is not accidental, as this block is not particularly useful for a typical visitor

To do this, we need to create a template. These are the steps we'll take:

1. Create the template file.

    Make a copy of `page.php` within your theme and give it a new name. I like to prepend all my custom template files with `tmpl_` so that they are sorted separately from all the WordPress template files that I will create. I'll name this file `tmpl_archives.php`.

    In order for WordPress to be able to identify this file as a template file, we need to add a specially styled comment to the top of the page (just as we did with `style.css`). The comment needs to be formatted like this:

    ```php
    <?php
    /* Template Name: Blog Archives Custom */
    ?>
    ```

    In the WP Admin panel, the template will be identified by this template name, so make sure the name signals to you for what the template is used.

2. Add WordPress functions.

    This is a crucial part of the process, but thankfully not a complicated one at this stage. Look over your new template file and find the occurrence of:

    ```php
    <h1><?php the_title(); ?></h1>
    <?php the_content(); ?>
    ```

    Now erase those two lines and put this in their place:

    ```php
    <?php get_template_part('content', 'tmpl_archives'); ?>
    ```

    This is the result we're after; the middle part of your `tmpl_archives.php` file should now look like this:

    ```php
    <article id="post-<?php the_ID(); ?>" <?php post_class(array('post-detail')); ?>>
        <div class="entry clearfix">
            <?php while ( have_posts() ) : the_post(); ?>
                <?php get_template_part( 'content', 'tmpl_archives' ); ?>
            <?php endwhile; ?>
        </div>
    </article>
    ```

Next, create a completely new file called content-`tmpl_archives.php`
and put the following code in it:

```
<div class="post-item">
    <div class="post-title">
        <h2><a href="<?php the_permalink(); ?>"><?php the_title();
?></a></h2>
    </div>

    <div class="entry clearfix">
        <?php the_content(); ?>

        <div style="float: left; width: 50%;">
            <h2>Categories</h2>
            <ul>
            <?php wp_list_categories('orderby=name&title_li='); ?>
            </ul>
        </div>
        <div style="float: left; width: 50%;">
            <h2>Tags</h2>
            <?php wp_tag_cloud('smallest=8&largest=20'); ?>
        </div>
        <div style="clear: both;"></div><!-- clears the floating
-->

        <?php
        $how_many_last_posts = 15;
        echo '<h2>Last '.$how_many_last_posts.' Posts</h2>'; $my_
query = new
            WP_Query('post_type=post&nopaging=1');
        if($my_query->have_posts())
        {
            echo '<ul>';
            $counter = 1;
            while($my_query->have_posts() && $counter<=$how_many_
last_posts)
            {
                $my_query->the_post();
                ?>
```

```
            <li><a href="<?php the_permalink() ?>"
rel="bookmark" title="Permanent Link to <?php the_title_
attribute(); ?>"><?php the_title(); ?></a></li>
                <?php
                $counter++;
            }
            echo '</ul>';
            wp_reset_postdata();
        }
        ?>

        <h2>By Month</h2>
        <p><?php wp_get_archives('type=monthly&format=custom&aft
er= |'); ?></p>
    </div>
</div><!-- /.post-item -->
```

The preceding code includes some additional functionalities on our new archives template. Actually, because we are creating a custom template, we can add any of the WordPress functions we discovered earlier in the chapter, as well as any other WordPress function in existence (refer to *Chapter 12, Creating a Non-blog Website Part Two – Community Websites and Custom Content Elements*).

What we did here is the following. Here are some of the more interesting parts of the code. Starting with the first part:

```
<div style="float: left; width: 50%;">
    <h2>Categories</h2>
    <ul>
    <?php wp_list_categories('orderby=name'); ?>
    </ul>
</div>
```

It's about adding a complete list of categories that are present on the site. The div elements are responsible for displaying this block on the left-hand side and allowing the next block, tags, to be placed next to it (it's a more effective way of achieving such an effect than using HTML tables because it's a more cross-device-friendly approach).

The next part of the code:

```
<div style="float: left; width: 50%;">
    <h2>Tags</h2>
    <?php wp_tag_cloud('smallest=8&largest=20'); ?>
</div>
<div style="clear: both;"></div><!-- clears the floating -->
```

It has a very similar purpose, only this time we're displaying the aforementioned tag cloud. The last `div` element visible in the preceding code is meant to clear the `float` parameter used in the previous `div` elements.

Next, we have the part responsible for displaying the latest posts:

```php
<?php
$how_many_last_posts = 15;
echo '<h2>Last '.$how_many_last_posts.' Posts</h2>'; $my_query =
new WP_Query('post_type=post&nopaging=1');
if($my_query->have_posts())
{
    echo '<ul>';
    $counter = 1;
    while($my_query->have_posts() && $counter<=$how_many_last_
posts)
    {
        $my_query->the_post();
        ?>
        <li><a href="<?php the_permalink() ?>" rel="bookmark"
title="Permanent Link to <?php the_title_attribute(); ?>"><?php
the_title(); ?></a></li>
        <?php
        $counter++;
    }
    echo '</ul>';
    wp_reset_postdata();
}
?>
```

Currently, the code displays 15 latest posts, but this can be adjusted if you just change the value of the `$how_many_last_posts` variable.

Finally, there's the block that displays a traditional monthly archive, where every month is represented as a standard link:

```php
<h2>By Month</h2>
<p><?php wp_get_archives('type=monthly&format=custom&after= |');
?></p>
```

At this point, you can save the file and proceed to the next step.

3. Apply the template to a page.

    Leave your HTML editor, and log in to your WP Admin. You need to edit or create the page in which you want to use this template. In this case, I will create a page and name it `Archives`.

On the **Edit Page** page, look for the **Template** menu within the **Page Attributes** box (at the right, by default).

Change it from **Default Template** to **Blog Archives Custom**, and click on **Update** (note that you can also change a page's template using Quick Edit by navigating to **Pages | Edit**). Now, in order to see the page somewhere, you have to add it to one of the menus. We already covered this in *Chapter 4, Pages, Menus, Media Library, and More*, so I'm sure you can get it done quickly. Once you have this handled, you can return to the frontend of your website and click on the **Archives** page. However, because your site is not that content-heavy at this point, you won't get a staggering effect:

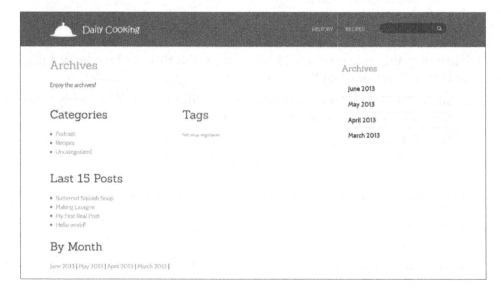

You'll have to wait a while to get the full value of a custom archives page. For example, here's what the preceding code delivers on one of my sites that has more than 200 posts published:

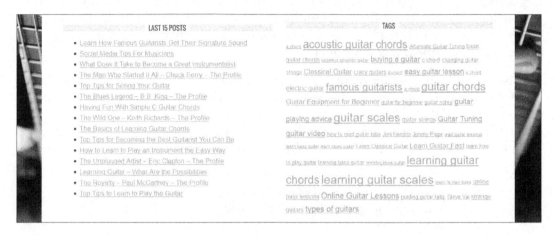

There is no limit to the number of custom templates you can make in your WordPress theme.

Now that we are done making templates for the `conexus-kitchen` theme, the theme directory has grown quite a lot.

Making your theme widget friendly

If you want to be able to use the widgets in your theme, you will need to make your theme widget friendly (also known as **widgetizing** your theme). Widgetizing is actually pretty easy, and involves just the following three steps:

1. Go back to your "static" sidebar.
2. Add some specific functions to the `functions.php` file.
3. Add conditional code to your sidebar.

Nearly all the PHP code you need to add in steps 2 and 3 can be pasted from already existing files, so the nonprogrammers out there shouldn't be too intimidated! Let's get started.

Going back to our "static" sidebar

The use of quotation marks probably makes you wonder what this is all about. The fact is that even though we have a sidebar at this stage, which is a static one, we're only using it as a placeholder—content that's going to be replaced with our dynamic widgets. In its final form, the static sidebar content will only be used if no widgets are selected in **Appearance | Widgets**.

This is actually not a requirement, per se, but it's always good to provide some "just in case" content like this. Now, the best part is that we already have this sidebar content created. We've been doing this a number of pages earlier when we were discussing the basic structure of a standard WordPress theme. Just to remind you what I'm on about, this is the structure we're working with:

```html
<div class="sidebar" role="complementary">
    <div class="widget-container widget_archive">
        <h3 class="widget-title">Archives</h3>
        <ul>
            <?php wp_get_archives(); ?>
        </ul>
    </div>
</div>
```

The first step to widgetizing such a sidebar is to register some standard widget areas. We're going to start with three new such areas. This is all done in the `functions.php` file.

Working with functions.php

As I said earlier, the `functions.php` file can contain many different elements, so now, it's about time to focus on how to actually enable dynamic sidebars also known as **widgets**. In order to do that, go back to your `functions.php` file and add the following lines of code:

```php
function ckitchen_register_sidebar($name, $id, $before_widget, $after_widget, $before_title, $after_title) {
    register_sidebar(array(
        'name' => stripslashes($name),
        'id' => $id,
        'before_widget' => $before_widget,
        'after_widget' => $after_widget,
        'before_title' => $before_title,
        'after_title' => $after_title
```

```
            )
        );
    }
    function ckitchen_register_sidebars() {
        ckitchen_register_sidebar('Post Sidebar','post-
    sidebar','','','','');
        ckitchen_register_sidebar('Page Sidebar','page-
    sidebar','','','','');
        ckitchen_register_sidebar('Main Sidebar','main-
    sidebar','','','','');
    }
    add_action('widgets_init', 'ckitchen_register_sidebars');
```

In the preceding code, I'm using two functions to register three separate widget areas. The main `ckitchen_register_sidebar()` function is just a container function that calls the WordPress' `register_sidebar()` function for registering the widget areas. The `ckitchen_register_sidebars()` function (the second one) is where the actual registration happens. In this function, there are three separate calls to `ckitchen_register_sidebar()` with different parameters for specific widget areas. As you can see, the widget areas that have been enabled are called **Post Sidebar** (the sidebar for individual posts), **Page Sidebar** (the sidebar for pages), and **Main Sidebar** (the sidebar used in all other situations, including the front page—index.php).

Now, the final `add_action('widgets_init', 'ckitchen_register_sidebars')` function call is what actually registers the widget areas (it's the most important line of code here).

Adding conditional code to sidebar

The third and final step is to add conditional code to your sidebar.php file. This code says, "If the person using this theme wants to use widgets, don't show this stuff. If he or she doesn't want to use widgets, do show this stuff." That way, a person not using widgets will see whatever default items you put into the sidebar.php file (in our case, the archives).

This is how the sidebar.php file looks with the widgets enabled:

```
    <div class="sidebar" role="complementary">
        <?php
        $show_default_sidebar = false;
        if(is_page()) {
            if(!function_exists('dynamic_sidebar') || !dynamic_
    sidebar('page-sidebar'))
                $show_default_sidebar = true;
```

```
        }
    elseif(is_single()) {
        if(!function_exists('dynamic_sidebar') || !dynamic_
sidebar('post-sidebar'))
            $show_default_sidebar = true;
    }
    elseif(is_archive() || is_search() || is_front_page() || is_
home()) {
        if(!function_exists('dynamic_sidebar') || !dynamic_
sidebar('main-sidebar'))
            $show_default_sidebar = true;
    }

    if($show_default_sidebar) {
    ?>
    <div class="widget-container widget_archive">
        <h3 class="widget-title">Archives</h3>
        <ul>
            <?php wp_get_archives(); ?>
        </ul>
    </div>
    <?php } ?>
</div>
```

There are some differences between this code and the code listed a couple of pages ago (our static sidebar). As you can see, the static sidebar is still a part of this new version, but it has been surrounded with some additional PHP code. Our widget-enabled `sidebar.php` file starts by defining a new variable `$show_default_sidebar`, which is set to `false`. This variable is then used to determine if any widgets have been assigned to its respective widget area. The main `if{}` conditional statement checks what kind of page we're dealing with (whether it's a post, a standard page, or something else), and then selects the correct widget area that should be displayed. In case there are no widgets assigned to that widget area, the `$show_default_sidebar` variable is set to `true` and the default sidebar appears (the one containing only the archive listing).

To make things clear, let me just admit that the only line of code WordPress needs to recognize and display a specific widget area (in this case, `page-sidebar`) is this one:

```
if(!function_exists('dynamic_sidebar') || !dynamic_sidebar('page-
sidebar'))
```

Adding some widgets

At this point, your theme is ready for widgets! You can now go to WP Admin, navigate to **Appearance | Widgets**, and add widgets (when you do, the default archive listing will disappear). For example, as you can see in the following screenshot, I added three widgets to one of the widget areas:

Be sure to click on **Save** and then return to your website and reload the page. The default items you had placed in the sidebar have been replaced with widgets, as shown in the following screenshot:

Further widgetizing options

What we just covered is the simplest way to widgetize a theme. There are actually a lot of options that you could utilize while adding the code to your `sidebar.php` and `functions.php` pages. For example, there are options that allow you to do the following: widgetizing more than one sidebar giving each a name, widgetizing a part of your sidebar but leave in some default items, customizing the search form widget, and many, many more.

 To learn about the variety of options available and how to take advantage of them, take a look at the codex: `http://codex.wordpress.org/Widgetizing_Themes`.

Enabling a menu in your theme

As of WordPress 3, users can now control more easily what appears in menus. Instead of having to show all the pages in the menu, you can choose to show a selection of pages, and/or categories, and/or other options (as we saw in *Chapter 4*, *Pages, Menus, Media Library, and More*).

The good news I have for you right now is that menus are already enabled in the structure of the theme we're creating here. Because we used the `wp_nav_menu()` function in the header of the site (in the file `header.php`), if the user creates a menu in **Appearance | Menus** and then assigns it to the area indicated as `primary`, it will show up in that spot. The same goes for the other menu area, `footer_menu`, which is placed in the footer.

If you want to have more than one navigation menu in your theme, you can register multiple navigation menu locations and let the user create multiple menus and choose which menu goes in which location. To learn more about that, check out this page of the codex: `http://codex.wordpress.org/Navigation_Menus`.

The `wp_nav_menu()` function is quite powerful, and can take a number of parameters that will let you control the classes and IDs, the name of the menu, and more. Take a look here in the codex for details: `http://codex.wordpress.org/Function_Reference/wp_nav_menu`.

Creating a child theme

If you can find an existing theme or theme framework that you like, and you just want to use your CSS and HTML skills, you can create a child theme. A child theme uses the parent theme as a starting point and, without changing the theme framework itself, alters just the bits you want to alter.

As a matter of fact, using child themes is the recommended way of making modifications to any theme. The rule of thumb is simple: if you want to change anything at all about a stock theme (either inside the source code, graphics, or template files), do it through a new child theme.

In plain English, a child theme inherits the functionality and features of the parent theme. The biggest value in creating child themes is that you can introduce any bells and whistles you wish without altering the structure of the parent theme. I know that this sounds like some additional work because if you just want to change a couple of lines of code, it's always going to be quicker to do it directly within the theme. However, taking the longer, child theme way has its benefits.

The main one is that if you were to modify the original theme directly, all your modifications would vanish the minute you updated the theme. However, if you're using child themes, you can take full advantage of any update that the original theme's authors release. Let me say this again, preserving your modifications after performing a theme update is impossible unless you're using a child theme.

Another benefit of working with child themes is that you have a very clear look over the modifications that you've introduced into your theme. Basically, every new thing that you're implementing through a child theme has to be placed in a new file; so even when you come back to review your child theme after a while, you can still easily identify every piece of your work.

The final benefit, actually, there's probably a lot more of them, but the final one on this short list is that it's very easy to revert every modification you've introduced through a child theme. In short, if something is causing some serious problems and you have to fix your site quickly (you know, an emergency), you can simply delete the files responsible. If you were modifying your original theme directly, going through every file individually would surely take much more time and would make any sort of quick recovery very difficult to achieve.

Let's take a quick look at how to make a child theme.

Creating the new theme directory

Just to make things easier to understand here, we'll take the theme that we've been creating in this chapter and build a child theme for it. The starting point is really simple. Create a new folder in `wp-content/themes/` and name it `conexus-child`.

Creating the stylesheet

The only file you need to start with in this directory is the stylesheet (`style.css`). The stylesheet needs the usual header and a new line:

```
/*
Theme Name: Conexus Child
Description: Child theme for the Conexus theme. Child themes are the
recommended way of making modifications to a theme.
Author: So and So
Author URI: http://yoursite.com
Template: conexus-kitchen
*/
```

The key line in that code is `Template: conexus-kitchen`. This tells WordPress that your new theme is a child theme of `conexus-kitchen`, the directory name of the `conexus-kitchen` theme (it's case sensitive). To make your child theme start out with the CSS from the parent theme, add this code below the comment:

```
@import url("../conexus-kitchen/style.css");
```

If you don't use the preceding line of code, your child theme will begin its existence on a blank stylesheet. In most cases, this is not a desirable scenario.

Using your child theme

That's it! Your new theme now shows up on the **Appearance** page:

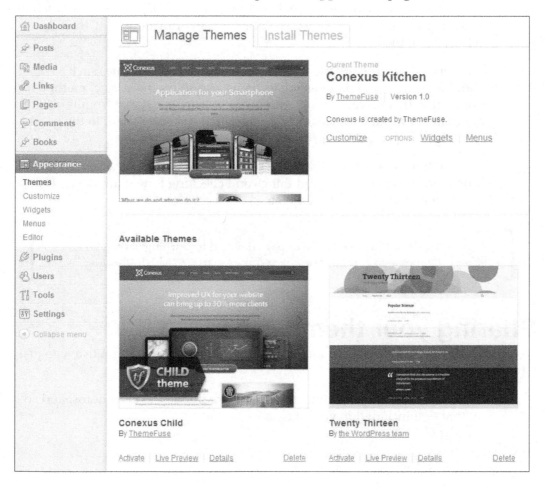

Well, okay, the theme is not really useful at this point, but it does exist and we can use it as the base for further modifications.

By default, it will use all of the main theme's styles, template files, functions, and everything else. If you activate it, it will present your site as if you were using your main theme.

If you want to change anything, do so in your child theme's folder. You will override the main theme's original template file if you create a template file (for example, `single.php`, `index.php`, and `archive.php`). The `functions.php` file works a little differently, however. If you create a `functions.php` file, it will be in addition to the main theme's original `functions.php` file; it will not override. In fact, your new file will be loaded first, right before the original file. If you want to override a specific function in the original `functions.php` file, just create a function with the same name. You can also create completely new functions that are not present in the parent theme.

Like I said, every other template file you create inside the child theme (such as `page.php` and `single.php`) will override its namesake so it's the perfect method to include a new, slightly different design or some new features. Apart from replacing existing template files, you can also add new ones that are not present in the parent (including custom page templates).

In the end, the whole topic of child themes is quite an easy one to grasp, once you spend a little while trying out different things and checking how your site reacts to the things you include in the child theme.

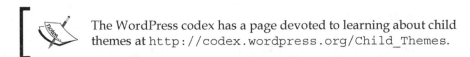

The WordPress codex has a page devoted to learning about child themes at `http://codex.wordpress.org/Child_Themes`.

Sharing your theme

If you want to turn your template into a package that other people can use, you just have to take the following steps:

1. Make sure you have the rights to redistribute images, icons, photos, and so on, that you included in your theme.

2. Remove all unnecessary files from your theme's folder. Be sure you don't have backup versions or old copies of any of your files. If you do delete any file, be sure to retest your theme to ensure you didn't accidentally delete something important.

3. Make sure the comment at the top of the `style.css` file is complete and accurate.

4. Create a `Readme.txt` file. This is a good place to let future users know with what version of WordPress your theme is compatible and if it has any special features or requirements.

5. Zip the folder and post your theme ZIP file on your own website for people to download, or post it directly in the WordPress **Themes Directory** at `http://wordpress.org/extend/themes`.

Even though the preceding process looks like a standard step-by-step one, it's actually nothing like it. To be honest, your theme has to be a really quality one if it's to be allowed into the directory. For example, every theme undergoes a human review, which often results in your theme not passing it. In this case, you just have to make the requested changes, resubmit your work, and keep trying until you get in.

These steps are outlined in a rather general way. If you'd like more details on the process of preparing and sharing your theme in the WordPress community, I highly recommend taking a look at the book *WordPress Theme Development Beginner's Guide Third Edition* by *Rachel McCollin* and *Tessa Blakeley Silver, Packt Publishing*. In this book, the author spends an entire chapter discussing the details involved with sharing your theme and makes recommendations regarding licensing, alternative packaging techniques, getting feedback, versioning, and tracking theme usage.

And speaking about licensing, by default, WordPress is available under the GNU General Public License (GPL). In plain English, this means that WordPress (the platform) is free and every derivative work that is built upon it has to be filed under GPL too—this includes themes. In short, every piece of PHP code you find inside WordPress, various themes, or plugins is GPL (that includes premium themes and plugins as well). When it comes to artwork and CSS, GPL might not apply. If you want to learn more about the GPL licensing, it's best if you go straight to the official legal opinion at `http://wordpress.org/news/2009/07/themes-are-gpl-too/`.

Now, apart from the official directory, you can also share your theme through other channels. First of all, you have to decide whether you want your theme to be available for free or not. In the case of the former, you can reach out to some popular blogs about WordPress and WordPress design, and simply let them know that you have a theme you'd like to share. Most of the time (if the theme looks attractive), they will have no problem notifying their community that there's a cool new free theme.

If you want to make your theme a premium one, you can go to ThemeForest (`http://themeforest.net/`) and try submitting it there. The only challenge is that your theme must really be a quality one if you don't want to get a lot of refunds.

I'm not forcing you to share your theme with the community right away, but once you build some expertise and build your themes to be really cool and useful, you really should reach out to the community and share your work.

Finally, if you're interested in creating an impact with your new theme in the community, consider launching a website dedicated to your theme. This website will be a place where you can publish a demo version, deliver some documentation, provide support forums, and other things to deliver great user experience.

Summary

You have now crossed to the other side of the "theming" world. You have learned how to make your own theme. With just the most basic HTML and CSS abilities, you can create a design and turn it into a fully functional WordPress theme.

In this chapter we saw how to do the following:

- Turning your HTML build into a basic theme
- Creating WordPress templates to influence the display of a variety of views on your site
- Creating custom templates to be applied to pages within your site
- Making your new theme widget-ready
- Creating a child theme
- Sharing your theme with everyone else in the WordPress community

In the next chapter, we'll discuss the topic of feeds, podcasting, and offline blogging. This information will allow you to expand your blogging habits and make your work more diverse.

8

Feeds, Podcasting, and Offline Blogging

Let's start off with a definition. For those of you who aren't sure, the following is what a **feed** is (when it comes to websites):

> "A **web feed** is a data format used for providing users with frequently updated content."
>
> —Wikipedia

Let's take a closer look at this concept. The key idea here is frequently updated content. A website that features a blog or updated news or any type of content that changes regularly will want to offer users a feed. This is because most users will not want (or remember) to visit every such website every day, and users will lose track of which websites have new content today, which don't, what they've already seen, and so on.

If you think about it, feeds are rapidly becoming the only sensible way of consuming content on the internet (no matter if it's written content, audio, or videos). With information overload being one of the most common problems that people experience online in the 21st century, visiting every website that we like manually is becoming quite unmanageable.

Instead, we can use a **feed aggregator** (or **feed reader**). The idea is simple, you can tell the feed reader about all of the regularly updated websites in which you are interested, and the feed reader will grab the updated content and display it all in one place. I, for example, used to enjoy one of the most popular feed readers of all time, that is Google Reader. The only problem was that it ceased to exist on July 1, 2013. Currently, there's a number of alternatives that grew strong after Google's moves.

I'm a **Feedly** user right now (http://www.feedly.com/), but you are free to choose your own favorite. Also, let me just tell you that for me, life without a feed reader would really be much more difficult. I know that it might sound very strange or like a big exaggeration, but I mean it. Just to give you some stats; currently, I'm subscribed to over 540 different feeds, and the best thing is that I only need a few minutes a day to catch up with the most important news and articles. How's that for time efficiency? Actually, I don't even need to visit all these sites directly, I can read every article inside the feed reader. This also adds up to a saving in terms of page load time, as feeds contain fewer advertisements and have only the textual content in which you'll be interested, you don't have to wait for website design elements or ads to render.

What this all boils down to is this: If you are going to create a website with frequently updated content, you'll want to offer your users a feed so that they can add it to their reader. Also, you'll want to be sure you are familiar with feeds and feed readers so that you can both understand what your users are seeing and also offer them everything they are likely to want.

In this chapter, you will learn about feeds, how to provide feeds for your own website's content, and some useful plugins to make all this happen.

But wait, there's more! We're also going to cover podcasting, which for some site owners is an important element of their online presence, and offline blogging apps, which is the best way to create a blog or a website content offline and then export it to the web with just a couple of clicks.

Feed basics

Feeds are pure contents (or just summaries of content) presented in a structured way via XML, and are usually organized with the most recent information on top. You can always stay up-to-date using feed aggregators (software that can read feeds). Using them, you can also have the content you want delivered or collected for you in the way and place you want. This applies not only to written content from blogs or new websites, but also audio and video content (that is, podcasts).

Typically, web feeds are either in **Really Simple Syndication** (**RSS**)or Atom format. RSS has changed over the past decade, and thus is often referred by a version number. The most up-to-date version of RSS is RSS 2.0.1. The older versions that are still somewhat in use are 0.91 and 1.0. However, to be honest, in my some-years' experience with blogging and WordPress, I can't recall a moment when I had to worry about or even be aware of the version I'm currently using. This is one of those things that goes unnoticed for the most part.

If you ever find that you have readers on your blog who write to you complaining that their feed reader can't read your RSS feed, then you could consider publishing links for the older formats (we'll review how to do that later in the chapter), or using a web tool such as FeedBurner. Tools such as these can serve up feeds in different formats, so your visitors can receive your content in whichever way they choose.

Feed readers

Your subscribers will read your content using a feed reader. Feed readers are either web-based or client-side software, which grab the XML content from all the feeds you want and format it legibly. WordPress was programmed with this need in mind and it automatically helps you format your posts so that they come in nicely through the feed readers.

Let me say this again, the functionality of content feeds is built in into WordPress by default. This means that you don't have to do anything at all to make it available. However, you may want to take a look at your blog in a few feed readers to see how your content looks. There are a few different basic types of feed readers, namely online, desktop, mobile, and so on.

As I mentioned a couple of pages ago, Google Reader which is the most popular feed reader in its time, is no longer available. In those last couple of months prior to its shutdown, most users shifted their subscriptions to other tools. Some of the popular solutions of today include:

- (The aforementioned) **Feedly**: http://www.feedly.com/
- **The Old Reader**: http://theoldreader.com/
- **NewsBlur**: http://newsblur.com/
- **Net News Wire**: http://netnewswireapp.com/
- **FeedDemon**: http://feeddemon.com/
- **RSS Bandit**: http://rssbandit.org/
- **Vienna RSS**: http://www.vienna-rss.org/

Every feed reader is constructed in a way that lets you add new feeds easily, organize them into folders and sections, see which feeds have been updated, and also see which items within each feed you have already read. The following is a screenshot of Feedly:

When it comes to desktop tools, they are usually easy to use and offer the same number of features. The only problem is that most desktop tools are not meant to work simultaneously on multiple devices. What this means is that you might experience some problems getting your feeds synchronized if you like to consume content on your desktop, laptop, smartphone, and other gear at the same time. At the end, for personal and professional use, web-based solutions tend to do a better job.

Learning more

You can find an extensive list of these and other feed readers on *Wikipedia* (`http://en.wikipedia.org/wiki/List_of_feed_aggregators`).

Your built-in WordPress feeds

Just as I've mentioned earlier, luckily for you, feed generation is automated in WordPress. The WordPress installation has a feed generator included. The feed generator generates feeds from posts, comments, and even categories. It also generates all versions of RSS and Atom feeds.

You can find the feed generator for your WordPress blog (that we created in the previous chapter) if you point your browser to any of the following URLs (replace `yoursite.com` with the URL of your WordPress installation), and if you have pretty permalinks turned on for your site:

- **RSS 2.0 feed**: `http://yoursite.com/feed/`
- **RDF/RSS 1.0 feed**: `http://yoursite.com/feed/rdf/`

- **RSS 0.92 feed**: http://yoursite.com/feed/rss/
- **Atom feed**: http://yoursite.com/feed/atom/
- **Comments RSS 2.0 feed**: http://yoursite.com/comments/feed/

If you do not have permalinks turned on for your site, you will need to use the following URLs instead:

- **RSS 2.0 feed**: http://yoursite.com/?feed=rss2
- **RDF/RSS 1.0 feed**: http://yoursite.com/?feed=rdf
- **RSS 0.92 feed**: http://yoursite.com/?feed=rss
- **Atom feed**: http://yoursite.com/?feed=atom
- **Comments RSS 2.0 feed**: http://yoursite.com/?feed=comments

The following screenshot is similar to what I see in my web browser when I navigate to the RSS 2 URL:

Adding feed links

WordPress automatically generates even the feed links that you see in the preceding screenshot, so you don't have to type them in or remember what they are for. If you're using an existing theme, there's a good chance it's already got the feed links in it, in which case you can skip the following section. If it doesn't, or if you want to learn more about adding feed links to your own templates, continue on here!

You can use handy built-in WordPress functions to add feeds to your theme. Actually, this is something we have partially done in the previous chapter. Just to remind you what I'm talking about, we used the following code to enable feed links in the `<head>` section of our custom theme. The following code was placed in the `functions.php` file of our theme:

```
functionckitchen_setup() {
  //Adds RSS feed links to <head> for posts and comments.
  add_theme_support('automatic-feed-links');

  /* other code */
}
add_action('after_setup_theme', 'ckitchen_setup');
```

The first instruction within the `ckitchen_setup()` function is exactly what makes sure that the automatic feed links are going to be included in the right place. The presence of these links in the `<head>` section allows various feed readers to pick up your feeds just by using the main URL of your site (in other words, visitors don't have to know the exact addresses of your feed URLs, instead they can subscribe through the main site's URL).

The only additional thing that we can do at this point to make our theme even more usable is to include some custom feed links in the footer, so that every visitor can click on them directly. This is exactly what I'm going to describe in the next section.

Feeds for the whole website

First, let's start by going back to the `footer.php` file that we created in the previous chapter. If you don't have it at your disposal at the moment, simply download the code bundle for *Chapter 7, Developing Your Own Theme*, and install it on your site.

Using your FTP software or the built-in WordPress theme editor, edit the `footer. php` file in your themes folder. Just after the **Proudly powered by WordPress** message, add the following code:

```
| <a href="<?= esc_url(get_bloginfo('rss2_url')) ?>"
  class="rss">Posts</a> | <a href="<?=
    esc_url(get_bloginfo('comments_rss2_url')) ?>"
      class="rss">Comments</a>
```

I've also added an RSS icon in PNG format to the theme's `images` folder, and the following CSS to the stylesheet:

```
.rss, p.rss a {
  background: url(images/rss.png) no-repeat;
  padding: 0 0 0 17px;
  color: #E69730;
}


p.rss { background: none; padding: 0; }
```

Now, when you reload your site, you'll see links for those two feeds in the footer. Have a glimpse at the following screenshot:

WordPress will generate the feed URLs for you based on your site settings so that you don't have to hardcode them into your template. If you want to add links for other kinds of feeds, replace `rss2_url` in the earlier mentioned link with the following text:

- **For RSS 1.0**: `rdf_url`
- **For RSS 0.92**: `rss_url`
- **For Atom**: `atom_url`

Feeds for comments

On the individual posts page, we can add a feed to allow users to subscribe to the comments on a particular post. Sometimes a single post on a blog can draw a lot of attention, with dozens or hundreds of people adding comments. People who comment, and even those who don't comment, may be interested in following the thread, or subscribing to it.

Using your FTP software or the built-in WordPress theme editor, edit the `single.php` file in your `themes` folder. If you're using the theme we built during *Chapter 7, Developing Your Own Theme*, find the code that we added in it, which includes the comments template `<?phpcomments_template('', true); ?>` and add the following code just before it:

```
<p class="rss">
  <?phppost_comments_feed_link('Subscribe to these comments'); ?>
</p>
```

If you are not using the theme we built in *Chapter 7, Developing Your Own Theme*, you can add the preceding code anywhere in `single.php` as long as it is inside the `if` and `while` loops of the loop. Now, when you look at a single post page, you'll see the subscription link just above the comments form, as follows:

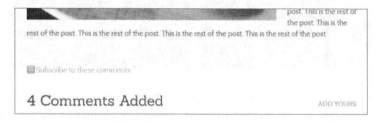

 More built-in feeds are available within WordPress. Learn about them at `http://codex.wordpress.org/WordPress_Feeds`.

Tracking subscribers with FeedBurner

Unlike visitors to your website's pages, your feed users cannot be tracked through normal site-tracking software, such as Google Analytics or Site Meter. The most popular way to track feed users is through the free services provided by **FeedBurner** (`http://feedburner.google.com`).

To use FeedBurner, you will need to divert all of your feed links through FeedBurner instead of sending people directly to your WordPress RSS feeds. FeedBurner will then keep a track of the number of subscribers for you and provide you with a separate dashboard, statistics, and other features.

Burning your feed on FeedBurner

You'll have to create a FeedBurner account before you can start using it. Just navigate to `http://feedburner.google.com/`, log in with your Google account, and follow the sign up instructions. You'll have the option to set up your feed there. Make sure that you select the correct feed that you want to connect to FeedBurner (usually, it's the main feed that is available at `http://yoursite.com/feed/`, not the comments feed that is available at `http://yoursite.com/comments/feed/`). Next, you can tweak your feed's title and set its custom URL, as shown in the following screenshot:

Feed Title:	
	Enter a title to help identify your new feed in your account.
Feed Address:	http://feeds.feedburner.com/
	The address above is where people can find your new feed.

Next » Cancel and do not activate

Then click on **Next**, and you're done.

If you want to, you can stay on the Feedburner options page and enable various stats and other features. But for now, you can just click on the **Skip directly to feed management** link and complete the setup process.

FeedBurner plugin

In order to complete the process on both sides (right now, we've only enabled Feedburner to work with our site, but we didn't let our site know about Feedburner's existence), we need an additional plugin. There are some alternate possibilities out there, but I advise you to use the **FD Feedburner Plugin**. This plugin will tell WordPress that when someone clicks on one of your feed URLs, which are generated by WordPress, redirect them through FeedBurner. You can download the plugin from `http://wordpress.org/extend/plugins/feedburner-plugin/`.

Upload and activate the plugin as you learned in *Chapter 5, Plugins and Widgets*. Then go to the configuration screen by navigating to **Settings | FeedBurner**. Enter your FeedBurner URL into the appropriate textbox (the one labeled **Redirect my feeds here**). You can add a comments feed if you want to track that as well. When it comes to the **Advanced Options** field, you can leave everything checked, as shown in the following screenshot. After all, it's the main feed we want to supercharge through Feedburner:

Advanced Options

☑ Do not redirect category or tag feeds

☑ Append category/tag to URL for category/tag feeds (*http://url_category*)

☑ Do not redirect search result feeds

☑ Do not redirect author feeds

Starting immediately, the feed URLs that WordPress generates (though they appear to be the same) will actually redirect the user to FeedBurner so that it can collect stats.

You won't be able to see your user data right away. FeedBurner will take a few days to collect statistics on your subscribers. Once it has enough data, you'll be able to log in and see how many subscribers you have, which feed readers they are using, and a lot of other data.

Podcasting

A **podcast** is a special feed that includes a reference to an audio or video file instead of just a text. People use a podcasting client, such as iTunes or Juice to collect and listen to the episodes.

[**Fun fact**: The word podcast is a combination of iPod and broadcasting]

Have you ever considered creating your own podcast? It's like having your own radio or TV show. Your subscribers, instead of reading your posts at their computers, can listen through their headphones to your content at any time.

Adding a podcast to your WordPress blog is outrageously easy. While generating your blog's RSS feeds, WordPress automatically adds an <enclosure> tag, which is available in RSS 2.0, if a music file is linked within that post, and this tag is read by podcast clients. Therefore, all you have to do is make a post; WordPress will do the rest for you.

Creating a podcast

For basic podcasting, the following are just two steps you have to take:

1. Record.
2. Post.

Let's have a glimpse at these steps in detail.

Recording yourself

You can record your voice, a conversation, music, or any other sound you'd like to podcast using any commercial or free software and save it as an MP3 file. You may also find that you need to do some editing afterwards.

Some good free software to consider using is as follows:

- I recommend using **Audacity**, which is a free, cross-platform sound recorder, and editor. You can download Audacity from http://audacity.sourceforge.net/. You may have to do a bit of extra fiddling to get the MP3 part working, so pay attention to the additional instructions at that point. If you don't want to learn the basics of audio compression and equalization, you may also want to use a leveling tool such as the **Levelator**, which can be found at http://www.conversationsnetwork.org/levelator. Although it's no longer updated as of the end of 2012, it still works well for leveling the volumes in a simple audio file.

- If you are working on Mac OS and like to use free software, have a glimpse at **Garage Band**. It comes with the OS, so it will already be installed on your computer.

- If you want to examine some advanced pieces of audio software, named **Digital Audio Workstation (DAW)**, used by professional podcast producers and musicians, look into **Sonar X2**, **Studio One**, **Logic**, or **ProTools**.

- To learn more about the basics of audio recording and production for podcasters, which will make your podcasts sound professional, feel free to check the in-depth tutorial that is available at http://www.hongkiat.com/blog/audio-production-for-podcasters/.

Making a post

Now that you've created an MP3 file and it's sitting on your computer, you're ready to make a WordPress post that will be the home for the first episode of your podcast, as follows:

1. In the WP Admin, click on **New Post** on the topmost menu. Enter some initial text into your post if you want to provide an explanation of this episode. I suggest you also, at this point, to add a new category to your blog named Podcast.

2. Just so we learn the basics of including media files, let's upload your media file via the media manager. Later on in this chapter, I will explain why this is not always the most effective approach. But for now, we're here to learn. Start by clicking on the **Add Media** button and drag-and-drop your MP3. If all goes well, your file will be on the server shortly (remember that audio files are bigger than images so uploading will always take a little longer).

3. Next, insert the MP3 file into your post. The following screenshot is of the options screen:

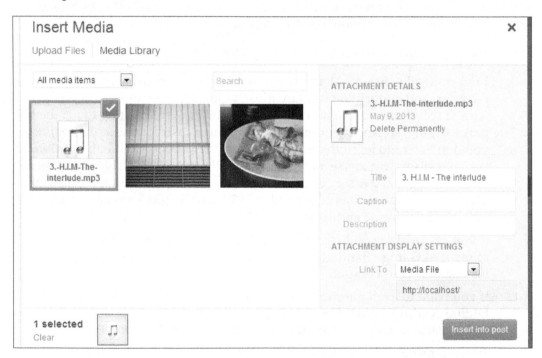

4. WordPress gives you three main possibilities under the **Embed or Link** section. The default one is **Embed Media Player**. If you select it, WordPress displays your audio file inside an interactive player, as shown in the following screenshot. However, here, we're going to select the second option, that is **Link to Media File**:

5. Click on **Insert into post**.
6. Make any other changes or additions you want to make to your post, publish the post, and you're done. The final result is visible in the following screenshot (it's just a standard link):

- one could refuse to pay expensive translators
- To achieve this, it would be necessary to have unifo
3. H.I.M – The interlude

That's it! Your website's RSS 2.0 feed and its Atom Feed can now be used by podcast clients to pick up your podcast.

You can use your own podcast client (iTunes, in my case) to subscribe right away. In iTunes, I navigate to **Advanced | Subscribe to podcast**, and paste in the RSS URL of the new Podcast category I just created, for example http://yoursite.com/category/podcast/feed/. At this point you (and your visitors) can enjoy the new podcast you've just created.

Dedicated podcasting

Setting up a dedicated podcast is easy; we already did it previously! You just need to use a separate category for all of your podcast posts. Whenever you post a podcast episode, be sure to assign it to this category only. Furthermore, in addition to providing a link to the podcast feed on the archive page, you'll want to make this link available in the sidebar of your site.

First, navigate to the archive page for your podcast category and copy the URL, for example http://yoursite.com/category/podcast/feed/. Also, to make things easier for iTunes users, you can add an iTunes-specific link. It is the same as your other link, but replace http:// with itpc://.

Now, create a new text widget for your sidebar and add this HTML to it (replace `yoursite.com` with your actual domain), as follows:

```
<ul>
  <li><a href="http://yoursite.com/category/podcast/feed">The
    Podcast</a></li>
  <li><a href="itpc://yoursite.com/category/podcast/feed">iTunes
    Podcast feed</a></li>
</ul>
```

That's it! The preceding simple lines of code will display two neat links pointing to the podcast.

 The WordPress codex has a section on getting started with podcasting. Have a glimpse at `http://codex.wordpress.org/Podcasting`.

Podcasting plugins

We just learned that it's quite easy to add a podcast to your WordPress website. However, if you want additional features, you may want to use a podcasting plugin. Some additional features might be as follows:

* Automatic feed generation
* Preview of what your podcast will look like in iTunes
* Download statistics
* Automatic inclusion of a player within your post on your website
* Support for separate category podcasts
* And many more features

There are a number of podcast-related plugins available in the WordPress plugin repository. The three most popular are as follows:

* **PowerPress**: `http://wordpress.org/extend/plugins/powerpress/`
* **PodPress**: `http://wordpress.org/extend/plugins/podpress/`
* **Podcasting plugin by TSG**: `http://wordpress.org/extend/plugins/podcasting/`

For an in-depth guide on how to use the PowerPress plugin, which is my favorite one on the preceding list, and how to configure it correctly, please visit this 30-minute video tutorial by *Pat Flynn* at `http://www.youtube.com/watch?v=Ei67QMWD4MA#!`

In it, you'll learn how to optimize your podcast and how to set it up properly so it can be picked up by iTunes, and then shared across the community.

Also there are hundreds more, which you can find by looking at all plugins tagged podcasting, `http://wordpress.org/extend/plugins/tags/podcasting`. You'll have to read the plugin descriptions and user reviews to decide which of these might be the best match for you.

Using a service to host audio files for free

Just as I mentioned a while ago, the old-school approach of uploading your podcast straight to your blog has its flaws, which doesn't make it the most effective way to handle things these days. First of all, if you want to host the media file on your main server (the one where your website is hosted), you can quickly encounter serious bandwidth problems, especially if your podcast becomes popular. Also, there's a problem with the maximum upload size in WordPress. Depending on your webhost, you might not be able to upload files larger than 2 MB, 8 MB, or 16 MB. The following screenshot shows how this problem looks like in the uploader:

Therefore, if you anticipate having a large number of subscribers, or if you plan on producing such a large volume that you'll run out of space on your own server, you can use an external hosting service that will host your audio files either for a fee or even free of cost. Some options to consider are as follows:

- **Libsyn**: It is an effective and affordable podcast hosting that is available at `http://www.libsyn.com/`
- **Archive.org**: Once you sign up for an account, you can contribute your audio files to be placed in the podcast directory. It is available at `http://archive.org/details/audio`
- **PodBean**: It is a free podcast hosting that is available at `http://podbean.com/`

If you choose to do this, first upload your file to the service you've selected and make a copy of the URL it gives you for the file. Now you need to insert it into your WordPress post by using one of the aforementioned plugins. After doing so, your podcast episode will become recognizable by podcast directories.

Offline blogging tools

Offline blogging tools or external blogging tools are some of the things I talked about briefly in *Chapter 3, Creating Blog Content*. Essentially, those tools allow you to create content for your site or blog offline, import it into the site and ultimately publish it for the whole world to see.

The more likely question that's on your mind right now is: Why not create the content directly in WordPress or even use software like Microsoft Word?

The benefits

Despite of the fact that internet access is widely available in the 21st century, you can still encounter some difficulties while travelling (scratch that, you surely will encounter them), or even occasional downtimes in your office, or at home. In such cases, connecting to the WP Admin of your site will be impossible, so you need to have some alternatives.

The first alternative that comes to mind is Microsoft Word or Open Office; it isn't really such a good solution. Although these tools are perfect for creating various documents, they use some specific methods of text formatting, which are not compatible with WordPress. As a result, if you try to copy and paste your post from Word to WordPress, you will get a lot of formatting garbage and the initial simple formatting you've had, such as bold fonts, italics, links, will get messed up.

With dedicated offline blogging apps, there's no such problem. Basically, they were created for the sole purpose of creating content offline (on your desktop computer, laptop, or mobile device), and then exporting it to a WordPress site.

Additionally, since the content is created offline, each post or article is kept as a single file, which you can easily send via e-mail, backup via Dropbox, or do anything else you'd normally do with a file.

To be honest with you, I do 100 percent of my WordPress blogging through an offline blogging tool. Again, that's 100 percent.

The tools

Offline blogging tools is an area where Windows users have it much better than their Linux or Mac friends. That's because some time ago, Microsoft released a tool named **Windows Live Writer** (it works on Windows only). And as far as I know, it's the best tool around. Additionally, there's something very "non-Microsofty" about it; it's free. You can get it at `http://explore.live.com/windows-live-writer`.

If you're mainly a Mac user, check out the following two editors: **MarsEdit** (`http://www.red-sweater.com/marsedit/`) and **Qumana** (`http://www.qumana.com/`)

Finally, for iOS, refer to the official WordPress app or an alternative app named **Blogsy**. They can be both used to write posts locally, on your iOS device, and then have them exported to your blog once you go online.

Using Windows Live Writer

As it turns out, the tool is very simple to use and that's one of the reasons why it's so great. It doesn't require any specific modifications to your WordPress site, which means that your blog is 100 percent ready to work with **Windows Live Writer** right from the get-go. The only configuration you need to take care of is within the Writer itself.

The installation process is pretty straightforward like all Microsoft's products, so I won't be describing it here. Also, you can have the Writer already installed on your Windows computer. This can happen if you've been using Microsoft's live package before as Writer is a part of it. The following screenshot shows how the main screen of Writer looks once you download and install it:

The design is really clear and at first, it seems like there's not much we can do inside this tool. It's probably the simplest text processing tool Microsoft has to offer these days. However, as you'll quickly realize, it has everything a blogger or a WordPress site owner might need. Let's start with the setup; how to connect Writer with your site.

When you attempt to use the tool for the first time, it will ask you about the kind of site you want it to connect to. If you've missed this automatic wizard, you can always click on the drop-down menu icon in the upper-left corner of the screen (visible in the preceding screenshot), navigate to **Options | Accounts**, and then click on the **Add...** button, which will have the same effect. The following screenshot is the place where you can set new blog accounts:

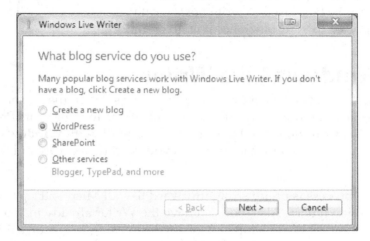

Writer can work with multiple WordPress sites at the same time, which makes it very useful for people managing websites professionally. Let's try setting up your first site. In the screen visible in the preceding screenshot, select **WordPress** and click on the **Next >** button. You will be taken to the next screen where you can input the address of your blog, your username and password. Once you click on **Next>** again, Writer will attempt to connect to your site. In the final step, you have the opportunity to set the blog's nickname, which will be visible only inside Writer.

If all goes well up to this point, you'll be taken back to the main screen. Let's take it apart and see what Writer has to offer. The top bar has only three tabs, namely **Home**, **Insert**, and **Blog Account** (plus the main drop-down menu and the help icon), as shown in the following screenshot:

The **Home** tab is where you can handle all the basic tasks of creating and formatting your content. You should be familiar with most of these features as they are quite similar to what you can find inside Microsoft Word:

The next tab is **Insert**; it offers a more in-depth look into all the things we can include within our content, as shown in the following screenshot:

The final tab, that is **Blog Account**, provides some additional options to view your blog's dashboard, update the theme, and adjust other parameters you might find important, as shown in the following screenshot:

Right under the main tabs, there's an additional section where you can set your post's categories, tags, and publication date (and when you click on the **View all** link, also things, such as the excerpt and slug), as shown in the following screenshot:

Finally, we have the status bar at the bottom. This is where, apart from the ability to edit your post, you can preview what it's going to look like on your site, view the HTML source code of it and check the current word count and post status:

Of course, as I said before, once you click either on the **Publish** button or the **Send draft to blog** button, your post is going to be exported directly to your site where you can perform some further fine tuning.

To be honest, that is all about Writer and the topic of offline blogging tools in general. In short, their purpose is to make your content creation process much quicker with much less hassle. Once you get to know Writer better (or any other similar tool), you will realize that working with WordPress can be as easy as creating a standard document in Word or Open Office.

Summary

There was a lot going on in this chapter. First, we focused on feeds (RSS) and their importance for every website that aims at being reader-friendly. Next, there was the topic of podcasting and a brief getting-started guide about it (how to configure your feeds, what plugins to use, and so on). Finally, we talked about offline blogging tools that can make your life a lot easier as an online content publisher.

In the next chapter, we'll discuss the topic of developing your own plugins and widgets, what the basics are and how to get your head around them.

9
Developing Plugins and Widgets

Earlier in this book, you learned how to install plugins. Plugins are essentially a way to add to or extend WordPress's built-in functionality. There are thousands of useful plugins (at the time of writing, the official counter at http://wordpress. org/plugins/ shows over 27,000 plugins) available from the online WordPress community, and they perform all different kinds of functions. In the earlier chapters, we installed plugins that catch spam, allow FeedBurner to track RSS followers, back up your site, give you basic SEO features, and more. You can also get plugins that manage your podcasts, create a Google XML site map, integrate with social bookmarking sites, track your stats, translate into other languages, and much more.

Sometimes, however, you'll find yourself in a situation where the plugin you need just doesn't exist. Luckily, it's quite easy to write a plugin for WordPress that you can use on your own site and share with the larger community if you want. All you need is some basic PHP knowledge, and you can write any plugin you want.

This chapter is divided into three major parts:

- In the first part, we'll create two plugins using an easy-to-follow step-by-step process
- In the second part, we'll create a widget using the built-in WordPress widget class
- In the third part, we'll look at shortcodes

Plugins

In this section, we'll create a plugin via a simple step-by-step process. We'll first see what the essential requirements are, then try out and test the plugin, and then briefly discuss the PHP code.

Building plugins from scratch

First of all, we're here to learn about WordPress, so in this particular case, we will indeed build things from scratch. This is always the best approach to get an in-depth look into how a particular technology works.

However, later on, once you're working with WordPress on a regular basis managing your own or other people's websites, I actually advise you to always look for an already existing plugin before deciding to write a new one yourself. As I said, there are over 27,000 plugins in the official directory alone, not to mention all the premium plugins available all over the web. In short, if you need some functionality, most likely, there's a plugin for that so you can just go out and get it.

Why is this the recommended approach? If I'm correct, you've chosen to use WordPress because you wanted to make your site as functional as possible with the least amount of effort possible. Following this line of thought, using an existing plugin simply requires much less effort than building one. Also, many existing plugins are already used by thousands of other people and have large communities supporting them. Choosing a quality plugin is, therefore, a lot safer path to take.

I feel that I should emphasize this clearly because experience tells me that many young WordPress developers tend to press their peers to create things from scratch just for the heck of it; despite the fact that there are other and better solutions available.

Moreover, please remember that everything that's a derivative work based on WordPress is available under GPL. So, there's nothing standing in your way to take an existing plugin, build upon it, make it better, and then reshare your version with the world. That way, we all win and there's no redundant work.

But before we can do that, we indeed must learn the craft by constructing something of our own from start to finish. Onwards then!

Plugin code requirements

Just as there were requirements for a theme, there are requirements for a plugin. At the very least, your plugin must:

- Be placed in the `wp-content/plugins` folder (inside the root folder of WordPress)
- Have a PHP file with a unique name (not used by any other plugin in the main `wp-content/plugins` folder)
- Have a specially structured comment at the top of the file (see at `http://codex.wordpress.org/File_Header`)

That's it. Then, of course, you must have some functions or processing code, but WordPress will recognize any file that meets these requirements as a plugin.

If your plugin is a simple one, you can just place a unique PHP file straight in your `wp-content/plugins` folder, so it can sit next to the default Hello Dolly plugin that WordPress comes with. However, a much better practice is to create a subfolder (again, unique) and place your PHP file there. It makes the `wp-content/plugins` folder seem much more organized. Plus, you never know when your plugin is going to need some additional files (it's always easier to simply add new files to a previously existing plugin folder than to restructure the plugin from scratch).

Basic plugin – adding link icons

As a demonstration, we will create a simple plugin that adds icons to document links within WordPress. For example, in *Chapter 8, Feeds, Podcasting, and Offline Blogging,* we added a link to an MP3 file. It looks like the following screenshot now:

- Everyone realizes why a new common language would be desirable
- one could refuse to pay expensive translators
- To achieve this, it would be necessary to have uniform grammar

3. H.I.M – The interlude

If several languages coalesce, the grammar of the resulting language is of the individual languages. The new common language will be more si

Once this plugin is complete, the link will look like the following screenshot instead:

To accomplish this, we have to do the following:

- Provide images of the icons that will be used.
- Have a PHP function that identifies the links to documents and adds a special CSS class to them.
- Have a stylesheet that creates the CSS classes for displaying the icons.
- Tell WordPress that whenever it prints the content of a post (that is, using the `the_content()` function), it has to run the first PHP function.
- Tell WordPress to include the new styles in the `<head>` tag.

Keep this list in mind as we move forward. Once all these five requirements are met, the plugin will be done.

Let's get started!

Naming and organizing the plugin files

Every plugin should have a unique name so that it does not conflict with any other plugin in the WordPress universe. When choosing a name for your plugin and the PHP file, be sure to choose something unique. You may even want to do a Google search for the name you choose in order to be sure that someone else isn't already using it.

Apart from the main plugin file itself, your plugin can contain any number of other files and subfolders. If the situation calls for it, you can even use media files such as audio and videos to go along with your plugin. Of course, additional CSS or JS files (or even full libraries) are allowed as well.

In this case, as my plugin will be composed of multiple files (a PHP file, a stylesheet, and some image files), I'm going to create a folder to house my plugin. I'll name the plugin Add Document Type Styles, and the folder name, ahs_doctypes_styles, will be prefixed with my initials as extra security to keep it unique. The PHP file, doctypes_styles.php, will live in this folder. I've also collected a number of document type icons.

The folder I created for my plugin now looks like the following screenshot:

doctypes_styles.css   doctypes_styles.php   icon-doc.gif
icon-mp3.gif   icon-pdf.gif   icon-zip.gif

 It is best practice to also create folders such as `images`, `css`, and `js` inside your plugin's folder if what you're building will consist of more files.

Now that I've got the images in my folder, I've taken care of the first requirement in the list of requirements my plugin has to meet.

 If your plugin has any unusual installation or configuration options, you may also want to include a `readme.txt` file in this folder that explains this. This readme file will be useful both as a reminder to you and as an instructional document to others who may use your plugin in the future. If you plan to submit your plugin to the WordPress plugin directory, you will be required to create a readme file. To get the template for such a file, please visit `http://wordpress.org/extend/plugins/about/readme.txt`.

As mentioned earlier, your plugin has to start with a special comment that tells WordPress how to describe the plugin to users on the plugins page. Now that I've got my folder and a blank PHP file created, I'll insert the special comment. It has to be structured like the following code. This really is fundamental (explained at `http://codex.wordpress.org/File_Header`).

```php
<?php
/*
Plugin Name: Add Document Type Styles
Plugin URI: http://springthistle.com/wordpress/plugin_doctypes
Description: Detects URLs in your post and page content and applies
style to those that link to documents so as to identify the document
type. Includes support for: pdf, doc, mp3 and zip; you can add more!
Version: 1.2.1
Author: <a href="http://springthistle.com">April Hodge Silver</a> & <a
href="http://karol.cc/">Karol K</a>
License: GPL2*/
?>
```

Another good piece of information to have in your plugin is about licensing. Most plugins use the **GPL** (**GNU General Public License**). This license essentially means that anyone can use, copy, and enhance your code, and that they are not allowed to prevent anyone else from redistributing it. I've also added a note about the GPL to my plugin's PHP file. Remember that all PHP code you encounter in any WordPress plugin is GPL by default. However, graphic files, CSS, JavaScript, and other elements might have a different license, so be careful when copying other people's work and making it part of your own.

That's all about the introductory code. Now we can add the meat.

Writing the plugin's core functions

The core of any plugin is the unique PHP code that you bring to the table. This is the part of the plugin that makes it what it is. Since this plugin is so simple, it only has a few lines of code in the middle.

The second requirement the plugin has to meet is have a PHP function that identifies links to documents and adds a special class to them. The following function does just that. In keeping with my efforts to ensure that my code is unique, I've prefixed both of my functions with `ahs_doctypes_`:

```
function ahs_doctypes_regex($text) {
    $text = preg_replace(
      '/href=([\'|"][[:alnum:]|[:punct:]]*)\.(pdf|doc|mp3|zip)
        ([\'|"])/', 'href=\\1.\\2\\3 class="link \\2"', $text);
    return $text;
}
```

When the function is given some text, it will perform a search for any HTML anchor tag linking to a PDF, DOC, MP3, or ZIP file, and replace it with a class to that anchor. Then, the function returns the altered `$text`.

The third requirement the plugin has to meet is have a stylesheet that creates classes for displaying the icons. The following function fetches our stylesheet:

```
function ahs_doctypes_styles() {
  wp_register_style('doctypes_styles',
    plugins_url('doctypes_styles.css', __FILE__));
  wp_enqueue_style('doctypes_styles');
}
```

As you can see in the preceding code, this function uses the same enqueue mechanism that we used in *Chapter 7, Developing Your Own Theme,* when registering the stylesheets for our custom theme. Here's the CSS file the preceding function fetches (inside `doctypes_styles.css`):

```
.link {
  background-repeat: no-repeat;
  padding: 2px 0 2px 20px;
}
.pdf { background-image: url(icon-pdf.gif); }
.doc { background-image: url(icon-doc.gif); }
.mp3 { background-image: url(icon-mp3.gif); }
.zip { background-image: url(icon-zip.gif); }
```

Indeed a very simple file, containing just a handful of styles and icons to distinguish our document links.

Adding hooks to the plugin

We get our code to actually run when it is supposed to by making use of WordPress **hooks**. The way in which plugin hooks work is—at various times while WordPress is running, it checks to see if any plugins have registered functions to run at that time. If there are, the functions are executed. These functions modify the default behavior of WordPress. The WordPress Codex says it best:

[…] There are two kinds of hooks:

1. Actions: Actions are the hooks that the WordPress core launches at specific points during execution, or when specific events occur. Your plugin can specify that one or more of its PHP functions are executed at these points, using the Action API.

2. Filters: Filters are the hooks that WordPress launches to modify text of various types before adding it to the database or sending it to the browser screen. Your plugin can specify that one or more of its PHP functions is executed to modify specific types of text at these times, using the Filter API.

This means you can tell WordPress to run your plugin's functions at the same time when it runs any of its built-in functions. In our case, we want our plugin's first function, `ahs_doctypes_regex()`, to be run as a filter along with WordPress's `the_content()` function. (This is the fourth requirement a plugin has to meet.)

Now add the following code to the bottom of the plugin:

```
add_filter('the_content', 'ahs_doctypes_regex');
```

This uses the `add_filter` hook that tells WordPress to register a function named `ahs_doctypes_regex()` when it is running the function named `the_content()`. By the way, if you have more than one function that you want added as a filter to the content, you can add a third argument to the `add_filter()` function. This third argument would be a number representing the load priority (the default value is `10`, highest priority is `1`, there are no particular limits for the lowest, you can even assign values such as `100` or `999`), and WordPress would run your functions in the order from smallest to largest.

All that's left in our list of requirements that a plugin has to meet is the fifth requirement: tell WordPress to include the new styles in the `<head>` tag. This is actually done the same way it's been done for themes, which is through the following hook using `add_action()` with the `wp_enqueue_scripts` handle:

```
add_action('wp_enqueue_scripts', 'ahs_doctypes_styles');
```

Here is the complete plugin PHP file (minus the license, which I removed for space considerations):

```php
<?php
/*
Plugin Name: Add Document Type Styles
Plugin URI: http://springthistle.com/wordpress/plugin_doctypes
Description: Detects URLs in your post and page content and applies
style to those that link to documents so as to identify the document
type. Includes support for: pdf, doc, mp3 and zip; you can add more!
Version: 1.2.1
Author: <a href="http://springthistle.com">April Hodge Silver</a> & <a
href="http://karol.cc/">Karol K</a>
License: GPL2
*/

// this function does the magic
function ahs_doctypes_regex($text) {
  $text = preg_replace('/href=([\'|"][[:alnum:]|[:punct:]]*)
    \.(pdf|doc|mp3|zip)([\'|"])/',
      'href=\\1.\\2\\3 class="link \\2"', $text);
  return $text;
}

// this functions adds the stylesheet to the head
function ahs_doctypes_styles() {
```

```
    wp_register_style('doctypes_styles',
      plugins_url('doctypes_styles.css', __FILE__));
    wp_enqueue_style('doctypes_styles');
}

add_filter('the_content', 'ahs_doctypes_regex', 9);
add_action('wp_enqueue_scripts', 'ahs_doctypes_styles');
?>
```

 Please make sure that there are no blank spaces before <?php and after ?>. If there are any spaces, the PHP will break, complaining that headers have already been sent. This is quite a common mistake developers stumble into during their initial attempts with WordPress plugins.

It's also a good idea not to use the PHP closing tags (?>) at all at the end of your PHP files. It saves you from some of the most unfortunate execution errors.

Make sure you save and close the preceding PHP file. You can now do one of the following two things:

- Using your FTP client, upload ahs_doctypes_styles/ to your wp-content/plugins/ folder
- Zip up your folder into ahs_doctypes_styles.zip and use the plugin uploader in the WP Admin to add this plugin to your WordPress installation

Once the plugin is installed, it will show up on the plugins page, as shown in the following screenshot:

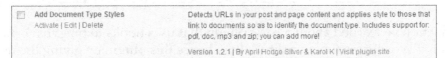

Now you can activate it. That's all you have to do! Let's take a look at the plugin.

 If you need more in-depth advice on installing and working with plugins then feel free to review *Chapter 5, Plugins and Widgets*, where we discussed plugins and widgets in detail.

Trying out the plugin

If you look at the podcast post we created in an earlier chapter, you'll notice that an MP3 icon has been added to it, as shown in the following screenshot:

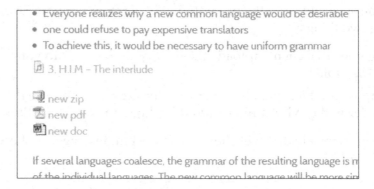

You can also try adding a new post with links to PDF, ZIP, or DOC files. This can be done by uploading the files and clicking on **Insert into Post**.

When you view this post, you'll see that icons have been automatically added to it by the plugin, as shown in the following screenshot:

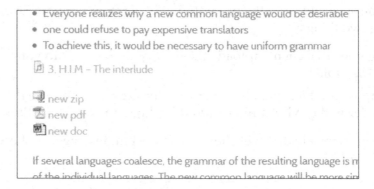

Now that you've learned about a basic plugin that uses hooks to piggyback on the existing WordPress functionality, let's enhance this plugin by giving the user some controls.

Adding an admin page

As you have already seen, some plugins add a page to the WP Admin where you or the user can edit plugin options. We've seen this with **Online Backup for WordPress**, **W3 Total Cache**, **FeedBurner**, **WordPress SEO**, and others. Now let's modify our plugin to give the user some control over which document types are supported.

First, deactivate the plugin we just wrote. We'll make changes to it and then reactivate it.

The following screenshot shows what the new management page will look like when we are done:

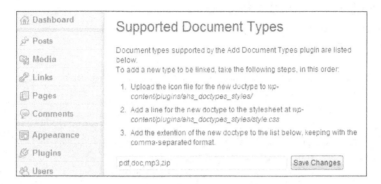

The following are the steps we'll carry out to modify the plugin in order to make this new page possible:

- Add functions that create an admin page and save the user's input in a new option

- Modify the ahs_doctypes_regex() function so that it retrieves the user's input

- Add hooks for the admin page functions

Let's get started!

Adding management page functions

The management page that we will create is going to add an option to the WP Admin. This uses the existing space in the WordPress options table in the database, so no database modifications are required. The name of the new option has to be unique. I'm going to call the new option ahs_supportedtypes, and I'll be sure to use supportedtypes_ in all of my function names to ensure that they are unique.

There are six functions we need to add to the plugin so that an admin page can be added to the WP Admin. Let's take a look at the first two:

1. The first function adds the new option, ahs_supportedtypes, when the plugin is activated, and also sets the default value.

```
function set_supportedtypes_options() {
    add_option("ahs_supportedtypes","pdf,doc,mp3,zip");
}
```

2. The second function removes the new option when the plugin is deactivated.

```
function unset_supportedtypes_options () {
    delete_option("ahs_supportedtypes");
}
```

3. Let's look at the new third function:

```
function modify_menu_for_supportedtypes() {
    add_submenu_page(
    'options-general.php',
    //The new options page will be added as a sub menu to
    //the Settings menu.
    'Document Types', //Page <title>
    'Document Types', //Menu title
    'manage_options', //Capability
    'ahs_doctypes_styles', //Slug
    'supportedtypes_options' //Function to call
    );
}
```

This function adds a new item to the **Settings** menu in the WP Admin using `add_submenu_page`. This takes six arguments, namely, where the options page should be placed, page title, menu link text, the user at the maximum level who can access the link, what file to open (none, in this case), and the function to call, `supportedtypes_options()`.

4. The `supportedtypes_options()` function is, in fact, the fourth new function we are adding:

```
function supportedtypes_options () {
    echo '<div class="wrap"><h2>Supported Document
        Types</h2>';
    if(isset($_POST['submit'])) {
        update_supportedtypes_options();
    }
    print_supportedtypes_form();
    echo '</div>';
}
```

This function actually displays our new page. It prints a title, checks to see if someone has clicked on the **Submit** button, and if it is clicked, the `supportedtypes_options()` function updates the options, and then prints the form.

5. The new fifth function we have to add is responsible for updating options if the **Submit** button has been clicked on.

```
function update_supportedtypes_options() {
  $updated = false;
  if ($_POST['ahs_supportedtypes']) {
    $safe_val = addslashes(strip_tags(
      $_POST['ahs_supportedtypes']));
    update_option('ahs_supportedtypes', $safe_val);
    $updated = true;
  }
  if ($updated) {
    echo '<div id="message" class="updated fade">';
    echo '<p>Supported Types successfully updated!</p>';
    echo '</div>';
  } else {
    echo '<div id="message" class="error fade">';
    echo '<p>Unable to update Supported Types!</p>';
    echo '</div>';
  }
}
```

6. The last function we need to add, the new sixth function, prints the form that users will see. Please make sure to have no spaces before, nor after the closing tag (EOF;).

```
function print_supportedtypes_form() {
  $val_ahs_supportedtypes =
    stripslashes(get_option('ahs_supportedtypes'));
  echo <<<EOF
<p>Document types supported by the Add Document Types plugin
are listed below.<br />To add a new type to be linked, take the
following steps, in this order:
<ol>
  <li>Upload the icon file for the new doctype to <i>
    wp-content/plugins/ahs_doctypes_styles/</i></li>
  <li>Add a line for the new doctype to the stylesheet at
    <i>wp-content/plugins/ahs_doctypes_styles/style.css</i>
      </li>
  <li>Add the extension of the new doctype to the list
    below, keeping with the comma-separated format.</li>
</ol>
</p>
```

```
<form method="post">
  <input type="text" name="ahs_supportedtypes" size="50"
    value="$val_ahs_supportedtypes" />
  <input type="submit" name="submit"
    value="Save Changes" />
</form>
EOF;
}
```

Those six functions together will take care of adding a link in the menu, adding the management page for that link, and updating the new option.

Modifying the ahs_doctypes_regex() function

Now that the users are able to edit the list of supported document types by appending the document types they want, we should have a way of telling the ahs_doctypes_regex() function to use the user's list instead of a built-in list. To do that, we need to use get_option('ahs_supportedtypes') in our ahs_doctypes_regex() function. The get_option() function will retrieve the value that the user has saved in the new option we just created. Modify your ahs_doctypes_regex() function so that it looks like, as follows:

```
function ahs_doctypes_regex($text) {
  $types = get_option('ahs_supportedtypes');
  $types = preg_replace('/,\s*/', '|', $types);

  // add the class to links

  $text = preg_replace('/href=([\'|"][[:alnum:]|[:punct:]]*)
    \.('.$types.')([\'|"])/i', 'href=\\1.\\2\\3 class="link \\2"',
      $text);

  return $text;
}
```

Adding hooks

We have added our management page functions, but now we have to tell WordPress to use them. To do that, we just need to add the following three new hooks:

```
add_action('admin_menu','modify_menu_for_supportedtypes');
register_activation_hook(__FILE__,"set_supportedtypes_options");
register_deactivation_hook(__FILE__,
  "unset_supportedtypes_options");
```

The first hook tells WordPress to add our link to the menu when it creates the menu with `admin_menu()`. The next two hooks tell WordPress to call the activation and deactivation functions when the plugin is activated or deactivated.

Trying out the plugin

We have added all of the new functions. Now it's time to save the file and see what happens. You can go ahead and reactivate the plugin. Now when you look at the **Settings** menu, you will see that the new link has been added:

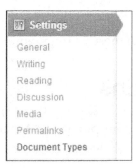

Click on the new link (**Document Types**) to see the management page.

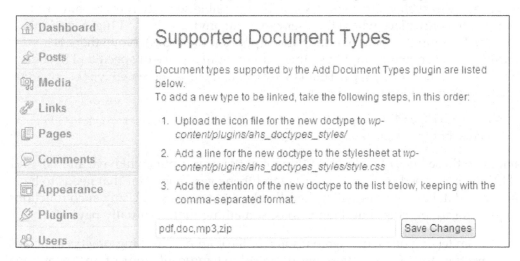

If you follow the three steps here on the management page (upload the file icon, add a new style to the stylesheet, and add the extension to the option), then that new document type will be supported.

There are already a number of ways in which this plugin could be improved. Some of them are:

- Instead of making the user upload his or her new icon using FTP, the plugin could allow the user to upload the new icon directly via the new management page

- The plugin could display the icons for the supported document types on the management page, so the users can see what they look like

- The plugin could check to make sure that for every document type in the option field there is an existing icon, else it displays an error to the user

Perhaps you'd like to try to make these changes yourself!

Testing your plugins

Just a minute ago, we tried out our new plugin, so it's probably a good moment to say a word or two about testing your plugins and making sure that they don't cause any problems for regular users in general.

Our particular plugin is a very simple one, the only thing it does is process each link it finds inside any post's or page's content and adds a custom icon next to it. However, even such a simple plugin can be a possible security breach point. For example, the only place where the user can input anything is the **Plugin** section in the WP Admin (the field handling the supported file types). Now, there is a possibility that someone might use this field to input a piece of specific PHP code instead of a standard file type. That is why our update_supportedtypes_options() function has the following two lines:

```
$safe_val = addslashes(strip_tags($_POST['ahs_supportedtypes']));
update_option('ahs_supportedtypes', $safe_val);
```

Thanks to those lines of code, everything that the user inputs will have all PHP and HTML tags stripped by strip_tags(), and then every character that needs to be quoted in database queries will be handled by addslashes(). Using such functions is a just-in-case practice, but it tends to be something that eventually pays off.

Apart from testing our work against some of the common hacking practices such as code injection and SQL injection, we also need to handle all kinds of unconventional uses we can think of. For instance, would anything bad happen if someone inputted a value that's not a standard file type? Or what if the CSS file goes missing all of a sudden? These are just some of the questions a good testing session should answer.

One more good way of testing plugins is to hand them over to a handful of trusted users and ask for feedback. Someone who's entirely new to your plugin will usually do a way better job at testing it than you – the author.

Of course, this short section here only scratches the surface of plugin testing and code testing in general, so I encourage you to give it a closer look on your own. There are many great resources on the Internet and in the nearest bookstore.

Plugin with DB access – capturing searched words

We're going to leave the doctypes plugin behind now, and create a new plugin, featuring active use of the database. Let's create a simple plugin that stores all the words that visitors search for using the blog's search function.

The database table structure for this plugin will be as follows:

Table wp_searchedwords

Field	Type	Null	Key	Default	Extra
Id	INT	NOT NULL	PRI		auto_increment
Word	VARCHAR(255)			NULL	
created	DATETIME	NOT NULL		Today 00:00:01	

Now, let's write the plugin code.

> Even though previously it says that the table is named wp_searchedwords, it won't always be the case. It's all based on the table prefix that's set on your site (the default one is indeed wp_). Here, I'm going to refer to the table as wp_searchedwords anyway, out of convenience.

Getting the plugin to talk to the database

The first part of this plugin has to be run only when the plugin is activated.
This will be the initialization function. One of its tasks is to create or update the
database table (the table will be created only if it hasn't been created before).

```
function searchedwords_init($content) {
  global $wpdb;
  $sw_table_name = $wpdb->prefix.'searchedwords';

  if (isset($_GET['activate']) && 'true' == $_GET['activate']) {
    $sql = 'CREATE TABLE ''.$sw_table_name.'' (
    id INT NOT NULL AUTO_INCREMENT,
    word VARCHAR(255),
    created DATETIME NOT NULL DEFAULT \''.date('Y-m-d').'
      00:00:01\',
    PRIMARY KEY  (id)
    )';

    require_once(ABSPATH.'wp-admin/includes/upgrade.php');
    dbDelta($sql);
  }

  // in case a search has just been performed, store the searched
  // word
  if (!empty($_GET['s'])) {
    $current_searched_words = explode(" ",urldecode($_GET['s']));
    foreach ($current_searched_words as $word) {
      $wpdb->query($wpdb->prepare("INSERT into '$sw_table_name'
        VALUES(null,'%s','".date('Y-m-d H:i:s')."')", $word));
    }
  }
}
```

This function connects to the database using various function calls such as dbDelta(),
$wpdb->query(), and $wpdb->prepare(). The dbDelta() function takes care of
creating the table or updating it (whatever is needed at the time; find out more at
http://codex.wordpress.org/Creating_Tables_with_Plugins). Apart from that,
when dealing with the WordPress database, you can utilize any database-related PHP
function in existence. Or you can use the WordPress' class member function, $wpdb-
>get_results(), as well. The function we're using here also stores the searched word
in the database table if a search has just been performed. This is done through the
$wpdb->query() and $wpdb->prepare() functions.

Adding management page functions

We now need a familiar-looking function that adds a management page to the admin menu. In this case, we're using `add_management_page()` instead of `add_submenu_page()` because this plugin is more of a tool than something that needs settings.

```
function modify_menu_for_searchedwords() {
  $page = add_management_page(
    "Searched Words",
    "Searched Words",
    'manage_options',
    'ahs_capture_searches',
    'searchedwords_page'
  );

  // Using registered $page handle to hook stylesheet loading
  add_action( 'admin_print_styles-' . $page,
    'searchedwords_admin_styles' );
}
```

The final line of the preceding function loads the stylesheet for the admin page. We'll need it to make the plugin's output look nice in WP Admin. There are two additional functions that make this possible, as follows:

```
function searchedwords_admin_init() {
  // registering the stylesheet for the admin
  wp_register_style('ahscapturesearchesstyles',
    plugins_url('ahs_capture_searches.css'));
}

function searchedwords_admin_styles() {
  // enqueue the stylesheet for the admin
  wp_enqueue_style('ahscapturesearchesstyles');
}
```

Finally, we also need a function that retrieves the information from the database and displays it on the new management page (again, everything done through the `$wpdb` object):

```
function searchedwords_page() {
  global $wpdb;
  $sw_table_name = $wpdb->prefix.'searchedwords';

  $searched_words = $wpdb->get_results("SELECT COUNT(word) AS
    occurrence, word FROM '$sw_table_name' GROUP BY word ORDER BY
      occurrence DESC");
  echo '<div class="wrap"><h2>Searched Words</h2>';
  echo '<table class="searchwords">';
```

```
    if($searched_words !== NULL) {
      echo '<tr><th>Search words</th><th># searches</th></tr>';
      foreach($searched_words as $searched_word) {
        echo '<tr><td>'.$searched_word->word.'</b></td><td>'.
          $searched_word->occurance.'</td></tr>';
      }
      $searched_perfomed = true;
    }
    else {
      echo '<tr><td colspan="2"><h3>No searches have been preformed
        yet</h3></td></tr>';
    }
    echo '</table></div>';
  }
```

That's it, only two. The previous plugin had more functions because data was being captured from the user and being saved. Here, that's not necessary.

Lastly, we just need to add three hooks:

```
add_filter('init', 'searchedwords_init');
add_action('admin_init', 'searchedwords_admin_init');
add_action('admin_menu', 'modify_menu_for_searchedwords');
```

The first hook tells WordPress to run the initialization function when the plugin is activated, or when a search is performed. The second hook takes care of the admin stylesheet. The third hook modifies the admin menu to add a link to the new management page.

Trying out the plugin

As with the last plugin, you can now either upload your plugin using FTP to wp-content/plugins, or you can turn it into a ZIP file and add it using the uploader in the WP Admin.

Once you've installed it, activate it. Look at the menu under **Tools** and you'll see a link to the new management page, as shown in the following screenshot:

When you click on **Searched Words**, you'll see a new page that the plugin created, as shown in the following screenshot:

The new page shows that no searches have been performed since the plugin was activated. Do a few searches on your site and return to the following page:

Learning more

There are hundreds of hooks available in WordPress—way too many to cover in this book. You can learn more about the hooks discussed in this book, as well as learn about all of the other hooks available, by going online. Start out at the following online reference sites:

- The **Plugin API** contains very thorough information about writing plugins and using hooks: http://codex.wordpress.org/Plugin_API
- For a complete list of action hooks: http://codex.wordpress.org/Plugin_API/Action_Reference
- For a complete list of filter hooks: http://codex.wordpress.org/Plugin_API/Filter_Reference
- You may also want to take a step back and look at the general **Plugin Resources** page in the WordPress **Codex**: http://codex.wordpress.org/Plugin_Resources
- If you want to submit your plugin to the WordPress Plugin Repository, you'll have to take steps similar to those you took when preparing a theme, and you'll also have to get hooked up to the WordPress SVN repository. Learn more about how to submit a plugin to the WordPress Plugin Repository at: http://codex.wordpress.org/Plugin_Submission_and_Promotion

Widgets

Writing a widget bears some similarities to writing a plugin, but in some ways it's easier because there is a widget class that you can leverage for some of the functionality. In other ways, it's a bit more time-consuming as there's a lot of mandatory code that every widget has to feature.

Custom tag cloud widget

In this section, we'll see how to write a widget that displays a custom tag cloud that we can then place in the sidebar. There will also be the possibility to change the title of the widget, and although this is a **tag cloud** widget, we'll be able to switch tags to categories and display them using a tag-cloud-style as well.

This isn't a complete from-the-scratch design, though. I'm actually using one of ThemeFuse's (`http://themefuse.com/`) widgets that came with the Conexus theme we were using in *Chapter 7*, *Developing Your Own Theme*, when learning how to build themes (also available in the code bundle for `Chapter 7`). The changes I'm making will give the widget a slightly different look. Again, it's the educational aspect we're after. In its final form, it will look like the following screenshot:

Just as a comparison, here's what the standard tag cloud widget (the native one in WordPress) looks like:

Let's get started!

Naming our widget

In this case, we're going to create the widget as a standalone plugin. So just like any other plugin, it needs a unique name and a unique appearance in the `wp-content/plugins` folder.

> Again, I encourage you to search the web whenever you're creating a new widget or plugin just to make sure that there's nothing out there going by the same name.
>
> That being said, there actually are two quite interesting plugins for custom tag clouds. Feel free to check them out: **3D Tag Cloud** (`http://wordpress.org/plugins/cardoza-3d-tag-cloud/`) and **Ultimate Tag Cloud Widget** (`http://wordpress.org/plugins/ultimate-tag-cloud-widget/`).

I'll name the new plugin file (which holds the widget) `kk_tag_cloud_widget.php`, and put it in its own `kk_tag_cloud_widget` folder inside `wp-content/plugins`.

This main PHP file starts just like any other plugin, with the following declaration:

```php
<?php
/*
Plugin Name: Karol K's Tag Cloud Widget
Description: Displays a tag cloud, ThemeFuse style.
Author: <a href="http://karol.cc/">Karol K</a> & <a href="http://themefuse.com/">ThemeFuse</a>
Version: 1.0
*/
```

Widget structure

When building a widget using the widget class, your widget needs to have the following structure:

```php
class UNIQUE_WIDGET_NAME extends WP_Widget {

  public function __construct() {
    $widget_ops = array();
    $control_ops = array();
    $this->WP_Widget('base id', 'name', $widget_ops,
      $control_ops);
  }

  public function form ($instance) {
    // prints the form on the widgets page
  }
```

```
    public function update ($new_instance, $old_instance) {
      // used when the user saves their widget options
    }

    public function widget ($args,$instance) {
      // used when the sidebar calls in the widget
    }
  }

  // initiate the widget

  // register the widget
```

My unique widget name for this project is KK_Widget_Tag_Cloud. Now, let's go over each of the preceding functions one by one and explain what's going on.

Widget initiation function

Let's start with the widget initiation function. Blank, it looks like as follows:

```
public function __construct() {
  $widget_ops = array();
  $control_ops = array();
  $this->WP_Widget('base-id', 'name', $widget_ops, $control_ops);
}
```

In this function, which is the constructor of the class, we initialize various things that the WP_Widget class is expecting. The first two variables, to which you can give any name you want, are just a handy way to set the two array variables expected by the third line of code.

Let's take a look at these three lines of code:

- The $widget_ops variable is where you can set the class name, which is given to the widget div itself, and the description, which is shown in the WP Admin on the widgets page.

- The $control_ops variable is where you can set options for the control box in the WP Admin on the widget page, such as the width and height of the widget and the ID prefix used for the names and IDs of the items inside. For my basic widget, I'm not going to use this variable (it's optional).

- When you call the parent class' constructor, WP_Widget(), you'll tell it the widget's unique ID, the widget's display title, and pass along the two arrays you created.

For this widget, my code now looks as follows:

```
public function __construct() {
  $widget_ops = array('description' => 'Your most used tags in
    cloud format; same height; custom background');
  $this->WP_Widget('kk-tag-cloud', 'KK Tag Cloud', $widget_ops);
}
```

Widget form function

This function has to be named `form()`. You may not rename it if you want the widget class to know what it's purpose is. You also need to have an argument in there, which I'm calling `$instance`, that the class also expects. This is where the current widget settings are stored.

This function needs to have all of the functionalities to create the form that users will see when adding the widget to a sidebar. Let's look at some abbreviated code and then explore what it's doing:

```
public function form( $instance ) {
  $instance = wp_parse_args( (array) $instance, array(
    'template' => '') );
  $current_taxonomy = $this->_get_current_taxonomy($instance);
  ?>
  <p>
    <label for="<?php echo $this->get_field_id('title');
      ?>">Title</label>
    <input type="text" class="widefat" id="<?php echo $this-
      >get_field_id('title'); ?>" name="<?php echo $this-
        >get_field_name('title'); ?>" value="<?php if (isset (
          $instance['title'])) {echo esc_attr( $instance['title']
            );} ?>" />
  </p>
  <p>
    <label for="<?php echo $this->get_field_id('taxonomy');
      ?>">Taxonomy</label>
    <select class="widefat" id="<?php echo $this-
      >get_field_id('taxonomy'); ?>" name="<?php echo $this-
        >get_field_name('taxonomy'); ?>">
    <?php foreach(get_object_taxonomies('post') as $taxonomy) :
      $tax = get_taxonomy($taxonomy);
      if (!$tax->show_tagcloud || empty($tax->labels->name))
        continue;
      ?>
```

```
            <option value="<?php echo esc_attr($taxonomy) ?>" <?php
                selected($taxonomy, $current_taxonomy); ?>><?php echo
                    $tax->labels->name; ?></option>
        <?php endforeach; ?>
        </select>
    </p>
    <?php
}
```

First you use a WordPress function named `wp_parse_args()`, which creates an `$instance` array that your form will use. What's in it depends on what defaults you've set and what settings the user has already saved.

Then you create form fields. For each form field, I make use of the built-in functions that will create unique names and IDs and input existing values, as follows:

- `$this->get-field_id()` creates a unique ID based on the widget instance (remember, you can create more than one instance of this widget)

- `$this->get_field_name()` creates a unique name based on the widget instance

- The `$instance` array is where you will find the current values for the widget, whether they are defaults or user-saved data

All the other code in there is just regular PHP and HTML. If you give the user the ability to set a title, and name that field title; WordPress will show it on the widget form when it's minimized. The widget form this will create will look like the following screenshot:

Widget save function

When a user clicks on the **Save** button on the widget form, WordPress uses AJAX to run your save function. You need to be sure to save whatever the user types in, which is all we're doing in this case, but you can put other functionalities here if it's appropriate for your widget (for example, database interactions, conversions, calculations, and so on). The final code for this function is as follows:

```
public function update( $new_instance, $old_instance ) {
    $instance['title'] = $new_instance['title'];
    $instance['taxonomy'] =
      stripslashes($new_instance['taxonomy']);
    return $instance;
}
```

Be sure this function is named `update()` and is prepared to accept two instances, one with old data and one with the just-submitted data. You can write your code to check the `$new_instance` array for problems, and thus return the `$old_instance` array if the new one isn't valid. The `$instance` array you return will be what's shown in the update widget form.

Widget print function

The third main function in your widget class is the one that is called by the sidebar when it's time to actually show the widget to people visiting the website. It needs to retrieve any relevant saved user data and print out information for the website visitor. In this case, our final print function looks like the following:

```
public function widget($args, $instance) {
  extract($args);
  $current_taxonomy = $this->_get_current_taxonomy($instance);
  if(!empty($instance['title'])) {
    $title = $instance['title'];
  }
  else {
    if('post_tag' == $current_taxonomy) {
      $title = 'Tags';
    }
    else {
      $tax = get_taxonomy($current_taxonomy);
      $title = $tax->labels->name;
    }
  }
```

```
$title = apply_filters('widget_title', $title, $instance,
  $this->id_base);

$before_widget = '<div class=
  "widget-container kk_widget_tag_cloud">';
$after_widget = '</div>';
$before_title = '<h3 class="widget-title">';
$after_title = '</h3>';

echo $before_widget;
if ( $title ) echo $before_title . $title. $after_title;
echo '<div class="kk_tagcloud">';
wp_tag_cloud( apply_filters('widget_tag_cloud_args',
  array('taxonomy' => $current_taxonomy) ) );
echo "</div>\n";
echo $after_widget;
}
```

The preceding function calls one more helper function responsible for fetching the current taxonomy. A very simple one, though, as shown in the following code snippet:

```
function _get_current_taxonomy($instance) {
  if ( !empty($instance['taxonomy']) &&
    taxonomy_exists($instance['taxonomy']) )
    return $instance['taxonomy'];

  return 'post_tag';
}
```

The first thing I do in the main function is extract the data in the instance, which has the information the website administrator had saved when filling out the widget form. Then, the widget takes a look into the selected taxonomy (tags or categories) and displays all individual items as a simple one-line list.

Custom widget styles

Our small widget has its own stylesheet that needs to be included in the current theme's head section, like any other stylesheet.

The file is named kk_tag_cloud_widget.css and contains the following:

```
.kk_widget_tag_cloud .kk_tagcloud {
    line-height:1.5em;
}
```

```css
.kk_widget_tag_cloud .kk_tagcloud a {
    background:#eee;
    color:#e8750f;
    display:inline-block;
    line-height:30px;
    margin:3px 2px;
    padding:0 11px;
    font-size:12px !important;
    border-radius:3px;
    -webkit-border-radius:3px;
    text-transform:uppercase;
}

.kk_widget_tag_cloud .kk_tagcloud a:hover {
    color:#f2f2f2;
    background:#404040;
}

.f_col .kk_widget_tag_cloud .kk_tagcloud a {
    color:#e6e6e6;
    background:#5a6164;
}

.f_col .kk_widget_tag_cloud .kk_tagcloud a:hover {
    background:#f2f2f2;
    color:#404040;
}
```

Nothing fancy, just a set of classes that will make sure that the widget looks great. Again, it's a slight customization based on ThemeFuse's original stylesheet.

The only thing we have to do with this stylesheet is enqueue it through a standard WordPress hook. Place this in your main plugin's file:

```php
function kk_tag_cloud_widget_styles_load() {
  wp_register_style('kk_tag_cloud_widget_styles',
    plugins_url('kk_tag_cloud_widget.css', __FILE__ ));
  wp_enqueue_style('kk_tag_cloud_widget_styles');
}
add_action('wp_enqueue_scripts',
  'kk_tag_cloud_widget_styles_load');
```

Initiating and hooking up the widget

That's it for widget functionality! Now you just need to add a little code that will hook the widget up to the rest of WordPress.

```
function KK_Widget_Tag_Cloud_Reg() {
  register_widget('KK_Widget_Tag_Cloud');
}
add_action('widgets_init', 'KK_Widget_Tag_Cloud_Reg');
```

This tells WordPress that when it initiates widgets, it should register our new widget.

 The entire code of this widget is available on the official Packt website. You can download it for free, along with the bundles for other chapters.

Trying out the widget

Your widget is ready to go! Save all of your changes, and upload your widget to `wp-content/plugins`. Go to the **Installed Plugins** page, and you'll see your widget waiting to be activated, as shown in the following screenshot:

Karol K's Tag Cloud Widget | Displays a tag cloud, ThemeFuse style.
Activate | Edit | Delete | Version 1.0 | By Karol K & ThemeFuse

Activate it, and then navigate to **Appearance | Widgets**. You'll see the widget waiting to be added to a sidebar, as shown in the following screenshot:

KK Tag Cloud

Your most used tags in cloud format; same height; custom background

Links

Your blogroll

Drag the widget to a sidebar, and then click on the little down arrow to edit it. You'll see the options slide down, as shown in the following screenshot:

You can enter a title or leave it blank for the default, and choose the taxonomy to use. Then click on **Save** as you would with any widget. When you return to the frontend of the site and reload, the new tag cloud will be right there, as shown in the following screenshot:

Learning more

You can browse the following online reference sites to learn more about widgets:

- The WordPress **Widgets API** is located at: http://codex.wordpress.org/ Widgets_API

- WordPress lists a number of widgets on the following page: http://codex. wordpress.org/WordPress_Widgets

- If you want to find more widgets to install on your website, visit the widgets section of the Plugin Repository at: http://wordpress.org/ plugins/ tags/widget

Bundling a widget with an existing plugin

If you're writing a plugin and you'd like to make a widget available with it, you don't have to create a separate widget plugin. Just include all of the widget code, like what we created in the preceding section, in with your plugin's PHP file. When the user activates the plugin, the widget you created will automatically show up on the widgets page in the WP Admin. No need for a separate file!

Shortcodes

Shortcodes are a handy way to let a nontechnical person, that is, the editor of the website, include dynamic functionality within pages and posts, without having to actually use any PHP, complex HTML structures, or custom JavaScript. In other words, shortcodes are handy reusable pieces of code, yet they don't require any actual coding experience or knowledge on the end user's part.

Shortcodes and the way they work

The way a shortcode works is that you tell WordPress to look at text within square brackets (`[]`) and evaluate it by running a PHP function. That PHP function can live in your `functions.php` file of your theme, or in a plugin file, or in a widget file. Let's create a simple shortcode and include it in with our most recent widget, the one we were developing just a minute ago for showing a custom tag cloud.

Types of shortcodes

Shortcodes are a pretty simple concept by definition, but we can still distinguish three main types:

- **Single-tag shortcodes**: These shortcodes are executed with just a single tag, for example: `[my_first_shortcode/]`.

- **Double-tag shortcodes**: These shortcodes are executed with opening and closing tags, for example: `[my_2nd_shortcode]some text here[/my_2nd_shortcode]` (please notice that the closing tag has an additional `/`). As you can see, there's also some content within the tags. This content can be processed by the shortcode function.

- **Shortcodes with attributes**: These shortcodes can have one or two tags and also a number of attributes we can use to customize the output, for example: `[my_3rd_shortcode name="Karol" twitter="carlosinho"]some text here[/my_3rd_shortcode]`.

Creating a simple shortcode

Let's create a simple shortcode that will make it possible to use our widget's output inside any given post or page.

This is going to be a double-tag shortcode with one additional attribute, which we'll use to indicate whether the output should be formatted using our custom CSS or WordPress' native styling.

Let's start by creating a new function at the bottom of our `kk_tag_cloud_widget.php` file and then we'll go through each individual line, as follows:

```
function kk_tag_cloud_handler($atts, $content=null) {
  extract(shortcode_atts(array(
    'use_css' => '1',
    'taxonomy' => 'post_tag'
    ), $atts));

  $tax = 'post_tag';
  if(taxonomy_exists($taxonomy))
    $tax = $taxonomy;

  $result = '';
  if ('0' != $use_css) $result .=
    '<div class="kk_widget_tag_cloud"><div class="kk_tagcloud">';
  if (null != $content) $result .=
    addslashes(strip_tags($content)).' ';
  $result .= wp_tag_cloud(apply_filters('widget_tag_cloud_args',
            array('taxonomy' => $tax, 'echo' => false)));
  if ('0' != $use_css) $result .= '</div></div>';

  return $result;
}
```

First of all, note that this function does not echo or print anything. It just returns a string. If you let your function print, it won't look correct on the website.

Inside our function, the first line handles the custom attributes that the shortcode receives (in this case, just the `use_css` parameter for indicating whether the styles should be used or not, and the `taxonomy` parameter to indicate the taxonomy that should be shown in the shortcode). WordPress will hand off the `$atts` argument automatically and we only have to use the `extract()` function to turn the attributes the user submits into variables available in the function. The values in the array passed to `extract()` set the defaults, in case the user chooses no options. In general, there is no limit to the number of options that you can make available to shortcode users.

The next line extracts the taxonomy identifier and tries to turn it into a valid taxonomy. In case the user's input is not valid, the default `post_tag` taxonomy will be used.

The final part of the function handles the display based on the state of the `use_css` attribute. Pretty basic at this point.

There's also a possibility to include a custom text as the main content of the shortcode. This can be useful in some situations.

What we have to do now is tell WordPress that this function is a shortcode, and we tell it what the shortcode is using a hook. Be sure to choose something unique! I've chosen `kk_tag_cloud` as the name for this shortcode, so the hook looks like the following code snippet:

```
add_shortcode('kk_tag_cloud', 'kk_tag_cloud_handler');
```

To use this shortcode in our content, all we have to do is edit any given post or page and put a following line in it:

```
[kk_tag_cloud taxonomy="category"]choose one:[/kk_tag_cloud]
```

Such a usage will have the following effect:

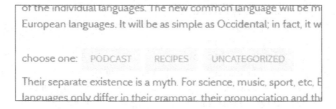

We can also use the shortcode, as shown in the following code snippet:

```
[kk_tag_cloud use_css="0" taxonomy="category"]choose
  one:[/kk_tag_cloud]
```

This will disable the custom styles and produce the following effect:

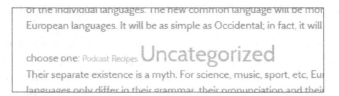

To display the tag cloud in its default form (showing the tags and using the custom stylesheet), all we have to do is execute the shortcode, as shown in the following code snippet:

```
[kk_tag_cloud][/kk_tag_cloud]
```

The effect is as shown in the following screenshot:

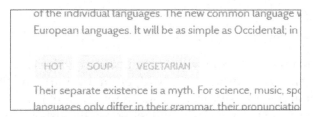

There are very few limitations regarding what you can and cannot do with shortcodes. However, the most common usages are for embedding online videos from sites such as YouTube, using the `[youtube]` shortcode, for example, or for showing various social media boxes and activity streams.

Enabling shortcodes in widgets

By default, shortcodes are ignored inside widgets. So, if you were to add a Text widget with your shortcode in it, as shown in the following screenshot:

Then all that would show is the shortcode itself:

```
Tags test

[kk_tag_cloud][/kk_tag_cloud]
```

This can be fixed by adding the following line just after our shortcode definition:

```
add_filter('widget_text', 'do_shortcode', 11);
```

And now all shortcodes on the site will be evaluated in widgets. In other words, you can place any shortcode inside a text widget. In this particular case, however, you can see that enabling our shortcode inside a text widget has very little sense, as we can clearly just use our tag cloud widget normally instead, but for other implementations (other shortcodes) it can indeed be useful.

Summary

In this chapter, you learned everything you needed to know about creating basic plugins and widgets. Now you know how to structure the PHP file, where to put your functions, and how to use hooks. You also learned about adding management pages and enabling plugins and widgets to have database access. On top of all that, you learned how to create shortcodes, a powerful tool that lets you make dynamic functionality available to all WordPress users. With your already-existing knowledge of PHP and HTML, you now have tools to get started with writing every plugin and widget your heart may desire.

The next chapter will be all about community blogging: running multiuser blogs, and other aspects of turning your site into a serious online magazine.

10
Community Blogging

So far in this book, we've focused on looking at a personal website, one that belongs to and is used by just one person. However, many blogs are used in a different way — there may be a single blog or website with a variety of writers, editors, and administrators. This makes the site more like a community project or even an online magazine.

Furthermore, it's by no means uncommon for bigger online publishers to use WordPress as the base for their websites. In which case, the site has a number of authors, editors, reviewers, and overall contributors with varying responsibilities. Not to mention the technical staff or designers.

In this chapter, we'll discuss allowing a blog to have multiple authors with differing levels of control over blog administration and content. We'll explore user management for multiple users on one blog, as well as other aspects of blogging as a member of a community. We'll also take some time to look at using a non-blog website with multiple users.

Concerns for a multiauthor blog

A multiauthor blog is useful when a group of people with similar interests wants to collaborate and share space to publish their writing, or if an organization or company wants to have an online magazine. If that group wants to publish news on a particular topic, or on many topics in a broad sense, then they'll each need to be able to log in and post their content, update their profile, and so on. For example, I can decide that I want every member of my family to be able to contribute to my Daily Cooking blog. Each of my sisters, brothers, cousins, aunts, and uncles can add their recipes and discoveries regarding food, which has the potential to make my food blog a richer and more exciting place for visitors.

However, content moderation is also of essential importance to a multiauthor blog. The best way to keep a blog clean and on topic is by using a moderation flow that restricts the display of content until it travels through an approval process. Such practice is usually called workflow, and it makes working in large groups much easier and more manageable.

User roles and abilities

WordPress includes the ability to have an unlimited number of users. Each of the users can be assigned one of the five (or six) roles. Let's look at these roles one at a time, starting with the most powerful.

Super Admin

Even though it sounds very appealing, the Super Admin (aka Network Admin) role isn't actually that fancy. Basically, WordPress has now allowed users to build a multisite setup (mentioned a couple of pages ago). This is a scenario where you have more than one site built on just a single WordPress installation. Now, the Super Admin is a role that has complete administration access to all websites that are part of a given multisite network.

Honestly speaking, if you don't have any multisite structure set up on your WordPress installation then you won't even see the Super Admin role in the WP Admin.

 The presence of the multisite structure itself reduces some of the capabilities of other user roles described in the following section, so the following list should be treated as a resource for single-site installations.

Administrator

When you installed WordPress, it created a user for you with administrative powers. This role is called administrator, and every WordPress site must have at least one admin (you will not be allowed to delete them all). As you have already seen in the earlier chapters, administrators can do everything.

The administrator's primary purpose is to manage everything about the website.

In general, you're not going to want to have a lot of administrators on a single blog or website. It is best to keep just one administrator for a blog with 10 to 20 authors and editors or perhaps up to three administrators for a blog with dozens of users.

Some examples of actions that only a user with an administrator role can take are:

- Switching blog theme
- Adding, editing, activating, or deactivating plugins
- Adding, editing, or deleting users
- Managing general blog options and settings

When creating more administrator accounts (or managing the main one), make sure to use only complex passwords that are hard to break using any sort of brute-force methods. In a nutshell, use as many numbers, special characters, combinations of uppercase and lowercase letters as you can. A lot of hacking attempts revolve around password guessing, so the more complex your password is, the tougher it will be to break.

Editor

After the administrator, the editor has the most powerful role. This role is for users who need to manage everything about the content of a website, but don't need to be able to change the basic structure, design, or functionality of the blog itself (that's for administrators).

 The editor's primary purpose is to manage all of the content of the blog.

To get an idea of how the screen looks when a user logs in as an editor, let's take a look at the editor's menu (on the right-hand side) in comparison with the administrator's menu (on the left-hand side):

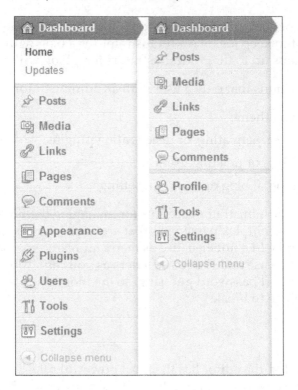

As you can see, the top section is unchanged (apart from the **Updates** link). However, nearly the entire bottom menu, with **Appearance**, **Plugins**, and **Users** (which is replaced by **Profile**), has disappeared. We can see that the editor is left only with the ability to edit his or her own profile, and to access the **Tools** section, which includes any plugin pages that allow editor-level access (for example, **Searched Words**, **Document Types**).

The examples of actions that a user with an editor role can take are:

- Managing all posts
- Creating and editing pages
- Moderating comments
- Managing categories, tags, and links
- Editing other users' content

There's one very useful aspect of the editor role. If you give it a closer look, you'll realize that it has all the credentials one would need to publish any piece of content on a given WordPress site. This makes it perfect for everyday use, even for single-author blogs or sites. Therefore, what I actually encourage you to do is set a separate editor account for yourself, and then use it for posting and editing content, instead of working with the default administrator account. Such a setup is a lot safer, particularly if someone tries to hijack your password or if any other bad thing happens to your account. The site itself won't get harmed (considering the fact that editors can't install new plugins or delete any existing ones).

For multiauthor blogs or sites, the editor role is meant to be assigned to users who are in charge of the content published on the site. Essentially, as the name itself indicates, the editor role is perfect for editors.

Author

Authors have much less access than editors. Authors can add and edit their own posts, and manage posts made by their subordinates. However, they can neither edit posts made by other authors, nor manage comments on posts that don't belong to them.

 The author's primary purpose is to manage his or her own content.

To get an idea of the experience of a user with the role of an author, let's take a look at the author's menu (on the right-hand side) in comparison with the editor's menu (on the left-hand side):

As you can see, the **Links** and **Pages** sections have disappeared, and so has the management page (under the **Settings** menu), which was available to editors (**Document Types**). Additionally, if the author looks at the complete list of posts, he or she will only have the ability to **View**, and not **Edit**, **Quick Edit**, or **Delete**, posts that he or she did not author (highlighted):

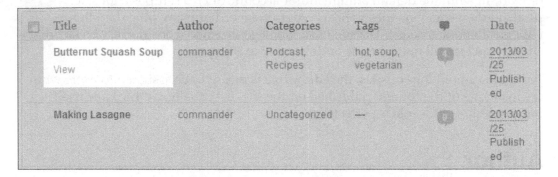

	Title	Author	Categories	Tags	💬	Date
☐	Butternut Squash Soup View	commander	Podcast, Recipes	hot, soup, vegetarian	4	2013/03 /25 Publish ed
	Making Lasagne	commander	Uncategorized	—	0	2013/03 /25 Publish ed

As you would imagine, the author role is perfect for, well… authors—users who are actively involved in creating content for your site. Authors can, for example, do the following:

- Submitting and publishing their posts
- Managing their posts after the publication
- Moderating comments under their posts

Contributor

Contributors are only able to write posts and submit them for review. These posts will be in the **Pending Review** status until an editor or administrator agrees to publish them. Contributors cannot upload images or other files, view the media library, add categories, and edit comments, or any of the other tasks available to more advanced users.

 The contributor's primary purpose is to submit content for consideration.

One important thing worth mentioning is that although contributors can create and submit their work for review, once the article is published, they no longer have the possibility to edit it in any way. However, they do get access to the comments section (for moderation).

When it comes to the real-world applications of this role, it's most commonly used when working with guest bloggers or posters, or any other regular contributors that are not part of your in-house team. Guest posting is really popular nowadays and handling it through contributor accounts is much less labor-intensive than receiving articles via e-mail and then having to copy-and-paste them to WordPress.

Subscriber

Subscribers have no ability to do anything at all. They can only log in and edit their profile, that's it (adjust their first name, last name, password, biographical info, and so on). Depending on the permissions set in **Settings | Discussion**, blog visitors may have to sign up as subscribers in order to be able to post comments. Also, there are some plugins that handle sending informational updates to subscribers, such as newsletters or e-mail notifications of new posts.

Most of the time, this role is used as a placeholder. Take, for example, a specific author who had been contributing to your site regularly in the past, but hasn't submitted anything in months. Instead of deleting his or her account completely, you can simply change his or her role to subscriber.

Managing users

To manage users, log in (as an administrator, of course) and navigate to **Users**. You'll see a list of your existing users:

When we installed WordPress, it created only your first user (which is how you've been logging in all this time). Let's create a new user, and assign that user the next most powerful role, that of an editor. To do this, navigate to **Users | Add New**. You'll see the **Add New User** form:

As you can see, only the **Username**, **E-mail**, and **Password** fields are required. You can also change the **Role** from the default (**Subscriber**) to one of the other roles. In this case, I've selected **Editor**. Then, I click on the **Add New User** button.

Apart from the required fields, it's also good practice to fill in **First Name** and **Last Name**. This can make the task of further managing the user accounts much clearer.

I can repeat this process to add an author, a contributor, and a subscriber. When I'm done, the **Users** page (where the users can be managed) will look like the following screenshot:

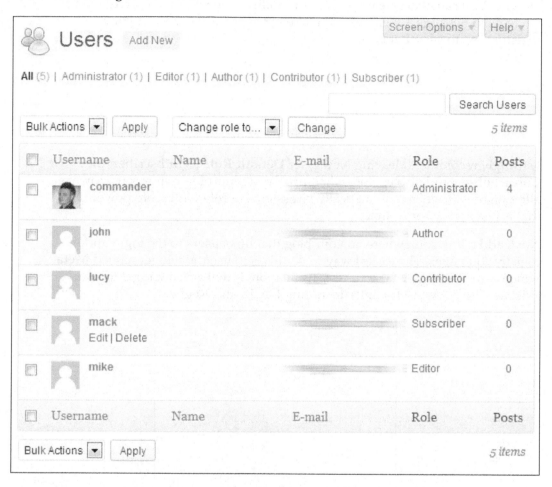

As with any other management list in WP Admin, you can roll over a row to see the management links (visible in the preceding screenshot). In this case, you can **Edit** or **Delete** users. You can use the checkboxes and the **Bulk Actions** menu, or use the filter links to view only users with particular roles. You can change the role of one or more users on this page by checking the box (or boxes) and using the **Change role to...** drop-down menu.

Enabling users to self register

Adding users yourself is not the only way to add users to your WordPress website. You can also give your users the ability to register themselves. First, navigate to **Settings | General** and make sure you've checked **Anyone can register** next to **Membership**:

I strongly recommend leaving **New User Default Role** as **Subscriber**; though **Contributor** could also be fine if the purpose of your blog requires it. However, allowing new users to automatically be assigned a role with more power than that is just asking for trouble.

Next, add a link somewhere on your blog that links users to the login and registration pages. The easiest way to do this is to use the widget named **Meta**, which comes with your WordPress installation. It will add a widget to your sidebar with a few useful links, including **Log in** and **Register**.

Of course, if this is not exactly the collection of links you want, you can create your own widget (we talked about widgets in *Chapter 5, Plugins and Widgets*)! Users clicking on **Register** will be taken to the following basic registration page that asks for only **Username** and **E-mail**:

After submitting this form, the user will be e-mailed a password, and the main site administrator will be sent an e-mail notification of the new registration. The user can now log in and edit his or her profile, or do more if an administrator changes his or her role.

Learning more

You can learn more about the built-in WordPress roles and capabilities here: http://codex.wordpress.org/Roles_and_Capabilities.

User management plugins

At the time of this writing, there were over 200 plugins tagged users in the WordPress **Plugin Directory**: http://wordpress.org/plugins/tags/users. We can actually divide those plugins into a handful of groups as the functionality offered is exceptionally wide. For example, there are plugins for:

- Dealing with various author accounts, co-authoring posts, and multi-author sites

- Constructing membership sites around WordPress where members can get access to premium packages of content based on their subscription model

- Building a classic e-commerce store where everybody can make a purchase from the available directory of "things"

- Building an online forum based on WordPress

- Building an e-mail newsletter sent to given site's users directly from within WordPress, instead of using external services

- Launching a social network on WordPress

- Managing user profiles for registered users

As you can see, the number of possibilities is really striking. If we want to, we can do essentially anything with a WordPress site and its users. Our imagination is the only limit.

There are three plugins that people often find useful when a number of people edit a website, especially if they have a range of authority over final website content.

- **Peter's Post Notes**: http://wordpress.org/plugins/peters-post-notes/ allows each user to add a note whenever they edit a post. Such a note can, for example, inform the editor that the post needs an image before it can be published.

- **Peter's Collaboration E-mails**: http://wordpress.org/plugins/peters-collaboration-e-mails/ (another plugin by the same developer) allows you to set up sending of e-mails (along with the note that has been included, via the first plugin above) whenever a contributor authors a new post, when the post is published, and if the post's status is changed again.

- **Edit Flow**: http://wordpress.org/plugins/edit-flow/ is one of the bigger editing plugins and it offers a ton of features. Basically, it's a complete-package kind of plugin for large publishing teams that need to set up a custom workflow to improve their writing and publishing processes. Even more powerful are the plugins that let you control what certain users are allowed to do within the WP Admin if the exact structure of the five roles WordPress offers you by default aren't quite right. The two most commonly used are:

- **Adminimize**: http://wordpress.org/extend/plugins/adminimize/. Without digging too deeply into the backend of roles and capabilities, this plugin lets you streamline the administration interface. You can hide certain menu items and also some boxes on the Add/Edit screens.

- **Membership**: http://wordpress.org/plugins/membership/. This one is among the top membership plugins on the market and probably the best free plugin available. In short, it's a complete membership site solution that allows you to publish members-only content, manage user accounts and even handle online payments for your premium memberships.

Finally, let's not forget about one of the more popular areas in modern website launch — social networks (such as Facebook). As it turns out, you don't need a huge budget at your disposal to launch such a network. A plugin such as **BuddyPress** (http://buddypress.org/) has all the functionality you'd need and best of all, it's free. We'll actually give BuddyPress a closer look in the next chapter where we'll focus on building non-blog websites, but I just wanted to mention it here to keep the message complete.

Creating a multisite website

In the past, there used to be a separate version of WordPress named **WordPress MU** (pronounced as myoo) that allowed you to create a master blog with many sub-blogs — essentially giving each user their own (limited) blog.

Well, as of WordPress 3.0, this capability is a built-in feature in WordPress, and just needs to be enabled. If you go to the old WordPress MU URL (`http://mu.wordpress.org/`), you'll see the following:

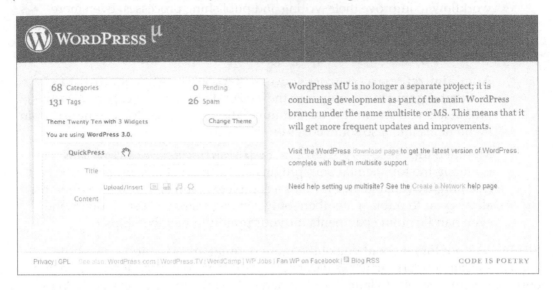

You may be wondering what makes a WordPress site, which can have multiple authors, different from a WordPress MU site. Here's the official definition from `wordpress.org`:

> *A multisite network is a collection of sites that all share the same WordPress installation. They can also share plugins and themes. The individual sites in the network are virtual sites in the sense that they do not have their own directories on your server [...] and they do have separate tables in the database.*

In other words, the multisite structure allows you to have a main website and for every user to have their own subsite, which gets its own subdomain or subdirectory. As the administrator of the site, you can choose how much flexibility to give users:

- How much control they have over their own sidebars and widgets
- How many themes they can choose from (if any)
- How many plugins they can choose from (if any)

Apart from that, you can also choose to launch a number of sites under a single domain for yourself, rather than handing them over to the users on your site. This can be a good idea for large online publishers with a couple of branches focusing on different topics and niches.

Websites that use WordPress MS include:

- wordpress.com
- blogs.nytimes.com
- metblogs.com
- trueslant.com
- blog.mozilla.com and more

As I mentioned earlier in the chapter, when you create a multisite structure, you'll get one more user account role called the Super Admin. This is the main administrator account for the whole network. The sole presence of this account reduces some of the capabilities of the standard administrator account. For example, in a multisite structure, standard administrators can no longer do the following:

- creating or editing users
- installing, editing, deleting, or updating themes
- installing, editing, or updating plugins
- updating core

The other roles retain their standard capabilities. Additionally, every user account, apart from the Super Admin, is assigned to a single subsite and not the network as a whole.

A full discussion on setting up and administering the WordPress MS capabilities is outside of the scope of this book. However, you can find a thorough and helpful tutorial in the WordPress codex at http://codex.wordpress.org/Create_A_Network.

Summary

In this chapter, we learned how to manage a group of users working with a single blog, which is a community of users. Community blogging can play an important role in a user group or a news website. We also learned how to manage the different levels of privileges for users in a community.

In the next chapter, we'll walk through the process of creating a complete non-blog website from scratch.

11
Creating a Non-blog Website Part One – The Basics

As you have seen while reading this book, WordPress comes fully equipped to power a blog with all of its particular requirements of post handling, categorization, chronological display, and so on. However, powering blogs is not WordPress' only purpose. In fact, there are millions of websites out there right now running WordPress, where blogging is not the primary focus of the website. I myself have built many such sites.

Just to give you a general idea of what's possible, here's a list of popular non-blog type websites that you can build and launch using WordPress (we will cover some of them in more detail later in this and the next chapter):

- **Static websites**: They feature just a handful of static subpages that are not meant to be updated very often. Also, the main content is not organized chronologically like blog posts.

- **Corporate or business websites**: They are similar to the previous type, but usually a bit bigger in size and in the number of subpages; additionally, most business sites have official or toned down designs.

- **E-commerce stores**: They are websites where anyone can browse through a number of products and then use a shopping cart to make a purchase. Apart from the shopping cart functionality, there's also online payment integration and often a backend inventory management system.

- **Membership websites**: They are websites where some of the content is available only to those users who have signed up for a membership and (often) paid a small fee for the privilege; such members-only areas can contain any type of content the site owner finds suitable. However, WordPress doesn't limit this in any way.

- **Video blogs**: They are just like standard blogs; only instead of text-based posts, the blogger publishes video-posts.

- **Photo blogs**: They are just like the previous type of blog, only revolving around photos; a common type of blog for photographers, graphic designers, and other people of similar professions.

- **Product websites**: In short, it's a similar type of site to an e-commerce store, only this time, we're usually dealing with just a single product on sale. It's a popular type of website for all kinds of web apps, iOS, or Android apps.

- **Social networks**: They are just like Facebook, but only run on WordPress.

- **Niche business websites**: Some examples of such sites are local restaurant websites, hotel websites, coffee shop websites, personal portfolio websites, art gallery websites, and so on.

Again, if I were to explain shortly what a general non-blog website is, I'd say that it's any kind of website where the blog is not the main functionality used by the website owner. And of course, non-blog websites make up the majority of the internet as a whole. However, since we're discussing WordPress here, which many still believe to be a blog system only, I just want to assure you that it's no longer the case. These days, WordPress can be used for virtually anything.

In this chapter and the next chapter, we will go through some of the types of websites mentioned earlier and present an effective way of building them with WordPress. We'll also use the knowledge we've acquired in the previous chapters, so it's best that you get familiar with everything that's been going on so far before consuming the information on the following pages.

Also, there are a number of new pieces of functionality we have not explored in previous chapters, and this is on what we will be focusing. These include:

- Designating a standard page to be the front page of the website

- Creating a custom post type with a custom taxonomy

- Altering the custom post type display in the WP Admin

Let's get started!

The must-do tasks

Even though there are many different types of sites one can build with WordPress, there are some steps that are mandatory for all of them.

For instance, no matter what type of website you want to launch, you always have to start by installing WordPress properly. This is exactly what we talked about in *Chapter 2, Getting Started*. Nothing is different in this case. The installation process is the same, all of the steps are the same, and the final result is the same too; you end up with a clean, blank WordPress installation. Also, whenever installing specific themes and plugins, make sure to follow the same guidelines we discussed in *Chapter 5, Plugins and Widgets* and *Chapter 6, Choosing and Installing Themes*.

Last but not the least, to ensure that your site is secure and has a good user management structure, you have to keep in mind all the best practices revolving around user accounts, and editorial workflow (publishing new content).

Basically, the only element that's different when building a non-blog website is the process of picking the theme and selecting the exact plugins for the site. Additionally, if you want to take it to the next level, you'll have to look into implementing various functionalities by hand or getting a custom solution made for you by a professional.

Luckily though, the process itself is not much more difficult than working with a standard blog. So once you have some experience with WordPress under your belt, you'll be able to get it done just as quickly.

Static websites

Let's start with static websites as they are the simplest type of non-blog websites and also the easiest ones to create (which shouldn't be surprising).

The best part about static websites is that building such a thing doesn't require any specific themes or plugins. The secret is your mindset as the developer. In essence, to pull this off effectively, the only things you need to do are:

- Utilize the WordPress' pages functionality
- Tune up the default home page to create a more static experience

The process

Firstly, let's tackle one common misconception. The point of a static website isn't to make the content hard-coded into the HTML or PHP files at all. The actual point is to abandon the standard chronological organization of content (to abandon the blog functionality) and to focus on building a site where pages exist on their own, independent of one another. So, in the end, we can still edit everything pretty easily through the WP Admin, and the only difference is that we're not using the standard WordPress' posts for anything. Instead, we're focusing on the WordPress' pages.

During the setup process of a good static page you'll have to:

1. Pick a WordPress theme that fits your goals and one that looks attractive for your particular project (something we talked about in *Chapter 6, Choosing and Installing Themes*); this is a mandatory step for any type of non-blog website. Not every theme will fit every type of website. So whenever picking a specific theme, keep in mind what you want to use the website for. This is going to make your time easier as a developer and the future visitors' work easier once the site is launched.
2. Create a list of all the static pages that you want to make a part of your website. For instance, for a local pet grooming service, the pages could be: gallery, offer and pricing, testimonials, contact, and map.
3. Create each page in the WP Admin (section **Pages | Add New**).
4. Create one more page, call it **HOME** and tweak it to provide a good home page experience. For instance, start by focusing on the elements that a first-time visitor would consider useful on your home page. A good home page should answer the question of *what this site is about*.
5. Create easy-to-grasp menus to make the navigation a breeze.

Steps 1-3 are pretty straightforward, so let's just focus on the last two.

Building your home page

By default, WordPress takes the main blog listing (the chronological list of posts) and uses it as the home page. This is not a desired situation in our case since there will be no posts. What we'll do instead is create a custom page and then use it as a static front page (homepage).

We'll start by doing something that should be very familiar to us at this point—go to **Pages | Add New** and create a new page titled **HOME**. What you'll place on this page is up to you. Essentially, a home page should be a great starting page for anyone who visits a given site for the first time. For instance, I've decided to go with a short intro message, a list of some popular articles on the site, a contact form provided by the Jetpack plugin, and an interactive map from Google Maps.

Once you have your page ready, the only thing you have to do is assign it as the front page. Go to **Settings | Reading**, click the radio button next to **A static page** and select your new page as the **Front page**, like this:

The other setting, that is, **Posts page** is not important at this stage, as posts are not the focus of this particular project.

When I go to my main website now, the home page no longer presents the standard listing. Now I can see this:

I have to admit, the word **HOME** doesn't look that pretty, so I will probably change it to something like **Welcome** to make it more visitor-friendly, but this is only an example.

If you want to make your home page more fancy, you can create a custom page template (described in *Chapter 7, Developing Your Own Theme*), which will allow you to include any design elements you might need and also a ton of custom functionality. Again, it all depends on the project.

Creating easy-to-grasp menus

The last element of this static-website puzzle is a proper menu (or proper menus). Because our home page is just like any other page one can create in WordPress. It will appear in the default pages menu (Pages Widget), which isn't the most optimized situation.

Therefore, whenever working with static websites, make sure to use only custom menus created by navigating to **Appearance | Menus**. This gives you full control over what gets displayed either in the header, the sidebar, or anywhere else on the site. For example, you can see that I've added a new link pointing to the home page in the top header menu on my site:

Just like I said, nothing difficult here.

Corporate or business websites

When we look at the main idea of corporate or business websites, it becomes apparent that their construction is similar to static websites. The only difference is that they are much bigger (they have more pages and more content) and the design seems much more official. Also, most businesses like to publish some announcements occasionally, so a blog-like functionality is required too (but it still won't take the role of the main element on the site).

In essence, creating a quality corporate site with WordPress is all about picking (or building) the right theme. If you do a quick research on the Web, you'll see that most corporate sites (at least the good ones) feature hardly any design. The thing that makes them stand out is their very subtle branding (through a certain color scheme or clever use of logos) and stellar navigation layout. What this means is that the easiest way to build a great corporate site with WordPress is to:

- Pick a clean theme with good content organization and featuring almost no design bells and whistles
- Include specific branding elements and pick the right color scheme
- Build a nice user-friendly navigation structure through custom menus
- Construct a custom home page
- (Optional) Add one visual element in the form of a home page slider to make the site seem more alive

Let's take the list one by one.

Picking a clean theme

This is something we talked about in the previous chapters so let me just point you towards some of the top places where you can get WordPress themes real quick. They are: the official directory (`http://wordpress.org/themes/`), ThemeFuse (`http://themefuse.com/`), WooThemes (`http:// woothemes.com/`), and Theme Forest. The thing to keep in mind is to go straight to the business-related part of the theme directory we're browsing. For example, at Theme Forest, go straight to: `http://themeforest.net/category/wordpress/corporate`. This will make the selection process a lot quicker.

> Keep in mind that if it's a free theme you're after, you should always get it from the official directory (we discussed this in *Chapter 6, Choosing and Installing Themes*). Also, if you want to build a theme on your own, look into some of the free theme frameworks like Gantry (`http://www.gantry-framework.org/`), or Thematic (`http://thematictheme.com/`).

Features to look for in a quality corporate theme include:

- Minimal design that lets you include your branding elements
- Easy way of adding a logo and other graphics
- Custom header functionality
- Favicon support
- Responsive layout (meaning that it'll be equally as attractive on a desktop computer and on a mobile phone)
- Widget areas

- Breadcrumbs
- Customizable sidebars
- Customizable layouts (for example, full-width, 1-sidebar, 2-sidebar, and so on)
- Multiauthor support (there's usually a number of people taking care of a corporate site simultaneously)
- Built-in color schemes to choose from
- SEO-compatible
- Custom page templates for home page, contact page, FAQ, offer, gallery, team, testimonials, 404 error, portfolio, and so on.
- Cross-browser compatible

Now, your theme doesn't have to do all of the above, but this list should be a good benchmark in determining how suitable the theme you're about to pick is when it comes to running a corporate site.

Branding elements

From a business point of view, branding is the most important parameter of a recognizable site. Therefore, make sure that the logo and the corporate identity of the company both match the color scheme of the theme. Also, as I mentioned in the previous section, a good theme should allow you to pick the color scheme from one of the predefined ones.

Finally, turn the logo into a favicon and upload it to the site too (this can be done through your theme's built-in favicon functionality or via a plugin like All In One Favicon (http://wordpress.org/plugins/all-in-one-favicon/). This will give the site some additional visibility in the bookmarks menu (should any visitor bookmark it).

Good navigation

This is most likely the toughest part of the job when building a corporate site. Mainly because we can never be sure how much content the site is eventually going to feature. There's always the danger that our navigation will either be too much for those handful of pages of content, or too little for hundreds of pages. There are, however, some best practices you can follow:

- Focus on providing an extensive menu in the footer. This will make sure that every visitor will be able to find what they're looking for once they scroll down to the bottom of the page. This is easily doable with footer widget areas that every good corporate theme should provide you with. Here's an example by Samsung:

- Create a top menu with only a couple of the most essential pages. Sometimes only **News** and **About** will be enough:

- Create a sidebar menu linking to the important areas of the site, like specific categories, products, announcements, or other things the average visitor might find interesting.

- Use breadcrumbs. Breadcrumbs are small links that present the path of the visitor in relation to the home page. Most themes provide this functionality by default. It's best to place them just below the header. Here's an example where breadcrumbs are used (highlighted):

- Display a visible search field. A large number of visitors coming to a corporate site are after a specific piece of information, so they naturally start looking for a search field right away. Therefore, making their life easier is a very good idea. A good placement for a search field is in the header and in the main sidebar (sidebar menu) for maximum visibility.

Custom home page

Just like with static websites, the default blog listing rarely makes a good home page for a corporate site. Going with a custom home page is always a better strategy and gives us a more optimized way of presenting the company, its goals, and field of expertise. To create such a home page, you can safely follow the instructions earlier in this chapter when we were discussing static websites.

Now, like I said, showing the default blog listing as the home page is not a good approach here. We should provide at least some integration with the blog-part of the website. The two most sensible solutions are to either link to a blog listing page in a visible place on the home page, or include a simplified listing as a widget in one of the available widget areas on the home page itself.

The latter can be done by a Recent Posts widget that's available in WordPress by default (we covered widgets and how to use them in *Chapter 5, Plugins and Widgets*). The former can be done as follows:

1. Create a new page (**Pages | Add New**) and name it **NEWS**. The page doesn't have to feature any content. It only needs to exist with a unique name. I'm suggesting **NEWS** because it gives a clear indication of what the page is for.

2. Go to **Settings | Reading** and set your new page as the default posts page. It will look as follows:

3. As you can see, there's also the old **HOME** page that's currently set as the **Front page**, we're going to leave it like that itself.

4. Place the link to the new blog section (**NEWS**) in the top menu (preferably). You can do it in **Appearance | Menus**.

5. Now, if you navigate to your new **NEWS** page (something like `http://yoursite.com/news`), you will see the default blog listing that the company—the owner of the website—can use to publish various announcements or other content.

Optional slider

The last element worth discussing here is a home page slider. Although most corporate websites are not about the graphics, introducing this single visual element is often in place. Animated sliders make every website seem more alive and attractive to the visitor. For a corporate site, the slider can present photos from events, individual announcements, product offers, contact details, and a number of other things.

Now, some themes will come with a slider functionality built in right from the get-go. If they don't, you can always get a plugin to handle the job. The only downside is that most slider plugins are not free. Among those that are free, I can point out two:

Meteor Slides

It is available at `http://wordpress.org/plugins/meteor-slides/`.

It allows you to pick specific images from the media library (or upload new ones), set them as slides, and then display them whenever you wish. You can display images either through a widget or by using a shortcode (`[meteor_slideshow]`). The slides themselves are actually organized as a new separate content type—**Slides**—right next to the default content types like **Posts** and **Pages** (more on custom content types in the next chapter).

This means that you can manage them just like you would manage your standard posts and pages.

The only downside is that the plugin in its current form doesn't allow you to display custom text content as a slide. You're basically limited to images only.

It's kind of difficult to show you what the slider looks like through a static screenshot, but anyway, just so you get the general idea, here's my current home page after using the `[meteor_slideshow]` shortcode at the top of the content block (please notice the navigation arrows on either side of the image):

SlideDeck 2 Lite Responsive Content Slider

It is available at `http://wordpress.org/plugins/slidedeck2/`.

This is the second free slider plugin I can recommend. Even though it's the light version, it still offers an impressive range of features and a lot of possible ways to create a slideshow. Right after installing the plugin and going to its section in the WP Admin (right below **Comments**), you'll see a rich user interface:

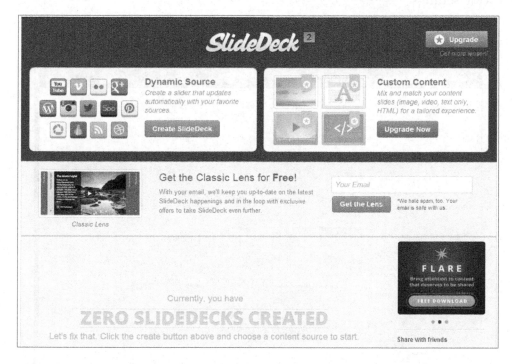

In the middle, there's a message that states **Currently, you have ZERO SLIDEDECKS CREATED**. Above the message, there's a **Create SlideDeck** button (visible in the preceding screenshot). Click on it to get started.

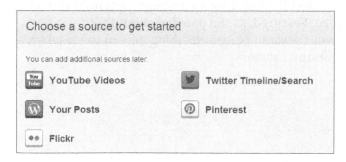

The window that will appear in the middle of the screen presents a number of possible ways to create a slider. You can, for example, fetch some content from Twitter, or even videos from YouTube. There's also the **Your Posts** link that we're going to use in this example. After clicking this link, you'll be redirected to another page where you'll be able to adjust the posts you want to have displayed in the slider.

One of the easiest ways to have specific content displayed in the slider is to use the following settings:

What I did here is select the **Filter by Taxonomy?** option, then **Categories**, and then pick a new category, **Featured**, as the one that should feed the posts for the slider. That way, whenever I want to place something new in the sidebar, all I have to do is assign it to the **Featured** category.

The plugin delivers a lot of customization features when it comes to the graphics and the overall presentation of the slider. I encourage you to play around with it for a while. Describing everything here would probably take a chapter of its own. Anyway, here's what I was able to get after some tuning up (the slider itself can be placed anywhere you wish with a simple shortcode):

Sliders are not a mandatory thing for corporate sites, but they might improve the user experience so they're probably worth a try.

E-commerce stores

As I said at the beginning of the chapter, e-commerce stores, in general, are websites where anyone can browse through a number of products and then use a shopping cart to make a purchase. Also, most e-commerce stores offer some kind of online payment integration, which allows every visitor to make and complete a purchase quickly. Additionally, sometimes there's even a backend inventory management system (an online warehouse of sorts) to make backend business management easier and integrated with the website.

Now, the best thing about this line of business is that you can actually launch an e-commerce store with WordPress, which, in my opinion, is simply incredible. As a former website developer, I remember how expensive and time consuming it was to build such a store from the ground up. Now, you can just install WordPress, get a proper theme, buy/download a specialized e-commerce plugin, and you're good to go. This is a prime example of how technology meets the expectations of running a business the modern way.

Okay, enough with the introduction. Now, let's focus on the actual process of building a quality e-commerce store.

First of all, the thing with e-commerce stores on WordPress is that they are extremely plugin-driven. What I actually mean is that if you want to launch such a website, you will need to get one main e-commerce plugin that's going to be responsible for the complete set of operations available in your store. In short, this plugin will run your store. For that reason, choosing the right plugin is extremely important, which is something I'm sure you understand.

There are numerous premium plugins in the market. They offer a ton of features and integrate with almost any online payment processing method possible. But what's actually quite surprising is the fact that some of the best plugins are completely free. Here's my favorite four:

- WP e-Commerce: `http://wordpress.org/plugins/wp-e-commerce/`
- WooCommerce: `http://wordpress.org/plugins/woocommerce/`
- eShop: `http://wordpress.org/plugins/eshop/`
- Easy Digital Downloads: `https://easydigitaldownloads.com/`
- Cart66 Lite: `http://wordpress.org/plugins/cart66-lite/`

Each of them offers an impressive range of features. I won't even attempt to list them here because it would take a chapter of its own. Instead, I will focus on one of them—my personal favorite, and use it to go through the whole process of setting up an e-commerce store that's optimized and ready to run any retail-based online business.

Without further delay, my plugin of choice is WooCommerce. It's beautifully designed and offers a truly exceptional range of features, which I will get into in a minute. But before I do that, if you're planning to launch your own store, it's advisable to test all of the plugins mentioned earlier and pick the one that you like the most. In other words, don't use WooCommerce just because I say it's cool. Make your own educated decision. After all, it's your business we're talking about here.

Now, let's talk about the plugin. The main reason why I like WooCommerce this much is because it can be integrated with any theme. And I really do mean any. However, for a real-life business website (not just a test website like we're going to build in a minute), I still think that you should use an optimized e-commerce theme. Again, feel free to visit one of the popular theme stores to get something of top quality. I listed a number of them in *Chapter 6, Choosing and Installing Themes*.

In short, a good e-commerce theme should:

- Have a clear design
- Present the center content block in an attention-grabbing way (this is where the products are going to be displayed)
- Allow you to tune the number of sidebars you want to display
- Be responsive (viewable on any device)
- Have a good navigation structure that's ready to house hundreds, if not thousands of subpages (product pages)
- Offer a built-in featured content slider, which you'll be using for showcasing promoted products
- Handle multilingual content
- Provide some level of social media integration (sharing product links on Twitter or Facebook)

In this chapter, for educational purposes, I will use the custom theme we were working on in *Chapter 7, Developing Your Own Theme*, the one for my cooking blog. But go ahead and feel free to use any theme you wish.

Standard setup

The initial part of the setup process is the same for all WordPress sites, including e-commerce WordPress sites. In other words, just proceed to installing the platform like you normally would. You can go back to *Chapter 2, Getting Started*, for more information.

As a result of this, you should have a nice blank WordPress site. Next, download and install the theme you'll use as the base of your store. As I said, I will go forward with my cooking blog theme.

Getting the plugin

To get WooCommerce, you can either go to `http://wordpress.org/plugins/woocommerce/` or install it straight from the WP Admin (**Plugins | Add New**). Just input `WooCommerce` into the main search field. Most likely, the first plugin on the list is the one you're looking for. Click on **Install Now** and when the process finishes, activate the plugin.

This is what you'll see after activating the plugin:

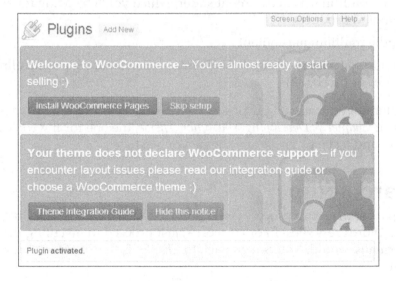

WooCommerce informs you right away about some of the actions you might have to take to be able to use the plugin to its fullest potential.

The first button in the preceding screenshot is a tricky one (labeled **Install WooCommerce Pages**). When you click on it, the plugin will create a range of pages that are meant to hold different parts of your new store. Although doing so might seem like cluttering the store right from get-go, it's actually a good idea because it provides a starter structure. I would therefore advise going ahead and clicking it after all.

When the process is done, you'll be redirected to the following page:

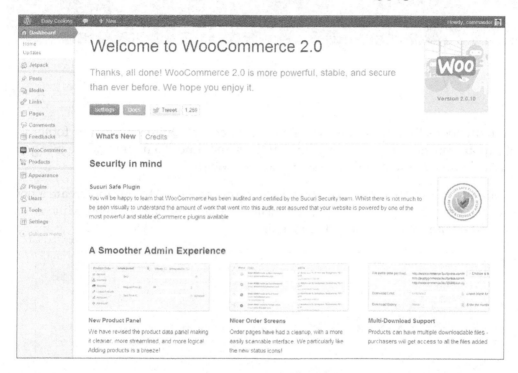

This page will guide you through a range a new and useful features and also list some of the under-the-hood elements, like custom functions and action handles. But let's not get into this right now. In this chapter, we're just going to implement some basic integration between the plugin and our current theme. Here's how to do that:

1. Create an additional custom menu to handle the new pages that the plugin created, and then assign the menu to the footer.
2. Adjust the main settings of the plugin.
3. Create a custom container page to handle the plugin's content.
4. Add some products and launch the store.
5. Check the stats: orders, coupons, and reports.

Custom menu for the store

Currently, the theme we're using takes all the pages we have on the site and displays links pointing to them in the footer. This doesn't look very nice though:

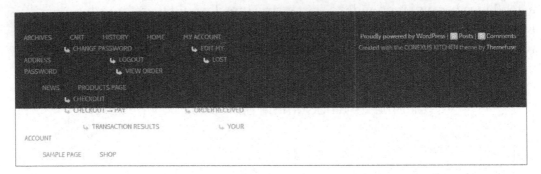

It actually looks like the design is seriously messed up. Quite simply, our footer is not capable of showing this many links at the same time. To fix this, we're just going to create a new menu and then assign it to the footer.

We already know how to do this. Just go to **Appearance | Menus** and create a new menu (as described in *Chapter 4, Pages, Menus, Media Library, and More*). Mine is called **Shop**, and there are just three pages in it:

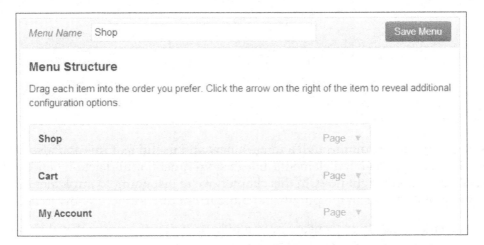

Next, the menu is assigned to the footer:

Finally, as a result, the footer looks much better now:

Main settings of the plugin

WooCommerce really is a complete solution when it comes to e-commerce, and the number of features scares even me. The following section presents some of the most crucial ones.

By going to **WooCommerce | Settings | General** you can set things like:

- **Base Location**: It is where your business is based. It is important for taxes, which the plugin helps you handle too.
- **Currency**: It shows what currency prices are listed in the store and which currency gateways will take payments in.
- **Allowed Countries**: It is the list of countries you're willing to ship to.
- **Coupons**: It shows if your store allows the use of coupons.
- **Guest checkout**: It shows if visitors have to register in order to make a purchase.
- **Basic styling of the core elements of the plugin**: It includes things such as call to action buttons, tabs, price labels, and so on.
- **Downloadable products support**: The plugin also lets you sell digital products and have them delivered right away through a secure download.

Apart from the **General** settings tab, you can also (and probably should) adjust other parameters in tabs like:

- **Catalog**: It shows various product options and product data parameters (like weight, size, and so on).

- **Pages**: It includes basic page settings. Here, you can assign the core pages of the store, for example, the page on your site that should hold the cart, and so on.

- **Inventory**: It includes various stock management settings.

- **Tax**: It is a handy section for tax handling and tax calculations.

- **Shipping**: It includes shipping and shipping rates.

- **Payment Gateways**: It includes payment collection settings.

- **Emails**: As in all e-commerce stores, e-mail is the main channel of communication with customers. In this section, you can set how your store should handle emails.

- **Integration**: This is where you can integrate your store with external solutions like Google Analytics or other tracking software.

Getting through all of these tabs and adjusting the settings will take a while for an actual e-commerce store. But here, we're just scratching the surface and finding out what's possible with a quality plugin like this. Therefore, don't spend too much time on all these settings tabs. Just glance over them, set the features that are the most interesting to you and proceed to the next step.

Custom container page for the store

Since WooCommerce is quite a popular plugin, some themes are advertised to be compatible with it right from the start. Unfortunately, ours isn't. You can see this by going to `http://yoursite.com/shop/` (the default subpage for the store). This is what you'll likely see:

Everything looks wrong. There's no sidebar and things are cramped up in the middle. This is very easy to fix though. And that's actually one of the strengths of WooCommerce. All you have to do is the following:

1. Create a copy of your `page.php` file.
2. Rename the copy to `woocommerce.php`.
3. Edit the new file, find the `<article></article>` block, erase it completely, and in its place put this single line: `<?php woocommerce_content(); ?>`
4. Save the file.

Now, your `woocommerce.php` file should look like this:

```php
<?php get_header(); ?>

<!-- middle -->
<div id="middle" class="cols2">
  <div class="container clearfix">
    <div class="content" role="main"><!-- content -->
      <?php woocommerce_content(); ?>
    </div>

    <?php get_sidebar(); ?>
  </div><!-- /.container -->
</div><!-- /.middle -->

<?php get_footer(); ?>
```

From now on, this file will be used to display any piece of content coming from WooCommerce.

> The preceding is the simplest way of integrating a theme with WooCommerce. If you want to learn more, feel free to visit:
> `http://docs.woothemes.com/document/third-party-custom-theme-compatibility/`

When we refresh the `http://yoursite.com/shop/` page now, this is what we'll see:

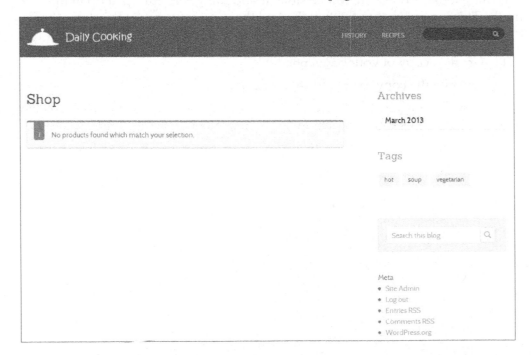

These changes make the page look a lot better. The sidebars are back and the main section is displayed neatly in the center. There's nothing else left to do now other than to add some products and start using the store.

Adding products

When it comes to products, WooCommerce follows the standard content organization method in WordPress. This means that you can manage products just like you'd manage any other piece of content (pages or posts).

What I've done here is added three products by going to **Products | Add Product** and filling out the product fields. Please notice that products also have their own categories and tags.

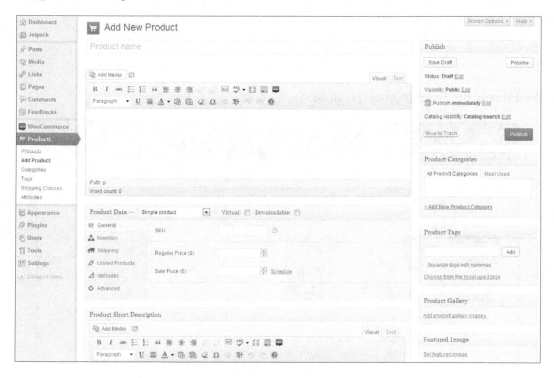

This is what my **Products** section in the WP Admin looks like right now:

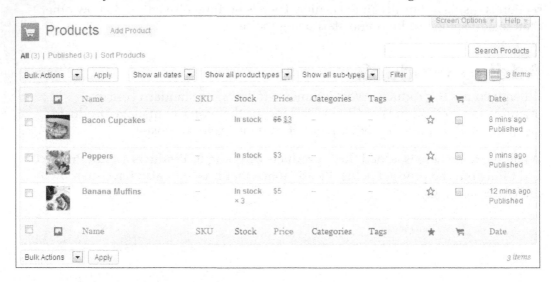

And this is the front page of the store:

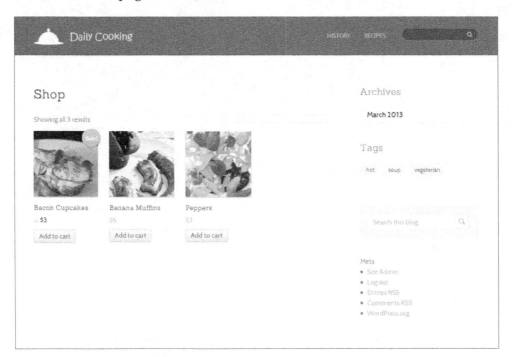

Finally, here are some screenshots presenting the individual areas of the store and of the transaction procedure. The product page appears as follows:

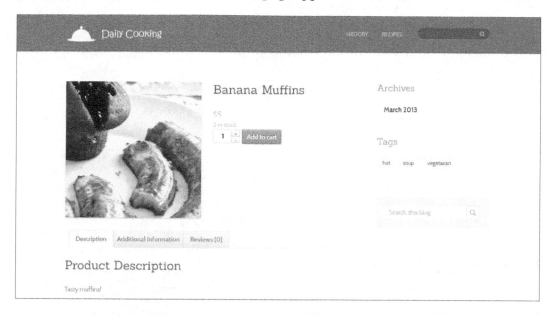

What happens when you add something to the cart? The following screenshot shows what you can expect:

The cart itself:

The checkout page looks like this:

Stats – orders, coupons, and reports

The last element of the plugin worth discussing here for a minute is the management backend—the orders, coupons, and reports sections.

Orders can be found by going to **WooCommerce | Orders**. You can manage them just like any other piece of WordPress content. There are a number of additional fields and parameters though, so there might be a slight learning curve. But still, a very friendly and easy to use environment.

To view reports, go to **WooCommerce | Reports**. There's a nice graphical representation of what's been going on in your store. You can view the sales, coupons used, customer activity, and your current stock. Right now, I don't have much going on in my store, so the graph looks like this:

You can add various coupons by going to **WooCommerce | Coupons** and then send them out to your customers. Or you can make them available on the Internet publicly as a promotional method.

That's pretty much it when it comes to using the plugin and launching a nice e-commerce store with WordPress. The most remarkable thing here is how easy it is to actually do it. Just imagine how much time it would take to create something with similar functionality from the ground up, or, better yet, the cost required to set it up. The possibilities that WordPress and various plugins deliver these days are really incredible. I'm sure that a couple of years ago, no one would have even believes that launching a quality e-commerce store could be done this easily.

One last thing, WooCommerce is not entirely free. If you want to install additional features, the official extensions are anything between USD 29 and USD 99. So for some specific, real-world applications, some financial investment might be required. This actually happens with most, if not all, e-commerce plugins.

Summary

We covered a lot of material in this chapter. We started by listing a number of popular types of non-blog websites that you can build successfully with WordPress. Then, we went through some of those types individually and discussed the specific elements to focus on in order to guarantee a quality final product.

The next chapter is part two of our guide on creating a non-blog website. In it, we'll go through some of the more user-centered types of websites, like membership sites, photo and video blogs, and finally, building your own social network.

12
Creating a Non-blog Website Part Two – Community Websites and Custom Content Elements

Let's get straight down to business here. In the previous chapter, we've seen different types of non-blog websites. This chapter is a continuation of the topic, so let's do two things. First, let's go through some of the more trendy uses of WordPress and focus on a step-by-step process of reaching a great final result. Second, let's discuss some of the custom content elements you can create in WordPress, such as custom post types, custom taxonomies, and customizing the admin display slightly.

Membership websites

When we're talking WordPress, from a technical point of view, a membership site is not very different from a standard blog site. The only thing that sets it apart is the fact that some of the content is protected by a level of access rights. In other words, the content is premium. And if anyone wants to get access to it, they usually have to take out their wallets and pay a small fee.

Even though membership sites might sound like a very niche thing to build with WordPress, there are actually more and more of such sites being launched every year. Many online businesses, especially in the educational niches, have realized that the membership model is one that provides very predictable profits and can be promoted in a variety of different ways.

But let's stick with WordPress as our main topic and leave the marketing issues aside, starting with some technical aspects of building a membership site. The following are the functionalities a membership site can/should offer:

- The possibility to feature various types of content, including text (standard articles), audio, video, PDF files, presentations, and photos
- An easy method of user registration and subscription
- Different levels of subscriptions (with different access rights)
- Integrated online payments (for premium subscriptions)
- Free trials
- Easy user account management and subscription management
- E-mail newsletter integration
- Teaser content (when you're showing part of the premium content to tease visitors into subscribing)
- Internal stats

The list of functionality is quite extensive, and some of it might not be that clear at first, but we're going to explain everything in just a while. Just like with our previous examples, we're going to build a functional membership site here and discuss some of the more important aspects of the process along the way.

For this purpose, let's use the theme from *Chapter 7, Developing Your Own Theme*. Like I said, membership sites are very similar in construction to standard blogs. And although you can look for specialized themes, often the default theme you're using right now will do the job well enough. The only requirement is that, from a user's/visitor's point of view, your membership site theme should provide good content presentation and should be able to handle various types of content. That is all.

Taking the simple approach

Even though the recommended approach to building a membership site is based on using specialized plugins, there's also an alternative path. But it's neither functional nor professional, so I'm mentioning it just to keep the message complete. I'm talking about using the simple password protection feature that's built into WordPress by default.

Basically, if you want to limit access to a given piece of content, all you have to do is go to the WP Admin, then to **Posts** or **Pages**, and click on the **Quick Edit** link beneath a given piece of content. There's a **Password** field at the bottom. After filling it out and clicking on **Update**, your content is no longer publicly visible from that point forward. Anyone who wants to view it has to enter the password.

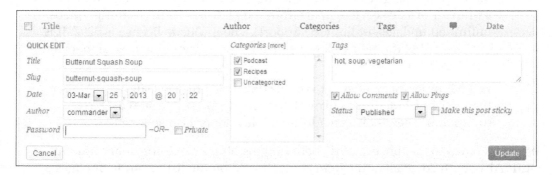

Although this simple method does work and it does the job of limiting access to specific pieces of content, it's not the prettiest one, at least not for serious membership sites. Besides, it doesn't handle the subscription process itself and forces you to find a way to deliver the passwords to your subscribers manually.

As it turns out, the simplest solutions are not always the best.

Using membership plugins

The only sensible method of building a membership site on WordPress is with the help of some specialized membership plugins. Of course, just like with any other type of site, you can still devote your time and effort to building everything from the ground up by hand. But similarly to e-commerce stores, it would take way too long before you could show any truly quality effects. So membership plugins it is!

As usual, there are many plugins available on the market, and finding the perfect one for your particular project might take a while, especially if you want to test every feature before making the site available to the world and your customers.

Now, the only downside is that most of those membership plugins are premium. Seriously premium, so to speak. Some price tags go as high as $297 (I'm going to point you to a free solution in just a minute).

Therefore, if you do have some money to invest in your membership site, I would advise looking into the following two plugins:

- **WishList Member** (`http://member.wishlistproducts.com`): This plugin is used by hundreds of sites worldwide; it's probably the most popular membership plugin available. The single site license is $97 and it provides a number of side services apart from the platform itself (training videos, unlimited updates, unlimited support). The multisite license is $297. It is not cheap, but it might be a great idea for professional web designers and developers.

- **WP-Member** (`http://wp-member.com`): This plugin is slightly cheaper than WishList Member, currently priced at $47 (single site) and $97 (multisite). There's also an additional developer license for $147.

When it comes to the functionality, both plugins offer an extraordinary amount of stuff. Also, both cover all of the items I mentioned on the list a couple of pages ago, plus some additional bells and whistles (for example, secure RSS feeds and data encryption).

Now, I'm not actually advising you to spend any money at this point, but we're here to learn, so I'm only mentioning these plugins because they are the top of the game in their field: membership plugins for WordPress.

Taking the free approach

This is probably a good moment to talk about a solution that's way cheaper to apply. Actually, the plugin I'm about to describe is free. It's simply named **Membership** and you can get it at `http://wordpress.org/plugins/membership/`.

The sole fact that it is free doesn't mean that it offers a poor range of features though, or that it isn't built with quality in mind. This is still one of the top membership site plugins available. Why is it free? It's based on a **freemium** model. This means that if you want to get more functionality or unlock some of the extra features, you'll have to get the Pro version, which costs $19.

Installing the plugin

This is a standard installation process. All you have to do is either go to `http://wordpress.org/plugins/membership/` to get the plugin and then upload it to your plugins folder. Or, you can fetch it straight from the **Plugins** | **Add New** section in the WP Admin.

When you activate the plugin, you will be prompted to enable the plugin's functionality. This can be done from the admin bar in your WP Admin, as shown in the following screenshot:

After doing so, you'll see a completely new section in the main sidebar, right below the **Settings** bar. It's named **Membership**, as shown in the following screenshot:

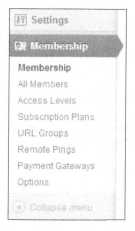

At this point, I advise you to go through the short user guide that will begin displaying automatically when you try to visit the **Membership** section. This will give you a basic overview of the plugin, as shown in the following screenshot:

The main block that's displayed right in the middle lets you get started quickly by creating your first membership site. We'll just select **Standard membership site** and proceed to the next step.

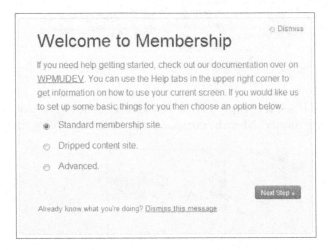

The free version of the plugin allows you to create two levels of access. Let's call ours Free and Premium. (I'm also selecting PayPal as the gateway for handling payments.)

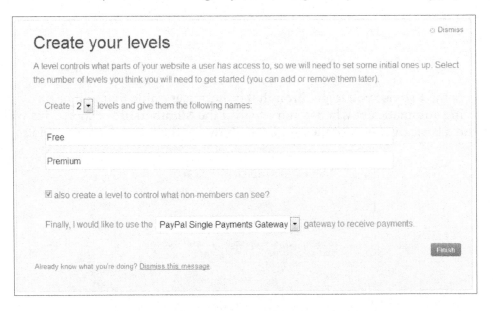

When I click on **Finish**, I'm basically done with the setup process. That wasn't hard, was it?

Using the plugin

Right after the setup process is complete, you will be presented with another on-screen user guide on how to use the plugin for doing the everyday work. This guide is quite a long one, 34 steps, but it does present all of the most crucial functionalities of **Membership**. So, in fact, I do advise you to go through it from start to finish.

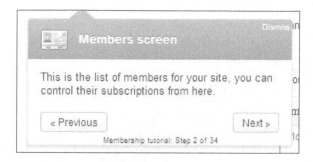

In short, the individual sections of the plugin allow you the following functionalities:

- **Manage subscribers** (navigate to **Membership | All Members**): With this you can assign subscribers to their subscription plans, manage subscription levels, and even check expiration dates

- **Manage subscription levels** (navigate to **Membership | Access Levels**): There's also one more level on top of the two we created during setup named **Visitors** and it controls what unregistered visitors see

- **Manage subscription plans** (navigate to **Membership | Subscription Plans**): This lets you control things such as descriptions, pricing, and the subscription levels that a specific subscription plan has access to

- **Manage payment gateways** (navigate to **Membership | Payment Gateways**): The plugin allows you to receive payments through various channels

- **Other options** (navigate to **Membership | Options**): This is where you can control other areas of the site that haven't been covered elsewhere

Now, let's talk about how managing your content actually works and what you can do to prevent some users from accessing the premium parts of it. Don't be afraid by the fact that the way this plugin handles content management is quite advanced. First, we have the access level settings available in **Membership | Access Levels**.

The following screenshot shows what we'll see after going there and selecting our **Free** level for editing:

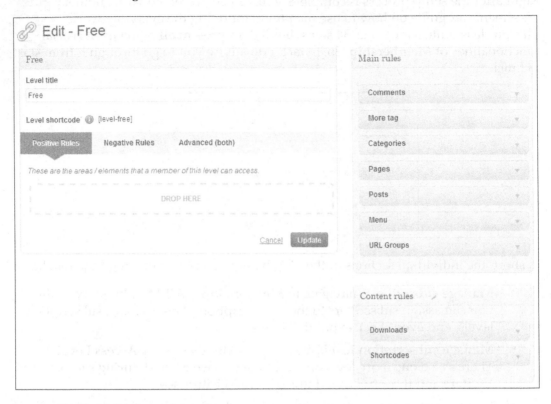

We can set each access level to utilize a set of **Positive Rules**, **Negative Rules**, or **Advanced (both)** rules. Basically, positive rules are how we can assign the content that a given access level can view, while negative rules do the opposite thing. For example, if I add all of my posts to the set of negative rules, I will effectively prevent every **Free** member from viewing any of them, as shown in the following screenshot:

Mind that this is just an example, and setting up everything properly so it actually makes sense in a real world application will take a significant while.

Apart from the basic access level settings, we can also use the shortcodes provided. For example, if we want to allow some content to be viewed by our **Free** members, the only thing we have to do is enclose it in the [level-free] shortcode. For example, as shown in the following code snippet:

```
[level-free]some content[/level-free]
```

As you can see, the plugin tries to make this as easy to grasp as possible.

There are a lot more features waiting for you inside **Membership** and I do encourage you to test it out for yourself if you're ever building a full-blown membership site. But for now, it's about time we switch to the next type of site on the list: **multimedia blogs**.

Video and photo blogs

Let's cover these two types of WordPress sites together because the individual goals for each are often very similar (although the designs might still be a bit different).

In short, a video blog is one where the author mainly publishes videos, instead of traditional text-based posts. A photo blog, on the other hand, is essentially the same thing, only revolving around photos.

Now, why would you even bother with a customized setup for a video blog or a photo blog in the first place, when you can just use a standard WordPress installation with a traditional blogging-optimized theme? Well, to be honest here, you can go with a standard setup indeed, and your video/photo blog will be just about fine. But with some additional work (not much) put on building something that's tailor-made for multimedia blogs, your site can get a big advantage over your competition. That's mostly in terms of usability and content presentation.

For instance, let's focus on some of the interesting features you can put on a video blog:

- Main blog listing built as a grid layout with big thumbnails, so every visitor can see the snapshots of the videos right away
- Videos on the main listing presented as concise blocks containing the thumbnail and a small amount of text to convince people to click over to the video
- Wide main blog listing with just a narrow sidebar on the left (or right)
- Integrated social media features (including the YouTube subscription buttons)
- Social media comments, fetched from the platform where the video is originally hosted
- Custom backend to host the videos on the blog (or on an external server)
- Shareable embed code, so your visitors can embed the videos easily
- Custom player to replace the native YouTube or Vimeo players

And for a photo blog, interesting features are

- Custom home page featuring one main photo (photo of the day)
- Automatic photo slider on the home page

- Lightbox functionality for viewing the photos in full size
- Wide main blog listing
- Integrated social media features
- Social media comments
- Custom backend to host photos
- Sharable embed code
- Custom photo controls (for example, save, view full size, share, and so on)

As you can see, most of these features can work equally well on both video blogs and photo blogs. As usual with WordPress, you can get most of them either by obtaining a quality theme, or by using some third-party plugins. Let's cover both approaches.

Exploring themes for video and photo sites

Being quite popular kinds of blog, both video and photo blogs have a very big number of themes available on the Internet. Be careful, though. Searching for a theme on Google can get you in trouble. Well, maybe not in trouble per se, but if you end up downloading a theme from a random site, you have no guarantee that it's a secure solution and that there's no malicious or encrypted code inside. A much better method is to either to go the official directory or to some of the recognized theme stores.

For starters, let's check out what's available in the directory:

- **Portfolio Press** (http://wordpress.org/themes/portfolio-press): This is one of the more popular portfolio themes in the directory, currently at over 240,000 downloads. It offers an optimized structure that allows you to publish photos, videos, art, or other types of graphics. Not much in terms of additional features, though.

- **Rustic** (http://wordpress.org/themes/rustic): This is another portfolio theme, based on a well-organized grid layout. It comes with some portfolio capability, and lets you add music, videos, or photos to your content. Additionally, there's an integrated Lightbox.

- **Photolistic** (http://wordpress.org/themes/photolistic): This is a neatly designed theme with clear content presentation and minimal structure. It is perfect for anyone who wants to focus more on showcasing content rather than guiding attention towards the theme itself.

  As you'd imagine, the premium side of the Internet—the theme stores—have a lot more to offer for video and photo bloggers.

- **VideoGrid** (`http://themefuse.com/wp-themes-shop/videogrid`): This is a great looking theme based on a grid layout. The main listing uses a number of square blocks optimized to host any sort of multimedia content. There are two color scheme variations: dark and light. There's also an advanced filtering mechanism to make the site user-friendly. In the end, the theme seems like a great solution for bloggers planning to publish a lot of content on a regular basis.

- **PhotoArtist** (`http://themefuse.com/wp-themes-shop/photo-artist`): This is another theme by ThemeFuse. This one is for photographers, artists, and anyone who wants to start publishing visual content. It offers a fullscreen slider, lightbox functionality, social media integration, and handy shortcodes for easier usage.

- **WooTube** (`http://www.woothemes.com/products/wootube`): As you can probably tell, this is a video theme. It features an automatic resize functionality to get your videos to look good on any device, an integrated embed code that you can share with the readers, and seven custom color schemes.

- **Chocolate WP** (`http://themeforest.net/item/chocolate-wp-responsive-photography-theme/299901`): This is a very nice photo blog theme with responsive structure (optimized for any device), a full screen photo or video home page, three home page sliders, nine custom color schemes, and an overall great design with a luxury feel to it.

Getting any of these premium themes will require an investment, so do it only if you're devoted to creating a really quality multimedia blog.

Getting plugins for video and photo sites

As I said, apart from video and photo optimized themes, you can also get a number of plugins that will make your site more functional. The good news is that we're only going to focus on free plugins.

Let's start with two plugins that I already mentioned in *Chapter 11, Creating a Non-blog Website Part One – The Basics*:

- **Meteor Slides** (`http://wordpress.org/plugins/meteor-slides/`)
- **SlideDeck 2 Lite Responsive Content Slider** (`http://wordpress.org/plugins/slidedeck2/`)

These are both great plugins for getting a nice slider functionality. This sort of thing does a good job at improving the overall user experience, especially when dealing with a multimedia-driven site. For a detailed description of these plugins, please review the previous chapter, the *Static websites* section.

Now, other plugins that can come handy are as follows:

- **WP Smush.it** (`http://wordpress.org/plugins/wp-smushit`): This plugin doesn't present any particular output on the frontend of your site because what it actually does is automatically optimize your images in the background. What happens is, whenever you upload a new image to the image library on your WordPress site, the plugin processes the image and compresses it to reduce the size. The important detail is that the image still looks the same with no loss in quality. This is a great plugin for saving your bandwidth, especially if you're publishing a lot of images.

  The installation process is quite standard. Once the plugin is activated, it starts working in the background with no supervision required.

- **WP jQuery Lightbox** (`http://wordpress.org/plugins/wp-jquery-lightbox`): This plugin delivers a really good looking lightbox functionality powered by jQuery, a popular Java Script library. The best thing about this plugin is that it's ultra easy to use. All you have to do is activate it and it will immediately start taking care of the images you're displaying on your blog. The plugin will intercept image clicks and show the image file in a nice lightbox instead of loading them individually (on a blank page).

  For example, the following screenshot is my **Making Lasagne** post and the image in it (image not particularly related to lasagne, so sorry about that):

Now, when I try to edit the image, all I have to do to enable lightbox is to click on the **Link to Image** button, which will place the direct address of the image file in the **Link URL** field, as shown in the following screenshot:

After clicking on the **Update** button and saving changes to the post, my lightbox is enabled, as shown in the following screenshot:

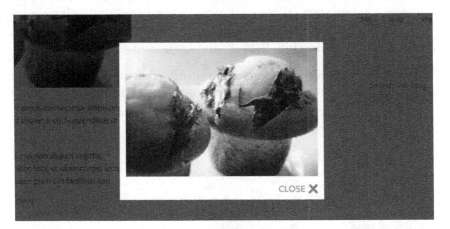

Lastly, I have two social media plugins I'd like to show you. The first one is named **Twitter Mentions As Comments** (`http://wordpress.org/plugins/twitter-mentions-as-comments/`).

It does exactly what the name says, which is scouting Twitter in search of any mentions of your content and then publishing those mentions as comments under given posts. In short, it's a great way to make your content seem more alive by showcasing some social media activity.

This plugin is very easy to use, with just one **Settings** section under **Settings |
Twitter | Comments**. Most of the time, the plugin works automatically.

The second plugin is simply named **Facebook** and it's the official Facebook plugin
for WordPress (`http://wordpress.org/plugins/facebook/`).

This plugin can give you a good level of integration between your main site and
your Facebook page or profile. With it, you can publish new posts on Facebook
almost automatically and also allow Facebook users to comment on your content
using their accounts. This is just a small part of the full functionality. I'd advise
you to give this plugin a closer look yourself. Since it's an official plugin, every
new functionality that Facebook makes available for WordPress blogs is sure to
be introduced as quickly as possible.

Just to sum up the topic of multimedia blogs, I have to point out that this is a very
crowded area among both theme and plugin developers. The plugins previously
mentioned will give you a good start, but having your finger on the pulse and
paying attention to what's new on the market (cool new plugins and themes) is the
actual best way to keep your photo or video blog on top of its game. That being said,
getting and testing every new plugin out there is not the recommended approach.
However, from time to time, you can find a true gem that's going to help you take
your blog to the next level.

Social networks

Finally, it's time to discuss one of the most surprising topics in relation to building
various types of websites with WordPress. As it turns out, the platform can be very
well used to run a fully functional social network. In other words, you can have your
own Facebook if you like to... at least when it comes to the functionality.

And speaking about functionality, in short, a social network built with WordPress
can offer the following:

- Support any number of user accounts
- Facebook-like publishing method for users (a "Wall" or an activity stream)
- Forums
- Blogs and micro blogs
- Friends
- Groups
- Private messages
- Comments
- Photo and video content
- And much, much more

That being said, building and then running a well-constructed social network utilizing all of the available features will require some serious work. This is way above the scope of this book. So here, we're only going to focus on the basic setup process and getting started. If you're planning to launch an actual social network and make it available to the world, you should probably get more info, either by going to the official online documentation or obtaining some publications on the topic.

Essentially, social networking on WordPress works through one specific plugin: **BuddyPress**, although calling it just a plugin is a massive understatement. BuddyPress is actually a whole online publishing environment on its own that integrates with WordPress. Unlike other plugins, it doesn't just display some custom content here and there. It actually changes the whole appearance (structure) of your WordPress site to make it look and operate like a social network.

Let's take the topic step-by-step, starting with the installation.

Installing a social network

Nothing fancy here, all you have to do is either go to `http://buddypress.org/`, download the main plugin, and then upload it to your WordPress site, or search for the plugin from within the WP Admin (**Plugins | Add New**) using the **BuddyPress** name. The installation process of the plugin itself is quite standard, meaning that after getting it on your server you only have to click on the **Activate** button. Right after doing so, you will see the following welcome screen:

It's actually advisable to go through the information in it to get a basic understanding of the platform and the things it has to offer.

Next, visit the **Settings** section under **Settings | BuddyPress**. First, pick the components you'd like to use on your new social network. For testing purposes, I just enabled all of them, as shown in the following screenshot:

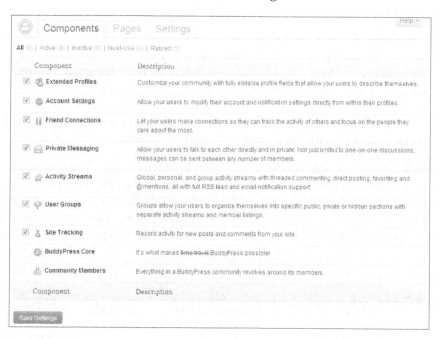

Remember that whenever you need any help working with BuddyPress, or any other element in WordPress, you can click on the **Help** drop-down section that's visible in the preceding screenshot. Also, to get more info about the available components, feel free to visit http://codex.buddypress.org/user/setting-up-a-new-installation/configure-buddypress-components/.

The second tab on this settings page, titled **Pages**, lets you assign the pages that will house some standard areas of your social network, for example, the activity stream, user groups, member profiles, and so on. You can create new pages here or use the ones that BuddyPress has already created during install.

Finally, there's the last tab, **Settings**, where you can adjust some of the other standard settings, such as the presence of the top toolbar, various profile settings, and group settings.

That's basically it when it comes to the main settings area. As you can see, the plugin is designed in a way that makes using it as easy as possible.

Designing your social network

In its current form, BuddyPress can work with any WordPress theme. That's right, you don't have to get an optimized social networking design if you don't want to. BuddyPress will manage to display its contents inside either the main content block of your current theme or the widget areas you have available (quite similar to WooCommerce, which we talked about in the previous chapter).

However, as usual, if you want to make your social network look more professional then you should probably look around and get something that's specially optimized for social networks. The best rule of thumb when searching for such themes, in my opinion, is to compare them against the biggest social network of them all: Facebook. Although some people don't enjoy the design that Facebook offers, it still is the most successful social network around, so they are clearly doing something right. Treating them as a benchmark of sorts is, therefore, a very good idea.

For my quick example in this chapter, I'm going to leave my cooking theme for a while and look for something more optimized to run a social network. And I don't have to look far because BuddyPress comes with its own default theme. Once you have the plugin installed, you can find the theme in **Appearance | Themes**. It's named **BuddyPress Default**. After activating it, my site looks like the following screenshot:

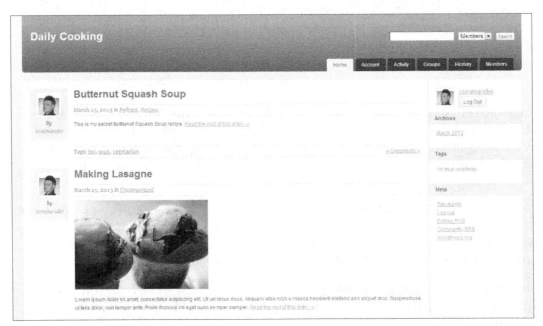

Really nothing that fancy. It's basically just a standard social network design with good focus on the person publishing the content in the main content block. We can give the site some flair by installing a free child theme named **Frisco for BuddyPress**.

You can get it by either going to **http://wordpress.org/themes/frisco-for-buddypress** or searching for Frisco in the **Appearance | Themes | Install Themes** section. The following screenshot shows what my site looks now after activating this new theme:

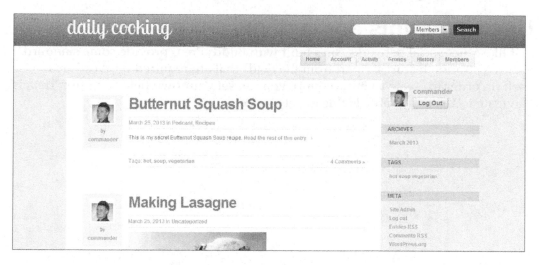

In my opinion, it's a more refined and modern design than the default theme. However, mind that this is a child theme, which means that you have to actually keep the default BuddyPress theme on your server for the new theme to work. Frisco also comes with some predefined color schemes to choose from. As you can see in the preceding screenshot, I went with the one named **Green**.

If you think that your site looks good enough at this point, then you can go straight to using it without focusing any more on the setup. However, if you really want to get to know the platform and the way it's built, I advise you to go to the official documentation, which is one of the best BuddyPress resources available (`http://codex.buddypress.org/`). It's also where you can learn all the ins and outs of BuddyPress development, creating your own themes or even BuddyPress extension plugins.

Extending the functionality

BuddyPress is constructed in a way that provides the basic social networking functionality and site organization. If you want to extend your social media site and give it some new features, you can install a number of BuddyPress plugins. You can find them at `http://buddypress.org/extend/plugins/`. Basically, they are just like other WordPress plugins (the installation process is the same), but instead of delivering some new functionality to WordPress, they focus more on BuddyPress.

One such plugin that I recommend you should get first is **BuddyPress Media** (`http://wordpress.org/plugins/buddypress-media/`). It lets your users add photos, music, and videos to their BuddyPress profiles.

User accounts and activity

Just like other social networks, sites built with BuddyPress provide some standard user registration features. Apart from the fields that are required by WordPress itself (in order to create a new account), you can set your own fields and user details. Navigate to **Users | Profile Fields** to get started.

Right now, there's just one field and one group of fields as shown in the preceding screenshot. You can add new groups by clicking on the **Add New Field Group** button, and add new fields by clicking on the **Add New Field** button for each group individually. Let's add just one additional field to test this. I'll call it `City`. Please keep in mind that this is just a simple field, so the user won't be allowed to choose a city, or to check if the city actually exists.

Each field has a number of parameters, such as description, whether it's required to fill it out or not, field type, and visibility.

After completing the procedure, I now have two custom fields on my registration page, which is available for the world to see under the default URL: `http://yoursite.com/register-2/` (this obviously can be changed).

Every user who registers gets access to a standard range of social networking features, meaning that users can manage their own profiles and also connect with other registered users.

When I try to visit the profile of one of my former editor accounts that I created as a test, I can see the following screenshot:

John doesn't have much going on in his profile yet, but I can still add him as my friend, send him a public message (which work very similarly to @mentions on Twitter), or a private message through the internal messaging system. When John publishes a status update, I can comment on it or mark it as my favorite. This is all very intuitive and in tune with the experience we're familiar with after years of browsing Facebook.

Additionally, just to mention one of the more general features, I can create groups and encourage users to gather around a similar interest. Finally, if you have some additional BuddyPress plugins installed, then you will obviously have many more features at your disposal.

There is a lot more stuff waiting for you inside BuddyPress and I actually encourage you to do some researching and learning on your own, especially if you're planning to launch a social network at some point. But for now, I think that we've got the topic covered, at least when it comes to giving you an introduction to social networking with WordPress and getting started with the best social networking plugin available: BuddyPress.

Introducing custom post types

While building some of the sites described in this and the previous chapter, you may stumble upon what's called custom post types. Or you may even decide to create them yourself for the purpose of your individual projects. But let's take it from the top. The custom post type functionality was added to WordPress in Version 3.0 because people wanted to be able to specify new objects.

The most commonly known objects are posts and pages, but there are actually already three other custom types in the WordPress backend: attachments, revisions, and navigation menus. However, if we feel that the situation/project calls for it, we can create any number of new post types by taking advantage of the custom post type functionality and its wide versatility.

For example, while building an e-commerce store using WooCommerce, you will find a new section in the WP Admin named **Products** (we talked about this in the previous chapter). These products are nothing else than a custom post type created by WooCommerce to make the store more functional and easier to grasp for the average user.

The need for custom post types can appear in other, even simpler, scenarios as well. For instance, when a writer is building a personal portfolio site, he or she might need a custom post type named book to present publications in an attractive way instead of just using standard posts. This is exactly what we're about to do in this section of the chapter. So, let's learn how custom post types work by building a new one named book.

For this purpose, we'll go back to our main cooking blog theme: **Conexus Kitchen**. In its default form, it doesn't feature any custom post types and that's a good thing, as we've got a blank canvas to work on.

To specify that you'd like to have a custom post type in your theme, you can add some code to your theme's functions.php file. This is what we'll be doing. However, keep in mind that you can also attach the custom post type to a plugin or a widget if you don't want it to be tied to a particular theme.

Registering a new post type

To register a new post type, all you have to do is add some simple code to your functions.php file. It's good practice to tie the creation of the new type to init of the theme, so that it gets called at a good point in the booting process, so we'll use the hook for init. Your initial custom post type code looks like the following code snippet:

```
add_action('init', 'book_init');
function book_init() {
    register_post_type('book');
}
```

The `register_post_type()` function takes an array as its second parameter, and in that array you can specify whether the object is public, whether it should be involved in rewriting the URL, what elements it supports on its editing page, and so on. Let's set up an array of all the arguments and then pass it to the function. Now our code looks like the following:

```
add_action('init', 'book_init');
function book_init() {
  $args = array(
    'description' => 'A custom post type that holds my books',
    'public' => true,
    'rewrite' => array('slug' => 'books'),
    'has_archive' => true,
    'supports' => array('title', 'editor', 'author', 'excerpt',
      'custom-fields', 'thumbnail')
  );
  register_post_type('book', $args);
  flush_rewrite_rules();
}
```

I've chosen each of these parameters because they make sense for the book custom post type. Let's take a look at them:

- `description`: This one's pretty self-explanatory.
- `public`: This means that the post type is available publicly, like posts and pages are, rather than hidden behind the scenes. It'll get a UI, it can be shown in navigation menus, and so on.
- `rewrite`: This specifies that the post type can be used in the rewrite rules for pretty permalinks.
- `has_archive`: This enables post type archives (a classic index page such as we can see for our standard posts).
- `supports`: This is an array of the capabilities users see when creating or editing an item. For books, we're including six of ten possible items.

The final function call, `flush_rewrite_rules()`, will allow us to show a standard archive listing of the books later on (just as for a standard post listing, but for our custom post type).

 These are just some of the arguments you can pass. Read about the others in the codex: http://codex.wordpress.org/Function_Reference/register_post_type.

Now that we've got the basic post type set up, let's add some labels.

Adding labels

You can add labels to your custom post type so that WordPress knows what to say when talking about it. First, let's simply create an array of all the labels. Put this as the first thing inside the `book_init()` function, as shown in the following code snippet:

```
$labels = array(
    'name' => 'Books',
    'singular_name' => 'Book',
    'add_new' => 'Add New',
    'add_new_item' => 'Add New Book',
    'edit_item' => 'Edit Book',
    'new_item' => 'New Book',
    'view_item' => 'View Book',
    'search_items' => 'Search Books',
    'not_found' =>  'No books found',
    'not_found_in_trash' => 'No books found in Trash'
);
```

Then add a single line of code to the `$args` array, telling it to use the labels, such as the following code snippet:

```
$args = array(
    'labels' => $labels,
    'description' => 'A custom post type that holds my books',
/* the rest of the function remains the same */
```

The next step is to add messages, which is what WordPress tells the user when they are doing stuff with books.

Adding messages

Whenever a user updates, previews, or does anything with a book, you'll want him or her to see an accurate message. All we need to do is create an array of messages, and then hook them in to WordPress. Here's the code:

```
add_filter('post_updated_messages', 'book_updated_messages');
function book_updated_messages( $messages ) {
  $messages['book'] = array(
    '' /*Unused. Messages start at index 1*/,
    sprintf('Book updated. <a href="%s">View book</a>',
      esc_url(get_permalink($post_ID))),
    'Custom field updated.',
    'Custom field deleted.',
    'Book updated.',
```

```
  (isset($_GET['revision']) ? sprintf('Book restored to revision
    from %s', wp_post_revision_title((int)$_GET['revision'],
      false)) : false),
  sprintf('Book published. <a href="%s">View book</a>',
    esc_url(get_permalink($post_ID))),
  'Book saved.',
  sprintf('Book submitted. <a target="_blank" href="%s">Preview
    book</a>', esc_url(add_query_arg('preview', 'true',
      get_permalink($post_ID)))),
  sprintf('Book scheduled for: <strong>%1$s</strong>.
    <a target="_blank" href="%2$s">Preview book</a>',
      date_i18n('M j, Y @ G:i', strtotime($post->post_date)),
        esc_url(get_permalink($post_ID))),
  sprintf('Book draft updated. <a target="_blank"
    href="%s">Preview book</a>', esc_url(add_query_arg(
      'preview', 'true', get_permalink($post_ID))))
  );
  return $messages;
}
```

This code creates a function named `book_updated_messages()` that sets up an array of messages and returns it. We call this using the filter for `post_updated_messages`.

Now, our custom post type is ready to use! Go to your WP Admin, and reload it. You'll see a new menu has appeared under **Comments**. It's named **Books**. Let's add a book:

I've given it a custom field named `book_author`, and I've also uploaded a featured image for the book cover.

I'll also add a couple more. Now, when you go to the main **Books** page, you'll see your books listed, as shown in the following screenshot:

If you click on **View** for one of these books, you'll see the book displayed using the `single.php` theme template, as shown in the following screenshot:

Let's make some new template files to display our books.

Creating book template files

WordPress needs to know how to display your new post type. We have to create a template for a single book and one for the list of books.

First, we'll make a book version of `single.php`. It must be named `single-post type name.php`, which in our case is `single-book.php`. Using `page.php` as our starting point (as it's already the closest to what we'd like our book page to look like), we're going to add displays of the custom field, `book_author`, and the featured image. So let's start by taking our `page.php` file, making a copy of it, and renaming it `single-book.php`. Then let's include the featured image functionality. After all these operations, the file looks like the following code snippet:

```php
<?php get_header(); ?>

<!-- middle -->
<div id="middle" class="cols2">
  <div class="container clearfix">
    <div class="content" role="main"><!-- content -->
      <article id="post-<?php the_ID(); ?>"
        <?php post_class(array('post-detail')); ?>>
        <div class="entry clearfix">
          <?php while ( have_posts() ) : the_post(); ?>
            <h1><?php the_title(); ?></h1>
            <?php if(has_post_thumbnail()) : ?>
              <div class="post-image alignleft">
                <?php echo get_the_post_thumbnail(); ?></div>
            <?php endif; ?>
            <?php the_content(); ?>
          <?php endwhile; ?>
        </div>
      </article>
    </div>

    <?php get_sidebar(); ?>
  </div><!-- /.container -->
</div><!-- /.middle -->

<?php get_footer(); ?>
```

Now, let's take our custom field, `book_author`, and display it right below the featured image. We can do that by adding one new line of code (highlighted) in between the featured image code and the main content code:

```php
<?php if(has_post_thumbnail()) : ?>
  <div class="post-image alignleft">
    <?php echo get_the_post_thumbnail(); ?></div>
```

```php
<?php endif; ?>
<p><em>by <?php echo get_post_meta($post->ID, 'book_author', true);
   ?></em></p>
<?php the_content(); ?>
```

Now when you visit a single book page, the author's name is displayed and the book's cover shows up automatically:

Our next task is a page that will show a listing of the books, like `index.php` does. If you go to `http://yoursite.com/books/` now, you'll see something like the following screenshot:

This is basically a standard archive listing. In fact, WordPress uses the default `archive.php` file to show the listing of every new custom post type. We can customize this by creating a new template file and calling it `archive-book.php`. To be more exact, every template file controlling the archive for any new custom post type has to be named `archive-post_type.php`. The easiest way of creating such a file is by making a copy of the standard `archive.php` file or the `index.php` file and renaming it `archive-book.php`. Then we can take it from there and modify the file to fit our requirements. So what I'm going to do here is use my `index.php` as the template and do some fine tuning around it.

Right now, my new `archive-book.php` file doesn't offer any custom way of displaying by books. Here's what the main loop looks like:

```php
<?php if (have_posts()) : ?>
<?php while (have_posts()) : the_post(); ?>
  <?php get_template_part('listing', 'blog'); ?>
<?php endwhile; else: ?>
  <h5>Sorry, no posts matched your criteria.</h5>
<?php endif; ?>
```

As you can see, the actual display is done by the `get_template_part('listing', 'blog')` function call. Let's change it so it fetches a new listing type, our books, and then create the listing file itself. Here's my new loop after the changes (the new part highlighted):

```php
<?php if (have_posts()) : ?>
<?php while (have_posts()) : the_post(); ?>
  <?php get_template_part('listing', 'book'); ?>
<?php endwhile; else: ?>
  <h5>Sorry, no posts matched your criteria.</h5>
<?php endif; ?>
```

(You can see the full code if you look at the code download for this chapter.)

Now, let's make a copy of the standard `listing-blog.php` file and rename it to `listing-book.php`. Right away, I'm going to erase the sections that handle the display of the post author link, the post date, and the comments (our custom post type doesn't support comments at the moment; you can enable them any time if needed). Next, I will make the thumbnail a bit smaller. Quite frankly, I don't have do this, but I believe that the book listing will look better with smaller thumbnails. Finally, I will add one line of code just above the `the_excerpt()` function call, in order to display my custom field, `book_author`. The finished file now looks like the following code snippet (new elements highlighted):

```php
<div class="post post-item">
  <div class="post-title">
```

```
        <h2><a href="<?php the_permalink(); ?>"><?php the_title();
            ?></a></h2>
    </div>

    <?php if(has_post_thumbnail()) : ?>
        <div class="post-image alignleft">
            <?php echo '<a href="'.esc_url(get_permalink()).'"
                >'.get_the_post_thumbnail($post->ID, 'thumbnail').'</a>'; ?>
        </div>
    <?php endif; ?>

    <div class="entry clearfix">
        <p><em>by <?php echo get_post_meta($post->ID, 'book_author',
            true); ?></em></p>
        <?php the_excerpt(); ?>
    </div>
</div><!-- /.post-item -->
```

And here's the final effect:

Registering and using a custom taxonomy

Just to follow the example given a while ago with our custom post type for books, let's now create a custom taxonomy. Essentially, you might not want to mix book categories and post categories, so we are going to create a custom taxonomy named **Book Categories**.

Add the following code to your `functions.php` file:

```
add_action( 'init', 'build_taxonomies', 0 );
function build_taxonomies() {
  register_taxonomy(
    'book_category',
    'book',
    array(
      'hierarchical' => true,
      'label' => 'Book Category',
      'query_var' => true,
      'rewrite' => array('slug' => 'available-books')
    )
  );
}
```

Like the `register_post_type()` function, the `register_taxonomy()` function allows you to register a new taxonomy within WordPress. You can read up on the details of all of the parameters you can add in the codex (http://codex. wordpress.org/Function_Reference/register_taxonomy). For now, you can see we're calling it a `book_category`; it belongs to the object type book, it's hierarchical, you can query it, and it needs to be included in the rewrite of URLs with a custom slug, `available-books`.

Next, we need to make this taxonomy available to books. Simply find the `$args` array we used when registering the book post type, and add the following item to the array:

```
'taxonomies' => array('book_category'),
```

When you return to the WP Admin and edit a book, you'll see that Book Categories have appeared on the right, and they are also in the main navigation pane on the left.

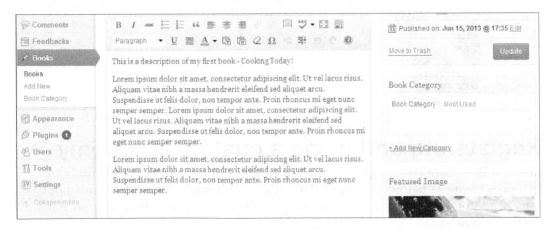

Now that you've added some categories and assigned them to the books, let's take a look at displaying those categories on the front of the website. First, we'll add them to the single book display. Open `single-book.php`, and add this code in an appropriate place within the loop, for example, just below the title:

```php
<?php echo get_the_term_list($post->ID, 'book_category',
  '<b>Categories:</b> ', ', ', ''); ?>
```

You're using the `get_the_term_list()` function, which takes the following arguments:

- ID of the post (`$post->ID`)
- Name of the taxonomy (`book_category`)
- Print before the list (`<b>Categories:</b>`)
- Separate items in the list with (`,`)
- Print after the list ()

Also, now that you've got categories, you can visit **Appearance** | **Menus** and add links to those categories to your header menu, and you can also create a custom menu with all the categories and add it to one of the sidebars.

> If, at any point during the creation of your custom post type and custom taxonomy, you get a 404 from WordPress when you don't think you should, then visit **Settings** | **Permalinks**. Sometimes WordPress needs to refresh the permalinks to make the new links work correctly.

Customizing the admin display

The final thing we can do to realize our new Book custom post type fully is to change its display in the admin. We don't need to know the WordPress user who created a given book, but we do want to see the book categories and the thumbnail. Let's go back to `functions.php`.

First, we'll change the columns that are displayed, as shown in the following code snippet:

```php
add_filter('manage_book_posts_columns', 'ahskk_custom_columns');
  function ahskk_custom_columns($defaults) {
  global $wp_query, $pagenow;
  if ($pagenow == 'edit.php') {
    unset($defaults['author']);
    unset($defaults['categories']);
    unset($defaults['date']);
```

```
      $defaults['book_category'] = 'Categories';
      $defaults['thumbnail'] = 'Image';
   }
   return $defaults;
}
add_action('manage_book_posts_custom_column',
   'ahskk_show_columns');
function ahskk_show_columns($name) {
   global $post;
   switch ($name) {
     case 'book_category':
       echo get_the_term_list($post->ID, 'book_category',
         '', ', ', '');
       break;
     case 'thumbnail':
       if (has_post_thumbnail($post->ID)) echo
         get_the_post_thumbnail($post->ID, array('40', '40'));
       break;
   }
}
```

The first bit says "don't show author, date, and categories, but do show book categories and thumbnail," and the second bit says "for the book categories column print the list of categories, and for the thumbnail column print the `get_post_thumbnail()` function."

Revisit the **Books** page in the WP Admin, and it now looks like the following screenshot:

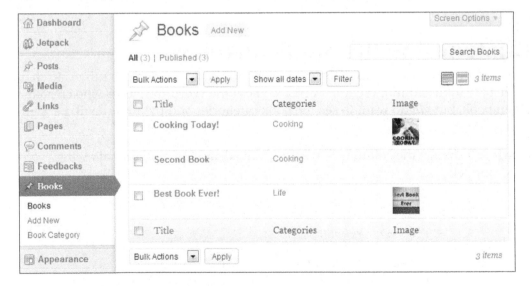

Summary

This chapter was part two of our non-blog website journey with WordPress. I hope you've enjoyed the material. Here, we went through the process of setting up video blogs, photo blogs, membership sites, and social networks. Along the way, we took a closer look at some interesting plugins and their functionalities, just to make our lives easier as WordPress developers. Finally, we created a custom post type and a corresponding custom taxonomy.

The next and final chapter of this book is available as a downloadable bonus on our website: http://www.packtpub.com/. You can get it for free through a standard download link. The chapter covers some general maintenance and troubleshooting for WordPress administrators, as well as providing a list of useful functions, CSS, and template files.

I believe that at this point, you are well-equipped to work with WordPress and use it to build your next great site! WordPress is a top-notch CMS that has matured tremendously over the years. The WordPress Admin panel is designed to be user-friendly, and is continuously being improved. The code that underlies WordPress is robust, and is the creation of a large community of dedicated developers. Additionally, WordPress's functionality can be extended through the use of plugins and themes.

I hope you have enjoyed this book, and have gotten a strong start to administering and using WordPress for your own site, whatever it may be. Be sure to stay connected to the WordPress open source community! Thank you for reading, you rock!

Index

B

b2/cafelog 8
blog
  about 9
  posting on 55, 57, 69, 78
Blog Account tab 253
blog engine 8
blog post 55
body_class() function 214
Book Categories 367
book_init() function 361
BuddyPress
  URL 303
BuddyPress Media plugin 356
build, converting into theme
  about 188
  loop 202-206
  theme folder, creating 189-191
  WordPress content, adding 191
BulletProof Security 144

C

caching 141, 142
Cart66 Lite
  URL 322
Categories box 59, 109
Categories page 92
category
  about 10
  adding 92
  managing 92, 111, 112
Category page 206
child theme
  about 159
  creating 229
  new theme directory, creating 230
  stylesheet, creating 230
  using 231, 232
Chocolate WP 348
Choose Image button 104
ckitchen_register_sidebar() 225
ckitchen_register_sidebar() function 225
ckitchen_register_sidebars() 225

ckitchen_setup() function 240
Codex
  about 19
  URL 19
Comment Blacklist box 85, 86
comment feeds
  about 241, 242
comments
  about 10, 82
  adding 82
  blacklisting 85, 86
  discussion settings 82
  moderating 85-88
Comment spam
  Akismet, activating 91
  Akismet API key 89, 90
  eliminating 88, 89
Compare any two revisions box 74
Conexus Kitchen blog theme 359
Configure/Deactivate button 148
content
  about 10, 123
  exporting 125
  importing 123-125
Content Management System (CMS)
  about 7
  advantage 155
contributor 296
corporate or business websites
  about 312
  building, steps 313
  clean theme, picking 313
  custom home page 316, 317
  elements branding 314
  features 313, 314
  good navigation 314-316
  Meteor Slides 318
  optional slider 317
  SlideDeck 2 Lite Responsive Content Slider
    319-321
Create a new gallery button 120
Create Gallery tab 115
Create secure.htaccess File button 145
Create SlideDeck button 319
CSS
  examining 181

excerpt
  about 69
  working 70
external blogging tools 80, 81
extract() function 287

F

Facebook plugin
  URL 351
featured image
  designating 65
feed
  about 235, 236
  burning, on FeedBurner 243
  feed readers 237, 238
  web feed 235
feed aggregator. *See* **feed reader**
FeedBurner
  about 264
  feed, burning on 243
  URL 242
  used, for subscribers tracking 242
FeedBurner plugin
  about 243, 244
  FD Feedburner Plugin 243
  URL 243
feed links
  adding 239, 240
  comment feeds 241, 242
  FeedBurner plugin 243, 244
  feed, burning on FeedBurner 243
  subscribers, tracking with FeedBurner 242
  website feeds 240, 241
Feedly
  about 12
  URL 236
feed reader
  about 235-238
  FeedDemon, URL 237
  Feedly 237
  list, URL 238
  Net News Wire, URL 237
  NewsBlur, URL 237
  RSS Bandit, URL 237

The Old Reader, URL 237
  types 237
  Vienna RSS, URL 237
Fetch
  URL 30
Filezilla
  URL 30
Filter by Taxonomy? option 320
footer.php 207-209
free approach
  about 340
  plugin, functionalities 343
  plugin, installing 340-342
  plugin, using 343-345
freemium model 340
Frisco for BuddyPress theme 355
functions.php file 192-194, 232

G

Gadgetry theme 170
Gantry
  URL 313
Generate strong password button 26
get_option() function 268
get_post_thumbnail() function 370
get_template_part() function 202
get_the_term_list() function 369
Globally Recognized Avatar. *See* **Gravatar**
GNU General Public License (GPL) 23, 233
Google Analytics
  enabling 140, 141
GPL (GNU General Public License) 260
Gravatar
  features 51
  getting 50, 51
  G rated 51
  PG rated 51
  R rated 51
  X rated 51

H

header
  about 103, 104
  Crop and Publish button 104

W

web feed 235
weblog. *See* blog
weblogger 9
weblogging 9
website feeds 240, 241
What You See Is What You Get (WYSIWYG)
    editor 15
widget form function 279, 280
widget initiation function 278
widgetizing 223
widget print function 281
widgets
    about 11, 150-153, 224, 276
    Available Widgets 153
    bundling, with existing plugin 286
    contents 150
    controlling 151
    custom tag cloud widget 276
    Inactive Widgets 153
    Main Widget Area 152
    Secondary Widget Area 152
widget save function 281
Windows Live Writer 81
    using 251-254
Wini themes
    URL 161
WooCommerce | Orders 335
WooCommerce plugin
    URL 322
    obtaining 324
WooCommerce | Reports 335
WooCommerce | Settings | General 327
WooThemes
    URL 161, 313
WooTub 348
WordCamp 18
WordPress
    about 8
    blog 18
    built-in feeds 238, 239
    choosing 13
    Codex 19
    comments 10

Custom Menus 12
features 13-17
forum 19
installing, through Softaculous 37-40
media library 112
news 18
online resources 17, 18
page 12
plugins 11, 255
post 10
recipes 10
reference links 17
RSS 12
tags 10
theme 11
users 12
using, for blog 8
using, for website 8
widgets 11
WordPress.com 14
WordPress.org 14
WordPress.com
    about 14
    first content, publishing 27, 28
    URL 26
    using 26, 27
    WordPress, manual installation 28
WordPress.com installation
    versus own server installation 25
WordPress content
    <head> tag 196
    footer 197-199
    functions.php file 192-195
    header 197-199
    sidebar 200, 201
WordPress Importer plugin 124
WordPress MS
    websites 305
WordPress MU
    about 303
    URL 304
WordPress.org 14
WordPress post
    creating 246, 247
WordPress SEO 264

Thank you for buying
WordPress 3.7 Complete *Third Edition*

About Packt Publishing

Packt, pronounced 'packed', published its first book "*Mastering phpMyAdmin for Effective MySQL Management*" in April 2004 and subsequently continued to specialize in publishing highly focused books on specific technologies and solutions.

Our books and publications share the experiences of your fellow IT professionals in adapting and customizing today's systems, applications, and frameworks. Our solution based books give you the knowledge and power to customize the software and technologies you're using to get the job done. Packt books are more specific and less general than the IT books you have seen in the past. Our unique business model allows us to bring you more focused information, giving you more of what you need to know, and less of what you don't.

Packt is a modern, yet unique publishing company, which focuses on producing quality, cutting-edge books for communities of developers, administrators, and newbies alike. For more information, please visit our website: www.packtpub.com.

About Packt Open Source

In 2010, Packt launched two new brands, Packt Open Source and Packt Enterprise, in order to continue its focus on specialization. This book is part of the Packt Open Source brand, home to books published on software built around Open Source licences, and offering information to anybody from advanced developers to budding web designers. The Open Source brand also runs Packt's Open Source Royalty Scheme, by which Packt gives a royalty to each Open Source project about whose software a book is sold.

Writing for Packt

We welcome all inquiries from people who are interested in authoring. Book proposals should be sent to author@packtpub.com. If your book idea is still at an early stage and you would like to discuss it first before writing a formal book proposal, contact us; one of our commissioning editors will get in touch with you.

We're not just looking for published authors; if you have strong technical skills but no writing experience, our experienced editors can help you develop a writing career, or simply get some additional reward for your expertise.

WordPress 3 Complete

ISBN: 978-1-84951-410-1   Paperback: 344 pages

Create your own complete website or blog from scratch with WordPress

1. Learn everything you need for creating your own feature-rich website or blog from scratch

2. Clear and practical explanations of all aspects of WordPress

3. In-depth coverage of installation, themes, plugins, and syndication

4. Explore WordPress as a fully functional content management system

WordPress Plugin Development Beginner's Guide

ISBN: 978-1-84719-359-9   Paperback: 296 pages

Build powerful, interactive plugins for your blog and to share online

1. Everything you need to create and distribute your own plugins following WordPress coding standards

2. Walk through the development of six complete, feature-rich, real-world plugins that are being used by thousands of WP users

3. Written by Vladimir Prelovac, WordPress expert and developer of WordPress plugins such as Smart YouTube and Plugin Central

Please check **www.PacktPub.com** for information on our titles

WordPress Plugin Development Cookbook

ISBN: 978-1-84951-768-3   Paperback: 318 pages

Over 80 step-by-step recipes to extend the most popular CMS and share your creations with its community

1. Learn to create plugins and configuration panels in order to bring new capabilities to WordPress

2. Tailor WordPress to your needs with new content types, custom widgets, and fancy jQuery elements, without breaching security needs

3. Detailed instructions on how to achieve each task, followed by clear explanations of concepts featured in each recipe

WordPress Theme Development
Third Edition Beginner's Guide

ISBN: 978-1-84951-422-4   Paperback: 252 pages

Learn how to design and build great WordPress themes

1. Learn how to design WordPress themes and build them from scratch

2. Learn how to create a WordPress theme design using HTML5 and CSS3

3. With clear and easy-to-follow worked examples to help you build your first WordPress theme if you've never done it before

CPSIA information can be obtained at www.ICGtesting.com
Printed in the USA
LVOW03s2013290115

424933LV00003B/12/P

9 781782 162407